About the Author

Born in Germany, Edgar Rothermich studied music and ... ous Tonmeister program at the Berlin Institute of Technolog... dK) in Berlin where he graduated in 1989 with a Master's Degree. He worked as a composer and music producer in Berlin, and moved to Los Angeles in 1991 where he continued his work on numerous projects in the music and film industry ("The Celestine Prophecy", "Outer Limits", "Babylon 5", "What the Bleep Do We Know", "Fuel", and "Big Money Rustlas").

For the past 20 years Edgar has had a successful musical partnership with electronic music pioneer and founding Tangerine Dream member Christopher Franke. Recently, in addition to his collaboration with Christopher, Edgar has been working with other artists, as well as on his own projects.

In 2010 he started to release his solo records in the "Why Not …" series with different styles and genres. The current releases are "Why Not Solo Piano", "Why Not Electronica", "Why Not Electronica Again", and "Why Not 90s Electronica". This previously unreleased album was produced in 1991/1992 by Christopher Franke. All albums are available on Amazon and iTunes, including the 2012 release, the re-recording of the Blade Runner Soundtrack.

In addition to composing music, Edgar Rothermich is writing technical manuals with a unique style, focusing on rich graphics and diagrams to explain concepts and functionality of software applications under his popular GEM series (Graphically Enhanced Manuals). His bestselling titles are available as printed books on Amazon, as Multi-Touch iBooks on the iBookstore, and as pdf downloads from his website.

(Languages: English, Deutsch, Español, and 简体中文)

www.DingDingMusic.com   GEM@DingDingMusic.com

About the Editor

Many thanks to Tressa Janik for editing and proofreading my manual.

Special Thanks

Special thanks to my beautiful wife, Li, for her love, support, and understanding during those long hours of working on the books. And let's not forget my son, Winston. Waiting for him during soccer practice or Chinese class always gives me extra time to work on a few chapters.

The manual is based on GarageBand for the iPad v2.0.1

Manual: Print Version 2014-0621

ISBN-13: 978-1482009187

ISBN-10: 1482009188

About the GEM (Graphically Enhanced Manuals)

> ### UNDERSTAND, not just LEARN
>
> What are Graphically Enhanced Manuals? They're a new type of manual with a visual approach that helps you UNDERSTAND a program, not just LEARN it. No need to read through 500 pages of dry text explanations. Rich graphics and diagrams help you to get that "aha" effect and make it easy to comprehend difficult concepts. The Graphically Enhanced Manuals help you master a program much faster with a much deeper understanding of concepts, features, and workflows in a very intuitive way that is easy to understand.

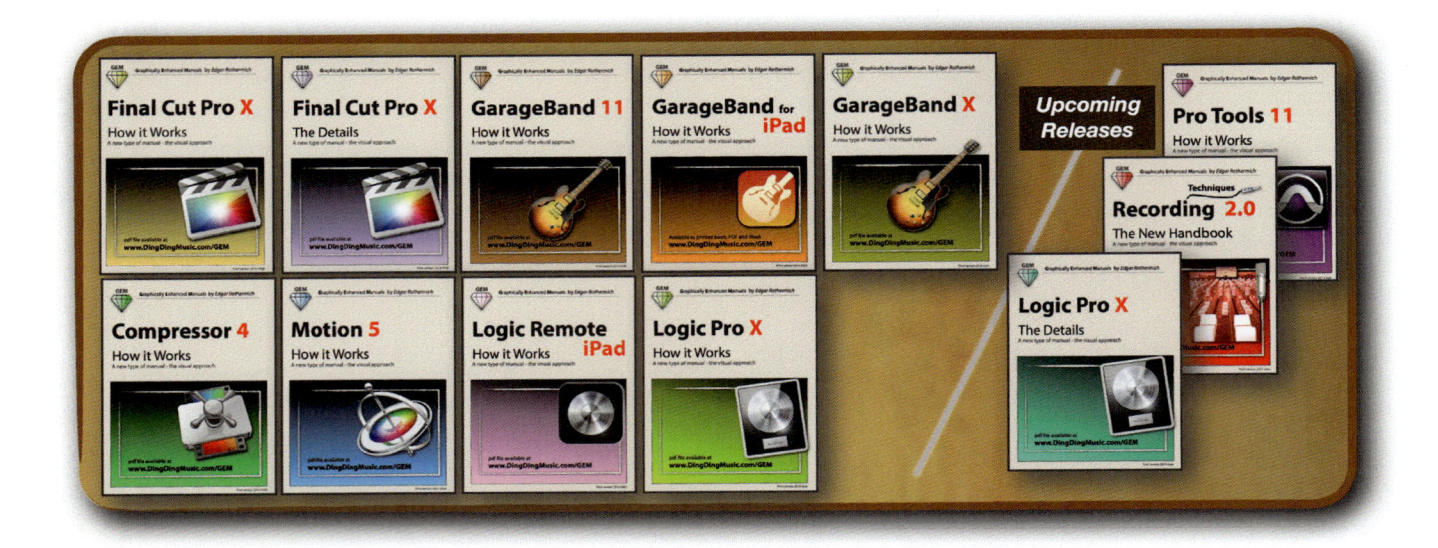

The titles are available in three different formats (languages: English, Deutsch, Español, 简体中文)

.... PDF downloads from my website www.DingDingMusic.com/Manuals

.... Interactive multi-touch iBooks on Apple's iBook Store.

.... Printed books on Amazon.com

For a list of all the available titles and bundles: www.DingDingMusic.com/Manuals

To be notified about new releases and updates, subscribe to subscribe@DingDingMusic.com

About the Formatting

Green colored text indicates keyboard shortcuts in all my other manuals for Mac applications. The iPad doesn't have keyboard shortcuts so here I just use the green font to indicate any touch gestures (tap, slide, etc.).

Blue arrows indicate what happens if you tap on an item or popup menu ●———➤

Table of Contents

Why a Manual?

GarageBand for the iPad is a very intuitive and easy to use little application, so why does it need a separate manual?

If you want to click around for fun and use the trial and error approach, then no, you might not need a manual. However, as I will show you, you can use GarageBand as a serious music production app. If you want to dive into it, find out every little detail and master its tools (while still having fun), then this manual is right for you. It is actually the only comprehensive manual for this app that covers all aspects and not just a quick start guide with a few highlights.

Please note that using the app requires some understanding in areas like iCloud, file management on an iPad, and some background about music production itself. As part of my approach to writing manuals, I will also provide that information at a level that is necessary to better understand a specific feature in GarageBand.

So in the end, your experience and use of the app will be more satisfying and ultimately even more fun. So let's get to it.

My Approach

If you've never read any of my other books and you aren't familiar with my Graphically Enhanced Manuals (GEM) series, let me explain my approach. As I mentioned at the beginning, my motto is:

"UNDERSTAND, not just LEARN"

Other manuals (original documentations or third party books) often provide just a quick way to: "press here and then click there, then that will happen ... now click over there and something else will happen". This will go on for the next couple hundred pages and all you'll do is memorize lots of steps without understanding the reason for doing them in the first place. Even more problematic is that you are stuck when you try to perform a procedure and the promised outcome doesn't happen. You will have no understanding why it didn't happen and, most importantly, what to do in order to make it happen.

Don't get me wrong, I'll also explain all the necessary procedures, but beyond that, the understanding of the underlying concept so you'll know the reason why you have to click here or there. Teaching you "why" develops a much deeper understanding of the application that later enables you to react to "unexpected" situations based on your knowledge. In the end, you will master the application.

And how do I provide that understanding? The key element is the visual approach, presenting easy to understand diagrams that describe an underlying concept better than five pages of descriptions.

Your Level

When writing a book, there is always the question of who is the audience. In the case of an instructional manual, this question is even more important. Here, the question is, who are the readers/students, and especially at what level are they?

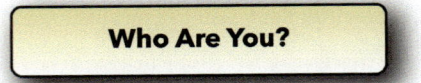

GarageBand is a so-called "content-creation" application and as any content creation app (Logic Pro X, Final Cut Pro X, Motion) it is a tool that allows you to create new content. However, there are two sides to the story. In order to learn the application (the tool), you have to be first somewhat familiar with the subject. Without an understanding of the specific field (music production, video production, animation), any manual for those software applications would be hard to comprehend.

When writing for a high-end application designed for professionals, the author can assume that the target audience is familiar with the material and the field it was created for (music production, video editing, animation, etc.). For example:

- You cannot pick up a manual for a fighter jet airplane, read it, and then climb in the cockpit and blast off into the sunset. It might require a little background knowledge about aviation and airplanes. If you are a pilot of a Jumbo Jet, or even if you are only a hobby pilot that has flown just a little propeller airplane before, then you might understand the manual.

- How about picking up a manual to create your first iPhone app. If you have no experience in writing Objective-C or any other computer programming code, you might have a hard time understanding what the manual is talking about if it assumes that you have basic programming skills.

Most applications require you to have a background in the field they cover (i.e. aviation, programming). A manual either assumes that the reader has that necessary knowledge and targets an experienced user, or it has to provide that basic background knowledge along with the teaching of the app if the potential user is a beginner.

In this manual, I teach the tool GarageBand. The field/subject is audio production and everything related to it.

Because GarageBand for iPad is free on the iTunes Store, everybody with an iDevice (iPad, iPhone, or even iPod Touch) has access to it and could start recording their own songs. However, not everybody might have prior knowledge in the field of music production and their related topics. I will cover some related topic or concepts in the book if they are necessary for a better understanding of how to use GarageBand.

What is GarageBand?

GarageBand is a software application for producing music. However, this is a very generic description that can include a lot of things. Usually such an application is called a DAW, a Digital Audio Workstation. Although this term is usually used for more complex apps like Logic Pro or Pro Tools, I still would call GarageBand a DAW, a mini-DAW.

- **Digital**: This means that we are working in the digital domain, using a computer (including iPads and iPhones). The opposite would be "analog" with analog tape machines, mixing consoles and effect racks, all connected with wires carrying analog signals. (WIKI-MOMENT: Analog vs. Digital)
- **Audio**: This word means that we are working in the audio field, dealing with music and sound, and not taking pictures or making a movie.
- **Workstation**: This word hints at the "Swiss army knife" aspect of the program. DAWs can usually perform a wide variety of tasks (recording, editing, mixing, mastering). In that aspect, GarageBand iPad is a mini-DAW.

D A W

There are other DAWs like Logic Pro, ProTools, Cubase, Live, and a wide variety of DAWs on the PC. Basically, they all provide the same tools for producing music. Their main difference is their feature set, different user interface, and specific workflows.

Feature Set

The question about how much "stuff" a software application provides comes down to how much stuff the user actually needs. You might not need a full blown word processor like Word to just write a few notes or a letter and you might not need the full version of Photoshop when a magic "enhance" button is enough to make your picture look better.

It is the same thing with DAWs. Logic Pro or ProTools might be too much for a user since all of their features and tools require a lot of time to learn and understand.

Here is a diagram that demonstrates the difference.

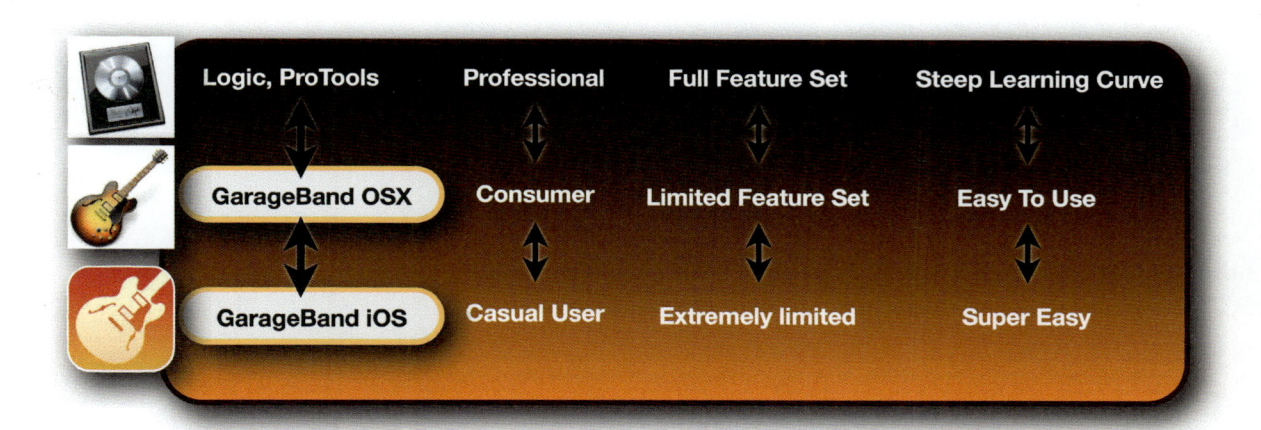

GarageBand X is a consumer product (with a consumer "price tag") designed for the entry level user with a stripped down feature set, limited in many areas. GarageBand for iPad takes it one step further. It is even more limited to the basic level of music production. As I mentioned in the introduction, you can use it as a little fun toy application, but it is still powerful enough to start creating a professional sounding song.

Specifications

Here is a list of the requirements and stuff that works and doesn't work in GarageBand for iPad v2.0:

▶ **Price**
- Free

This includes a starter set that contains the Audio Recorder, plus three Touch Instruments (Keyboard, Drums, and Smart Guitar), which come with eight preset sounds.

▶ **In-App Purchase**
- $4.99

With a one-time in-app purchase, you can add Guitar Amp, Smart Keyboard, Smart Bass, Smart Strings, Smart Drums, Sampler, and a total of 157 preset sounds (Patches).

If you previously purchased an earlier version of GarageBand for iOS, you will get the In-App Purchase content for free. To restore your purchase, you may need to tap "Already Purchased?" when you see the in-app purchase in GarageBand.

▶ **Supported Hardware**
- iPad 2, or later
- iPad mini
- iPhone 4, or later
- iPod Touch 5

▶ **System Requirement**
- iOS 7.0 or later

▶ **Project File Compatibility**
- Can be opened in GarageBand X (and GarageBand 11)
- Can be opened in Logic Pro X (and Logic Pro 9)

▶ **Specs**
- Sample Rate: 44.1kHz (fixed)
- Bit Depth: 16bit (fixed)
- Maximum Project length: 320 bars (4/4)
- Available Time Signatures: 4/4, 3/4, 6/8
- Maximum Tracks per Song: Depend on the iDevice:
  - ✦ 32 Tracks: Phone 5s, iPad Air, iPad mini Retina
  - ✦ 16 Tracks: iPad2, 3, 4, iPod Touch5, iPad mini, iPhone 4s, 5, 5c
  - ✦ 8 Tracks: iPhone 4

▶ **Audio Formats**
- Import AIFF, CAF, WAV, Apple Lossless, MP3, and AAC (except protected AAC files)
- Record AIFF (16bit)
- Bounce to AIFF, AAC

▶ **Support for**
- Inter-App Audio (IAA)
- AudioBus

What to do with it

Here is a list of things you can do with GarageBand on the iPad:

- ☑ Record your music with microphones, electric guitars, or MIDI keyboards
- ☑ Mix your music and add loop based audio files
- ☑ Create Ringtones
- ☑ Use it as a synthesizer instrument (sound module)
- ☑ Use it as a guitar amp with stompboxes to play your electric guitar
- ☑ Jam with others who use GarageBand on their iDevices

Regardless of what you use GarageBand for, you are dealing with a recording studio in a (tiny) box. To give you a little background about audio recording, I cover briefly the main components in a Studio in the next chapter.

New Terminology vs. different Terminology

As I pointed out in my GarageBand X manual "GarageBand X - How it Works", learning your first music production application has its advantage. You start with a clean slate, you are learning new terminology, and a new interface. You will have the same advantage if GarageBand for the iPad is your first "encounter" with such an application. However, if you already have experience with other music production applications already (Logic Pro, ProTools, or other PC based DAWs), then you are facing one common problem. You might have to re-learn or un-learn terminology or procedures.

The underlying concepts and procedures of the various music production applications are pretty much the same, but different apps have different ways of presenting the same thing, use different terms, icons, or just different layouts. GarageBand has its own unique way too. This re-learning of terms and workflows is sometimes more difficult than learning something new because with something new you don't have a specific expectation of how things work.

The good news is that GarageBand for the iPad has a very basic feature set so you, the user, are not confronted with too many technical terms.

The Learning Path

So with all that in mind, let's dive into GarageBand for the iPad.

- ▶ Imagine a full-blown recording studio in a little handheld device.
- ▶ Imagine a $100,000 recording studio for the price of a $5 app.

What you will Learn

Here are the topics and the roadmap of my book and how I will teach GarageBand step-by-step. I recommend that you go through the book in sequential order because I put a lot of effort into coming up with the right sequence of how and when to explain the specific features and related topics. Of course, if you have some previous knowledge, you can glance over specific sections and skip to the next one.

"GarageBand for iPad - How it Works"

1 - Introduction: This is the current chapter you are reading right now.

2 - Prior Knowledge: Here, you find an introduction to several topics related to music production and music software.

3 - Getting Started: Here, I show all the steps on how to acquire and install GarageBand with a detailed look at the download procedure, plus, a first look at the user interface.

4 - Instrument Browser: How to pick the various Instruments for your Song and why the Guitar Amp is considered an Instrument.

5 - Tracks View: This is the area where you might spend the most time in. So you better get yourself comfortable understanding all the necessary controls.

6 - Instrument View: A separate view dedicated to look at each Instrument in your Song. Here is where you perform your instruments, and here is where you record.

7 - My Songs: A unique (or should I say strange) way on how to manage your files, how to mix your Songs, and everything else related to file management.

8 - iCloud: A separate chapter just for iCloud. Is it necessary ... you bet it is. Everything you need to know about living "on a cloud".

9 - Create your Song: Now let's get down to business and create our own Song. Song creation the iPad way.

10 - Record your Song: No matter if it is Audio or MIDI, I will show you how to record it and how to get it into your Song. Don't play an instrument? Don't worry; I got you covered with Apple Loops and other stuff to import.

11 - Edit your Song: Need a little nip and tuck to polish your recording? Learn the tools and craft on how to get it right.

12 - Mix your Song: In case it doesn't sound right, there are remedies to make it right, pleasing to the ear and pleasing to your fans.

13 - Instruments: A closer look at all the available instruments, especially the magic world of Smart Instruments.

14 - More Stuff: And last but not least ... other stuff you also might need to know. How about the new kid on the block called "IAA".

Some topics I touch might require further reading beyond the scope of this manual. I mark them with *"WIKI-MOMENT"*. Think of them as suggestions to Google around or study on Wikipedia to get an even deeper understanding of the topic.

Next are a few topics that a GarageBand user should be familiar with before starting to use the application. Instead of assuming that you, the reader, has that knowledge, I will discuss these topics briefly. Maybe you are familiar with the topics already or maybe you find some a little bit too advanced. Either way, having that foundation and background information definitely helps you when using GarageBand.

Music Production in the Studio

Recording Music

● Tape Machine

This is the central element in a Recording Studio, the device that you record your music on. Some big studios still have the original type of device, a "Tape Recorder", that thing with the two reels and magnetic tape moving across. These are mostly analog tape machines that changed into cassette-based tape recorders using digital recording techniques. All those separate hardware devices are replaced nowadays by a computer that records your music onto a big hard drive (using a DAW).

Although the mechanics and the functionality of a computer-based recording device like GarageBand are quite different, the interface, the terminology, and its operations are based on those old Tape Machines.

● Transport/Navigation Control

Every kind of recording device has to have controls, the so-called Transport Controls or Navigation Controls. With tape-based devices, they let you move the tape to the specific position. Even though there is no tape moved around on a hard drive (or no parts at all with SSD drives), the control buttons are the same as in the old days.

● Reader, LCD Display

The essential part in a Navigation system is the readout that tells you where you are on the tape. When you want to record the 2nd verse of your song, you have to be sure that you are at the 2nd verse. Original Tape Machines had a simple time reader (sometimes even mechanical). Nowadays, you have some sort of digital LCD (Liquid Crystal Display) clock. Professional systems use the industry standard called SMPTE time to display time (WIKI MOMENT: SMPTE Time).

● Playhead

A Playhead on an original Tape Machine was a special magnet that picked up the recording in the form of magnetic fields from the tape that rolled by. This Playhead is now represented by a vertical line that represents the position where you play or record your music. That position relates to the number displayed on the LCD Display.

Tracks

One of the main characteristics of a Tape Recorder is the number of Tracks it can record. A track was originally the horizontal space on the tape where the Playhead reads the recorded information. The wider the tape (1/2 inch, 1 inch, 2 inch), the more separate tracks could fit on that tape. The more tracks a tape recorder provides, the more instruments you can record separately at the same time location. This has the advantage of being able to record an additional track later on (overdubbing) and also feeding those separate tracks to separate channels on a mixing board to treat those tracks (instruments) differently. Often you could see the number of available tracks on a machine by the amount of separate Meters on the machine.

Modern DAWs are not restricted by the width of a tape anymore. The number of tracks is determined by the software and often just limited by the capabilities of the computer (or iPad, iPhones) and the speed of your drive you are recording to.

Input

This element can be easily overlooked, but it might be the most important one. If you can't get any signal (instrument) into the recording device, then you cannot record anything, simple as that. A tape machine is usually hooked up to the mixing console and you record through it.

On a DAW the "first point of entry" is your computer. Although you can use your finger as an "input device" on the iPad to play many instruments, you still have to know how to get "external devices" into your iPad or iPhone if you want to use those.

Mixing Music

Mixing Console

The second most important element in a recording studio is the mixing console, or mixer. This is the tool you use to mix your recording. Although it is also used for the recording part, its main purpose is to create the final mix of your recorded song.

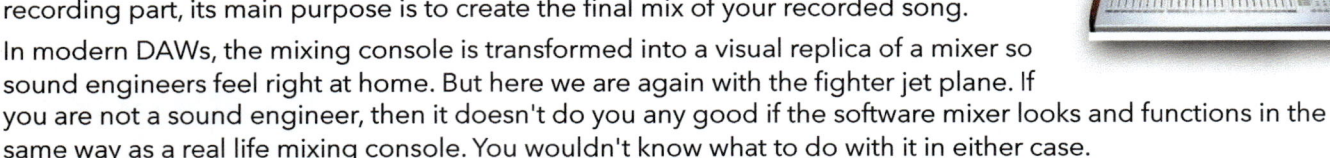

In modern DAWs, the mixing console is transformed into a visual replica of a mixer so sound engineers feel right at home. But here we are again with the fighter jet plane. If you are not a sound engineer, then it doesn't do you any good if the software mixer looks and functions in the same way as a real life mixing console. You wouldn't know what to do with it in either case.

That's why consumer DAW's like GarageBand try to simplify the part of the user interface that represents the mixing console. That could create a problem if you learned how to use a regular mixing board, but now have to re-learn the "simplified" version, which you might find strange.

Channels (Tracks)

The main elements of a mixing console are its Channels, or Channel Strips. These are the identical looking strips with a long fader and all kinds of knobs. The size of a mixer is usually determined by how many physical channel strips it has (8, 32, 64, …). The signal of each of your recorded Tracks from the recording machine is sent (routed) to their own channel strip so you can treat each instrument differently to achieve the right sound for your song.

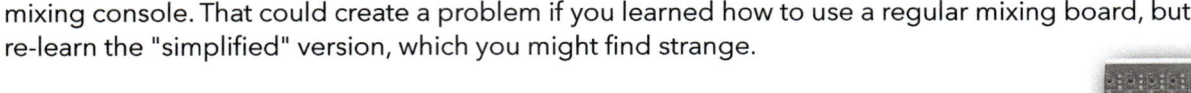

A modern DAW often has virtually an unlimited amount of those Channel Strips, although somehow limited again by the capability of the computer. Because the *Track* from the recorder is related to the *Channel* on the mixer, both terms (Channel, Track) are often used to describe the same component.

Outboard Effects

The basic step of mixing different Instruments (tracks) to get a great sounding song is to get the balance right. You set the correct volume for each instrument and position it in the stereo field, i.e. make the guitar come out of the left speaker and the keyboard from the right speaker. The singer comes from both speakers and, therefore, appears to come from the center (WIKI MOMENT: sound mixing techniques).

The interesting part of mixing, however starts when you add effects to an instrument like delay, reverb, or distortion. It would not be practical to build all those effects into a channel strip. There are too many of them and you might need some effects only on a few instruments. The channel strip would be too long and too expensive. This is where the outboard effects come in. A recording studio usually has a separate rack of effect modules that the engineer could use on specific channel strips.

A similar principle is used in a DAW, which often provides a set of effect Plugins (or you can add additional third party effects to your system). You can "use" those effects on an individual channel that you want an effect applied to. GarageBand for iPad also uses effect plugins, but in a very simplified and limited way.

 Channel Controls

The available Controls on a Channel Strip determine how you can alter the sound of the instrument that is assigned to it (runs through that channel). The main controls are the Fader (change the volume), Pan (change the stereo position left-to-right), Mute (turn it off), Solo (listen only to that instrument), and Meter (check the signal level). Depending on the mixing console (or DAW), the Channel Strips can provide even more controls.

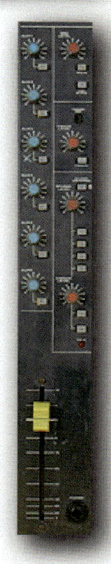

Master Channel

While each Channel Strip affects only the instrument it is assigned to, there is one additional Channel Strip on each Mixing Console and that is the Master Channel. The signals of all the Channels (and their instruments) are added together and go through that Master Channel. This Master Channel is used to do some final treatment to the mix, i.e. lower the overall volume or compress the mix to make it sound louder. This Master Channel is reduced in GarageBand for iPad to just one level meter. At least that is how it appears, but as we will see, GarageBand for iPad does not have a real Master Channel Fader.

Next are a few topics and procedures that are common in DAWs. They could be potential stumbling blocks if this GarageBand app is your first encounter with recording and mixing music on a computer. If you are familiar with GarageBand on the Mac or other DAWs, then you might already know the following concepts.

Audio vs. MIDI

GarageBand on the Mac doesn't use the standard terminology of *Audio* vs. *MIDI*. In an effort to "simplify" the user experience, the application uses some other terms (i.e. "Software Instrument" instead of MIDI). GarageBand for iPad continues to use those terms and avoids even more to mention the distinction between Audio and MIDI when it comes to recording songs.

I still believe that it is not complicated to introduce that concept to the user even in the context of a highly simplified mini-DAW like GarageBand for iPad.

➡ *Audio Signal*

This is a signal from a device that creates a sound in the form of a waveform. This can be any acoustic source like any acoustic instrument or vocals that are captured by a microphone. Also, electrical instruments like an electric guitar or synthesizer that produce sound (with the help of an amplifier). GarageBand uses the term *"Real Instruments"*, which makes sense for the guitar and synthesizer, but could be confusing when referring to a microphone as a Real Instrument.

➡ *MIDI Signal*

A MIDI Signal is a specific type of data stream that describes the musical notes (and controls) that you play on a MIDI keyboard or software keyboard on a computer and also on your iPad. The MIDI standard (Musical Instruments Digital Interface) is a specification that describes how musical notes are transferred into data. A MIDI signal can be recorded as data on a DAW and freely edited in different ways (Piano Roll, Score Editor). However, it contains only the "description" of the music (what note, how loud, how long) and the data has to be sent to a sound module in order to "play" and finally hear it also as sound. GarageBand contains a wide variety of those sound modules (Software Instruments) to choose from.

Always be aware of which of these two signals (Audio or MIDI) you are dealing with when you're recording, when you select a Track for recording, or when you edit your recordings. I will refer to those signals throughout the manual when explaining specific features. In my GarageBand X manual "GarageBand X - How it Works", I cover that topic in more details. (WIKI-Moment: MIDI)

The Arrange Window

The most important window in every DAW is the so-called *Arrange* Window. The layout of that window is similar in various DAWs and even our mini-DAW, GarageBand for iPad, follows that concept, although it is called the *Tracks View* window.

The Arrange Window is where you record and build your song (similar to the multi-track Tape Machine). The second most important window in a DAW is the Mixer Window, which is similar to a real mixing console with all its channel strips and controls. Both GarageBand apps, due to their simplicity, don't have a separate Mixer Window. The basic mixing functionality is done in the Arrange Window (plus a few additional windows).

Here is the basic layout of the Arrange Window:

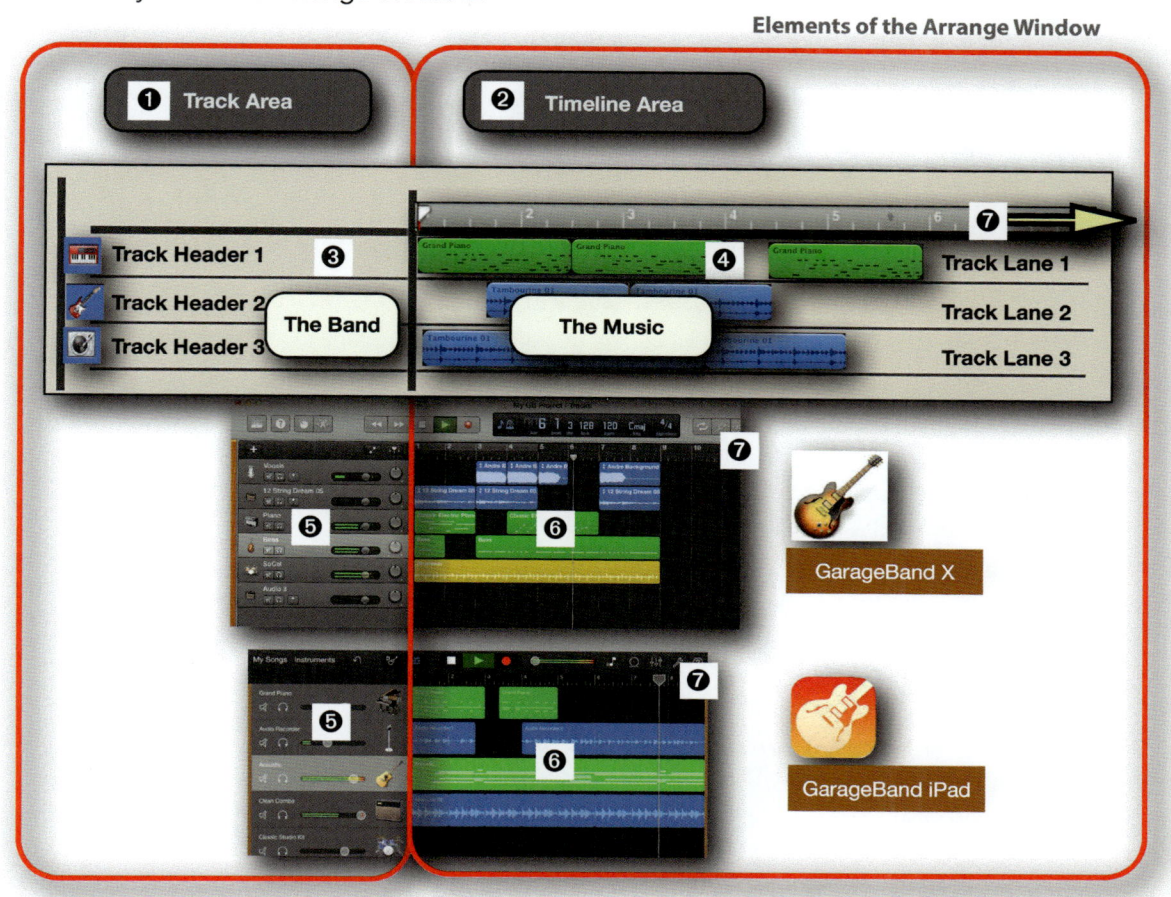

Elements of the Arrange Window

The Arrange window represents your song in the form of rows that are divided into two areas. Here is the terminology:

🏆 Tracks

Each row in the Arrange Window represents a single Track (Instrument) in your Song. The more Tracks in your Song, the more rows you got. GarageBand for iPad can have up to 32 Tracks.

The rows are divided into two sections:

🏆 Track Header ❸

This is the left section of the Arrange window, the **Track Area ❶**. Think of it as your band. The controls ❺ on the Track Header function as a mini-mixer.

🏆 Track Lane ❹

This is the right section of the Arrange window, the **Timeline Area ❷**. This is where your music is placed in the form of Regions ❻ along a timeline. The Timeline Area has a special header, the Time Ruler ❼, so you can see where in your Song the Regions are placed.

Tracks / Instruments

So what is the difference between Instruments, Tracks, and Channels? Is there a difference? Those three terms are often used to describe the same thing. This is not a problem as long as you understand their original meaning.

The following diagram shows the basic concept of a multi-track recording using those terms:

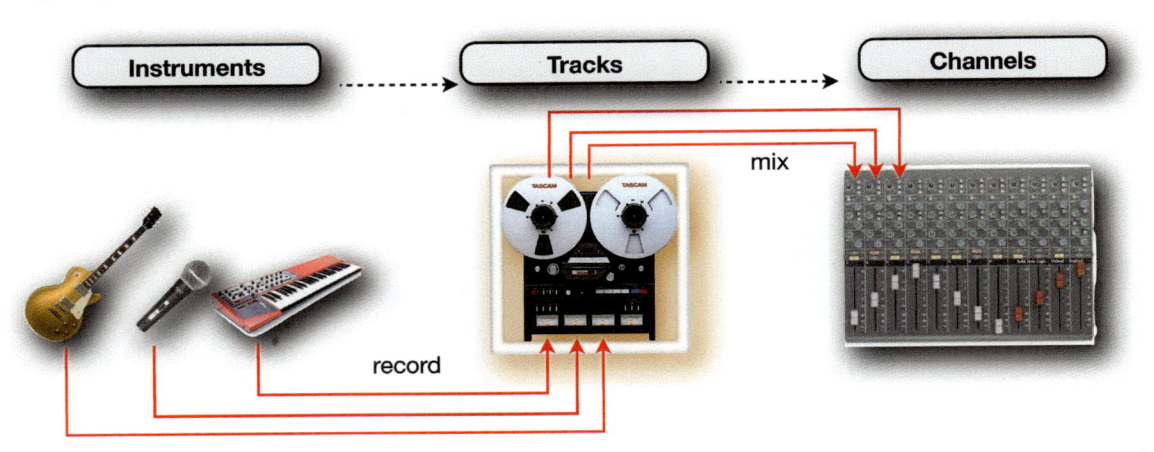

Instruments

The Instrument represents the source or the signal that you are recording. A few things to keep in mind:

- ▶ A tape machine can only record a "sound" source, which GarageBand 11 referred to as a "Real Instrument". But DAWs can also record a "data" source, the MIDI signal from a MIDI keyboard. This is what GarageBand refers to as a "Software Instrument".
- ▶ If the source is a microphone that records an acoustic instrument, then the term "Real Instrument" still makes sense.
- ▶ If the source is a microphone that records a vocalist or sound effects, then the term is still "Real Instrument" (although a little bit of a stretch).

Tracks

The signal from the Instrument (or mic) is recorded on separate Tracks on a multi-track tape machine. Now you have the relationship between Instrument-Track. A few things to keep in mind:

- ▶ On a tape machine, you have a specific amount of available Tracks and you can connect Instruments (source signals) to them. In a DAW you can create a Track when you need it, assign an Instrument to it, and record on that Track. In GarageBand, this is a single procedure. You select an Instrument, which automatically creates a Track for it.
- ▶ This close relationship explains why a row on the Arrange window (Tracks View) is referred to as *Track*, but also as an *Instrument*. It is the Instrument that is *assigned* to that Track.

Channels

Once you have recorded your Instruments onto the Tracks of the Tape Machine, you connect the individual Tracks to individual Channels (channel strips) of a Mixing Console to finally mix your Song. Now you have the connection between all three terms. A specific Channel represents a specific Track of a specific Instrument. A few things to keep in mind:

- ▶ A Mixing Console is also used during the recording process.
- ▶ The recording and mixing processes are usually different steps performed in different studios by different engineers. However, those different tasks often merge, i.e. mixing while still doing some recording.
- ▶ On a DAW, the virtual Track in the Arrange window is linked to a channel strip on its virtual Mixer window. GarageBand doesn't have a separate Mixer window and, therefore, the Track, a.k.a. the Instrument, is also the Channel where you mix the Track/Instrument.

As you see, Instruments, Tracks, and Channels are the same - kind of.

Regions

I already mentioned the term *Region* in the section about the Arrange window. Chances are that most readers know what a Region is, but let's review it.

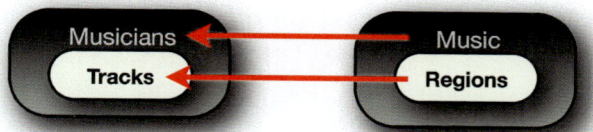

Regions are the building blocks of your song, similar to a score or lead sheet that has the music content written on it. The same way you put the score for each musician on his or her music stand, you put the Regions for each Track on its Track Lane. This way you determine what Regions are played by which Track.

Arrange Window (Tracks View)

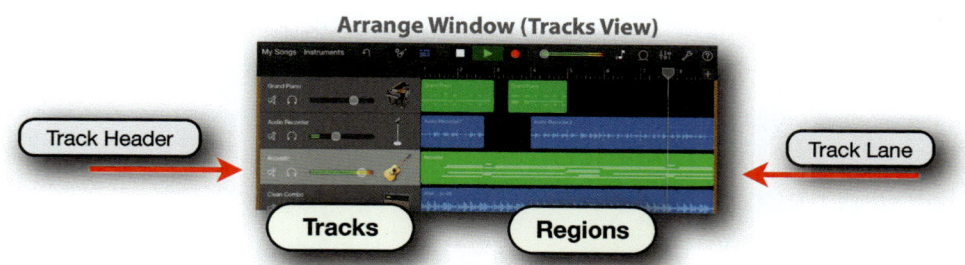

➡ What is a Region

The basic concept and use of Regions is pretty much the same with all the DAWs. Here are the basics:

- A Region is represented by a rectangle on the Track's Track Lane.
- You can think of the Region as a container that holds the information (music) for the Track, telling it what to play.
- The length of the Region defines the length of the "musical instruction" for the Track.
- The "musical instruction" for a Track can be one long Region or many shorter Regions that are placed on the Track Lane only at the position where the Track has to play something.
- Regions are created when you record an Instrument or when you drag an existing recording (audio file) onto a Track.
- Regions are color-coded.
- The most important thing, however, is to understand that there are two fundamentally different types of Regions.

➡ Types of Regions

As I pointed out earlier, there are two types of signals: Audio Signals and MIDI Signals. This distinction is important when it comes to Regions, the "container" that carries the recorded signal, because there are Audio Regions and MIDI Regions.

 **MIDI Regions**

The MIDI Region contains the MIDI data that you recorded from the onscreen Software Instrument or your MIDI keyboard. You can actually see those notes as tiny dots or lines (the" *MIDI Events*") on the Region and we will learn later how to open the MIDI Editor window to edit those notes.

 **Audio Regions**

An Audio Region is linked to an audio file, a recording of an audio signal. The Region displays a miniature waveform of that audio signal. Audio Regions are more restricted when it comes to editing (changing the recording) and GarageBand is even more limited, only allowing you to trim the Region, change the beginning and end of the Region, and move the Region to a different position or Track in your Song.

Color Code

When using GarageBand, you have to pay attention to the color code of Regions. They are not randomly picked to make the Interface look pretty. They have a meaning, which is similar to other music apps by Apple (GarageBand on the Mac, Logic Pro, Apple Loop Types). Green means MIDI, blue means Audio.

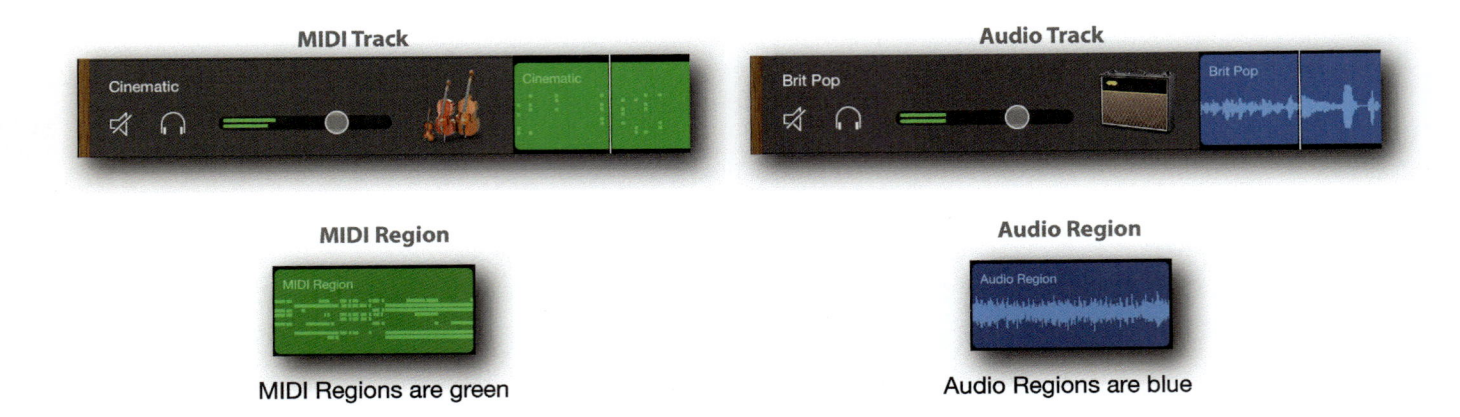

MIDI Regions are green

Audio Regions are blue

Playhead

As we have seen, the visual representation of your song (the music) is the Timeline Area in the Arrange window similar to a musical score. The ruler on top functions as the time axis that provides the orientation to see which elements of your song (the Regions) are placed at what section of your song. Now when you hit the Play Button, you want to know from what position GarageBand is playing your song.

This "play position indicator" is called the *Playhead*. It is a white triangle on the Time Ruler that marks the exact play position on the Ruler and extends as a vertical white line across the Track Lanes in the Timeline Area.

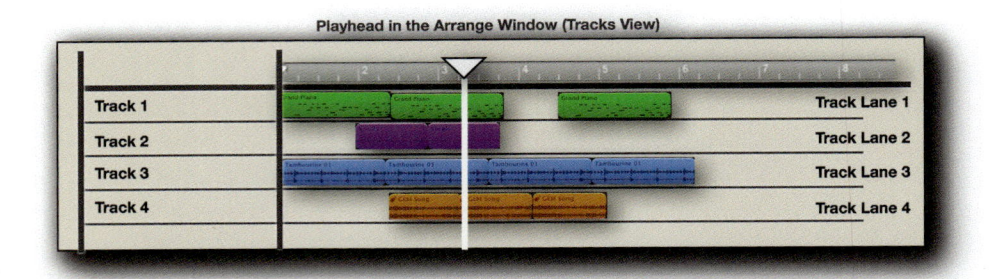

Here is the basic functionality:

- ▶ **GarageBand is not playing**: The Playhead shows the position from where GarageBand will play your Song when you *tap* the Play Button, or start recording when you *tap* the Record Button.
- ▶ **GarageBand is playing (or recording)**: The Playhead moves across the Timeline Area so you can see exactly which part of your Song is playing. It locks its position when reaching the middle of the Timeline Area and now the Timeline Area scrolls underneath the stationary Playhead. This is a feature called *Autoscroll*.
- ▶ **Touch**: The advantage of iDevices like the iPad is that you can touch the Playhead and move it directly along the Time Ruler or *tap* on a position on the Time Ruler to move the Playhead there.

The GarageBand apps

As you already know by now, there are two GarageBand apps with a slightly confusing naming convention.

➡️ ***Operating System (Computer Platform)***

The reason for the two different versions of GarageBand is the fact that Apple has two different types of operating systems, the brain running on those devices.

 Macs (iMac, MacBook, MacMini, etc.) use the operating system called **OS X**

🌐 **iDevices** (iPhone, iPad, iPod, etc.) use the operating system called **iOS**

Those two operating systems are not compatible, which means a software application has to be written for a specific system to run on a Mac or an iDevice. Many apps are now available for both platforms, i.e. Apple's iPhoto, iMovie, and Keynote, but also apps from other companies like Microsoft's Office. GarageBand is also available for both platforms.

The main difference between the OSX and iOS version of an app is often the feature limitation on the iOS app and GarageBand is no exception. When going through the various GarageBand features in this manual, I will occasionally point out how they compare to the GarageBand OSX version to see where the limitations are.

➡️ ***Naming***

The problem with those two GarageBand versions is how to name them properly. When you look at the Mac Store for OSX applications, the app is called "GarageBand" and when you look at the iTunes Store for iOS applications, it is also called "GarageBand". Now when you want to talk about a specific GarageBand app, you have to describe which one you are referring to because there is no standard naming convention that differentiates them.

Here are a few examples how they are named:

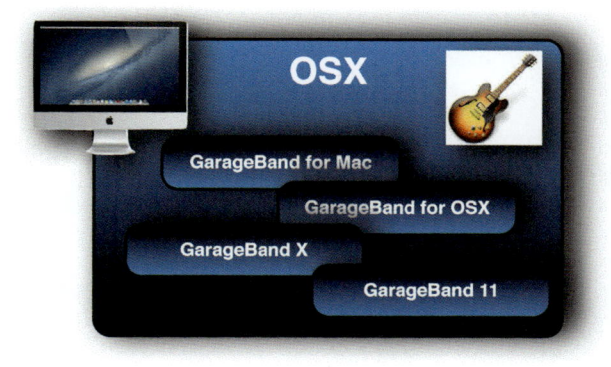

The term "GarageBand OSX" and "GarageBand iOS" would be the most accurate and shortest terms, but it is already too technical because it requires that the user knows what OSX and iOS stand for. The most common term is "GarageBand for iPad" and that's why I use it as the title of this manual. Keep in mind that the GarageBand for iPad app also runs on the iPhone and iPod (which is even more amazing when thinking about what a powerful app you have in the palm of your hand).

Throughout this manual, I will use "GarageBand" to refer to this "GarageBand for iPad" version and "GarageBand X" to refer to the new GarageBand v10 running on OSX.

➡ *Compatibility*

Let's have a quick look at the big picture.

The GarageBand app is part of an ecosystem of multiple audio apps from Apple. There are two aspects of compatibility:

🔘 Projects

You can start with a Project on GarageBand for iPad, or even on the iPhone (while waiting in line at the post office). Later at home, you can take that Project and open it in GarageBand on your Mac (requires GarageBand X) to continue to work on it. To take it to the next level, you can bring that Project to a friend or a studio and open it in Logic Pro to really get serious with it.

🔘 Sounds

There are two more apps in that ecosystem. *MainStage,* which is for live performance and *Soundtrack* (now discontinued), that was used mainly for audio post production together with Final Cut Pro. Those five applications share the same Apple Loops library, as well as software instruments and plugins and also various settings. For example, you can tweak the sound of a software synth or create a new Apple Loop in GarageBand and then have access to that setting and Apple Loop right away in Logic or MainStage.

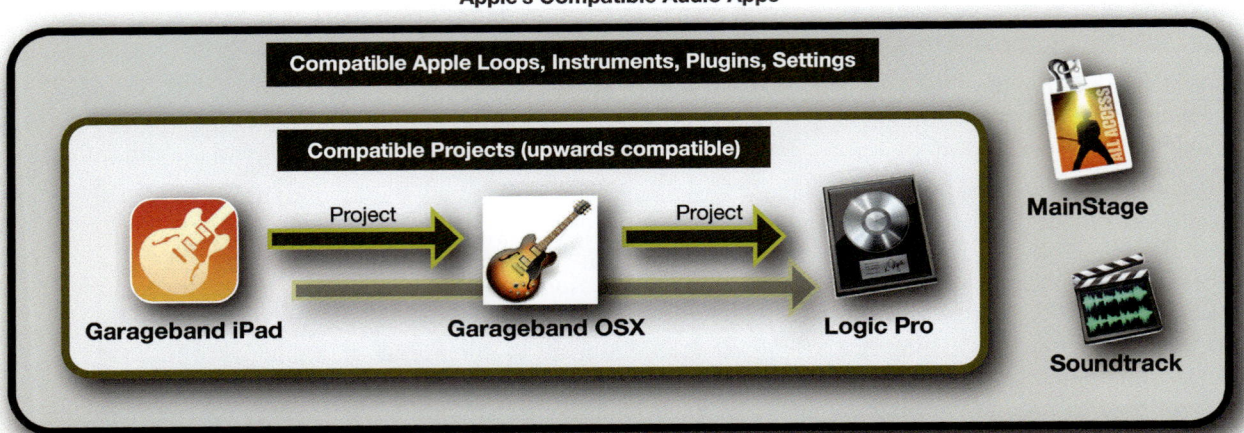

Apple's Compatible Audio Apps

➡ *iPad - iPhone - iPod*

Calling the app *GarageBand for iPad* is a little bit misleading. "GarageBand iOS" is more accurate because the application runs on all iDevices that meets the minimum requirement for the hardware and software (iOS 7). You purchase the app only once and it syncs to all your iDevices on your Apple ID account.

- ☑ **iPad**
- ☑ **iPad mini**
- ☑ **iPhone** (optimized for iPhone 5)
- ☑ **iPod touch** (4th generation and later)

Unlike other apps that blow up or shrink down the graphics to accommodate the different screen sizes, GarageBand uses two slightly different user interfaces. The regular interface for the iPad and an interface that takes the smaller screen size of an iPhone and iPad Touch into account.

All the screenshots in this manual refer to the iPad version. I have a separate chapter at the end of this manual that shows how some pages are different in the smaller iPhone version compared to the standard iPad version of GarageBand.

GarageBand is an iOS app that can be downloaded for free from the Apple iTunes Store. As with any other iPad app, you can download it from the iTunes App Store directly on your iPad or download it to your desktop Mac in iTunes first and then synchronize the app (copy it over) to your iPad.

Download to your Mac

❶ Launch the iTunes application on your Mac.

❷ Select" iTunes Store" in the Sidebar.

❸ Select the "App Store" tab in the header.

❹ Type "GarageBand" in the Search Field, hit *enter*, and select the app from the selection.

❺ Click the "Free" button below the app icon to download GarageBand.

❻ A Sign In Dialog will appear if you are not logged into the iTunes Store with your Apple ID yet. Enter your Apple ID and Password in those fields and click *Get*.

❼ If you don't have an Apple ID yet, click the "Create Apple ID" button to create a free Apple ID. There is no credit card required, only a valid email address to confirm the Apple ID and some other basic information.

iTunes Application

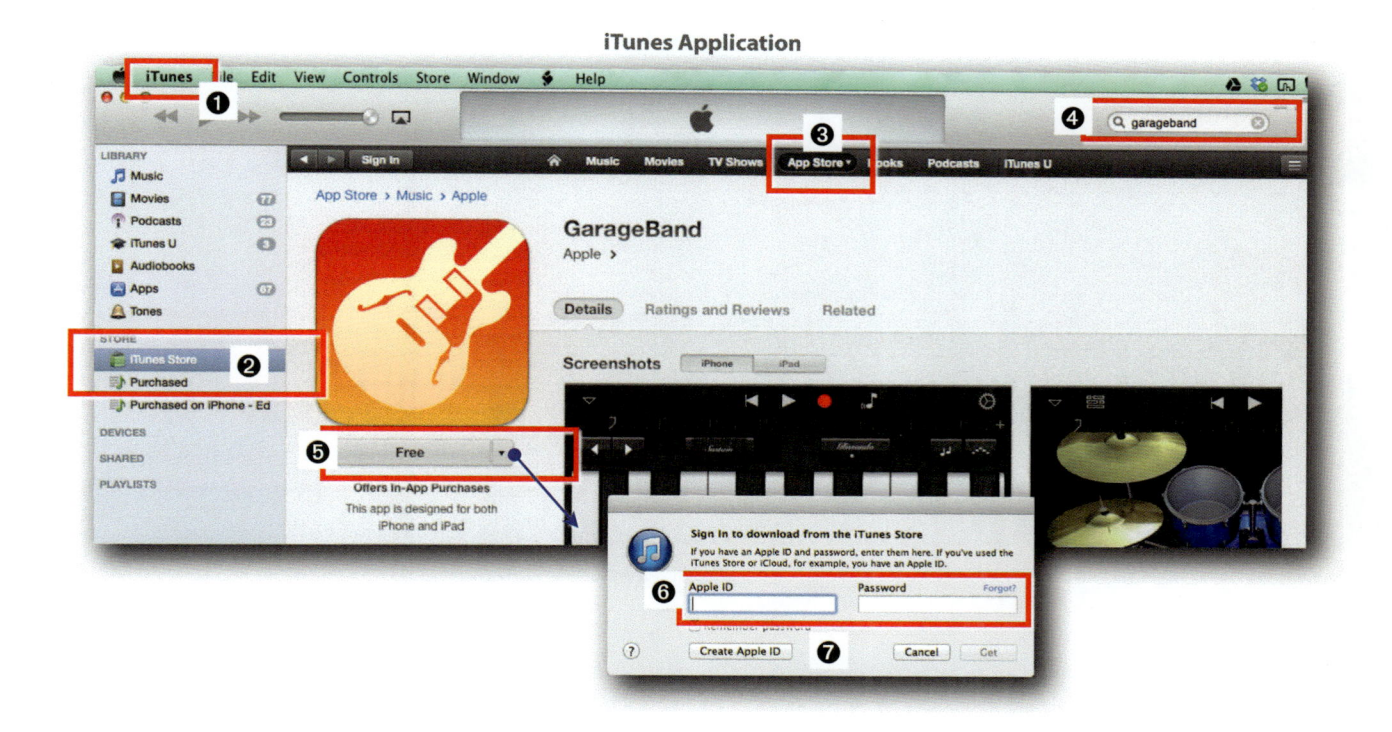

After you have downloaded GarageBand to your Mac, sync it to your iPad.

Download on your iPad

The procedure for downloading the GarageBand app directly to your iPad is the same as with any other iOS app:

❶ Open the App Store app on your iPad.

❷ Type "GarageBand" in the Search Field and *tap* search.

❸ The GarageBand app is displayed with a button next to it. What button is displayed depends on the status.

    ❹ **Free**: The app hasn't been downloaded yet with your current Apple ID. *Tap* the Free Button to start the download process. You will be prompted to enter your Apple ID in a Dialog window ❽.

    ❺ **iCloud Icon**: The app was already downloaded to your iCloud account that is linked to your current Apple ID but is currently not on your iPad. *Tap* the button to download the GarageBand app to your iPad. You will be prompted to enter your Apple ID in a Dialog window ❽.

    ❻ **Installing**: The app is currently installing on your iPad. Don't close your iPad during this process.

    ❼ **Open**: The app is already on your iPad. *Tap* the Open Button to launch GarageBand.

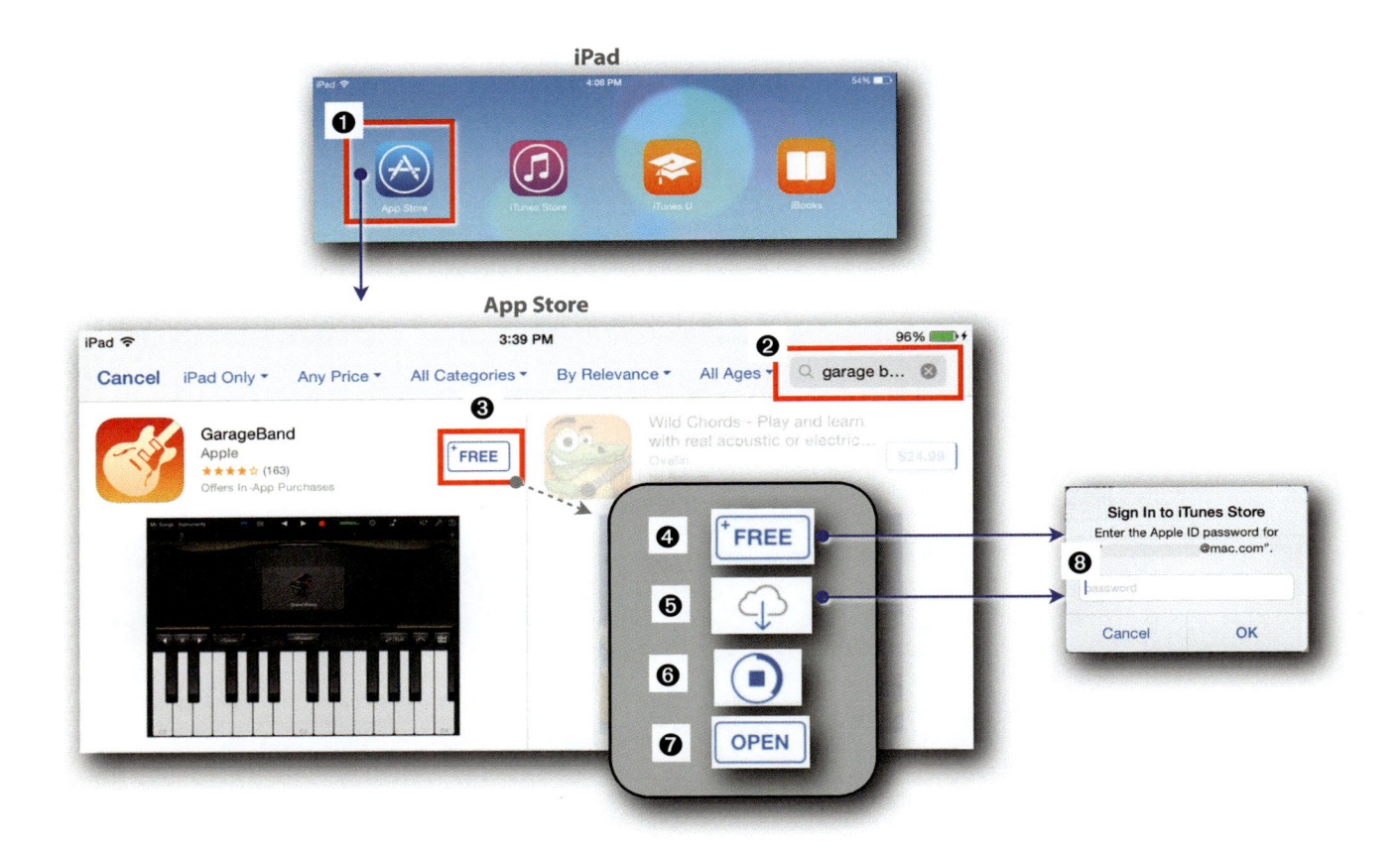

Once installed on your iPad, *tap* the GarageBand icon on your home screen to launch the app.

In-App Purchase (IAP)

When Apple upgraded GarageBand for iPad to version 2, it made it a free app to make it available to an even wider audience. However, this step towards a free app came at its "price".

The previous paid version of GarageBand included a complete set of instruments and sounds. Now the free version includes only, what Apple calls, a "Starter Set". The app is still fully functional, but you are limited in two areas: Available Instruments (only Keyboard, Drums, Smart Guitar, Audio Recorder) and available Patches (only 8 preset sounds for the instruments).

🟡 Starter Set

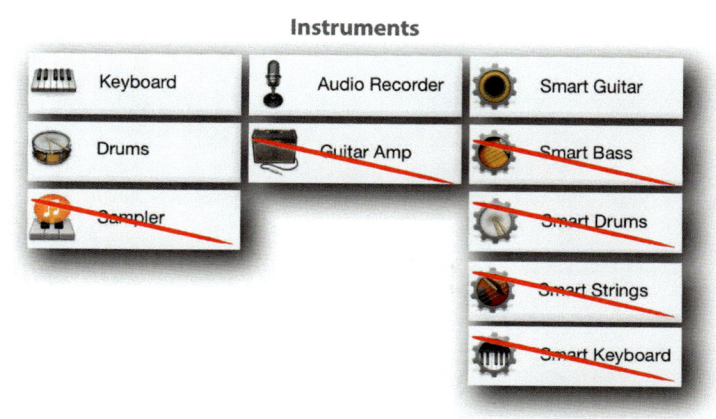
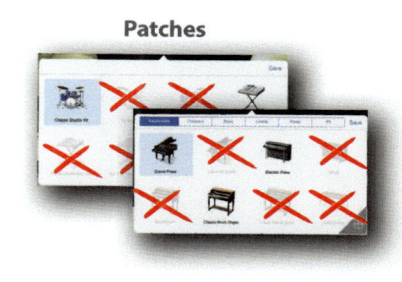

 All the Instruments and Patches are still visible in GarageBand, but they are marked with the download icon to indicate that the Instrument or Patch is not downloaded yet. If you try to open a Song that uses any of those Instruments or Sounds, you get a warning message ❺.

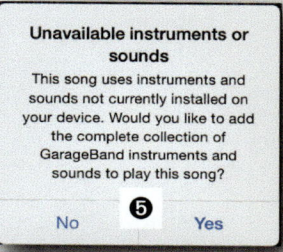

🟡 Complete Set

To get the complete set of all 10 Instruments and 157 Patches (preset sounds), you have to do the $4.99 In-App Purchase (this is still cheaper than the original $12.97 for GarageBand for iPad).

- ☑ **Tap** on any of the Instruments or Patches that display the download icon 🔽 ❶.
- ☑ On the next window, **tap** "Continue" ❷.
- ☑ On the next confirmation window, **tap** "Buy" ❸, enter your password ❹ for your iCloud account, and **tap** OK to start the download.
- ☑ If you previously purchased an earlier version (v1) of GarageBand for iOS from your iCloud account, then GarageBand remembers that you actually already paid for that content. In that case, instead of purchasing the content you just "restore" it, which means, you re-download the content for free. **Tap** on "Already purchased?" ❺ at the bottom of the page.

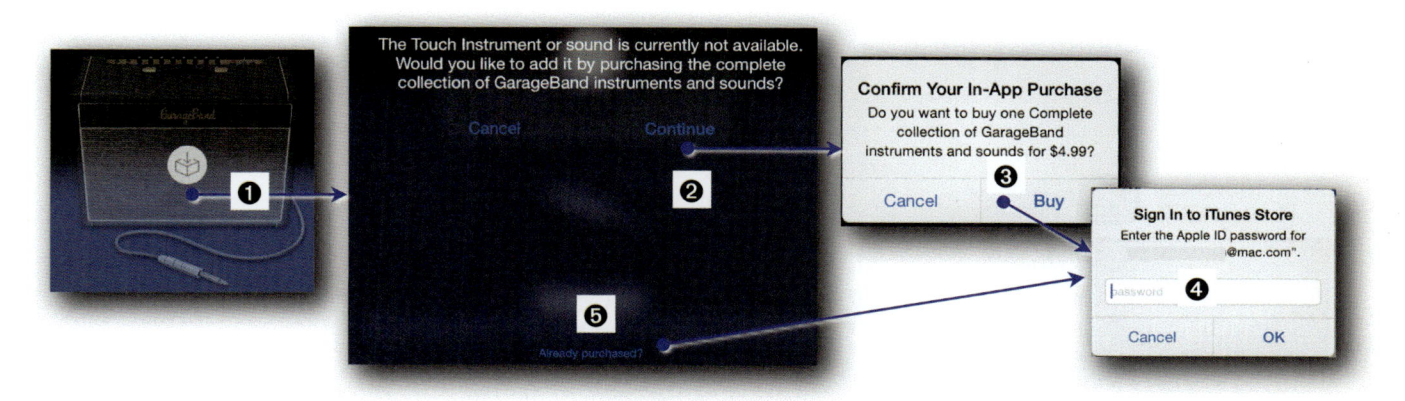

External Hardware

Once you have downloaded GarageBand to your iPad, you can start creating your Songs. However, to record external audio sources (i.e. microphone, electric guitars) you might need additional devices to connect those sources to your iPad in order to record them in GarageBand. There are many solutions and products from third party vendors to choose from. First, here is an overview about the three options how to connect a device to your iPad.

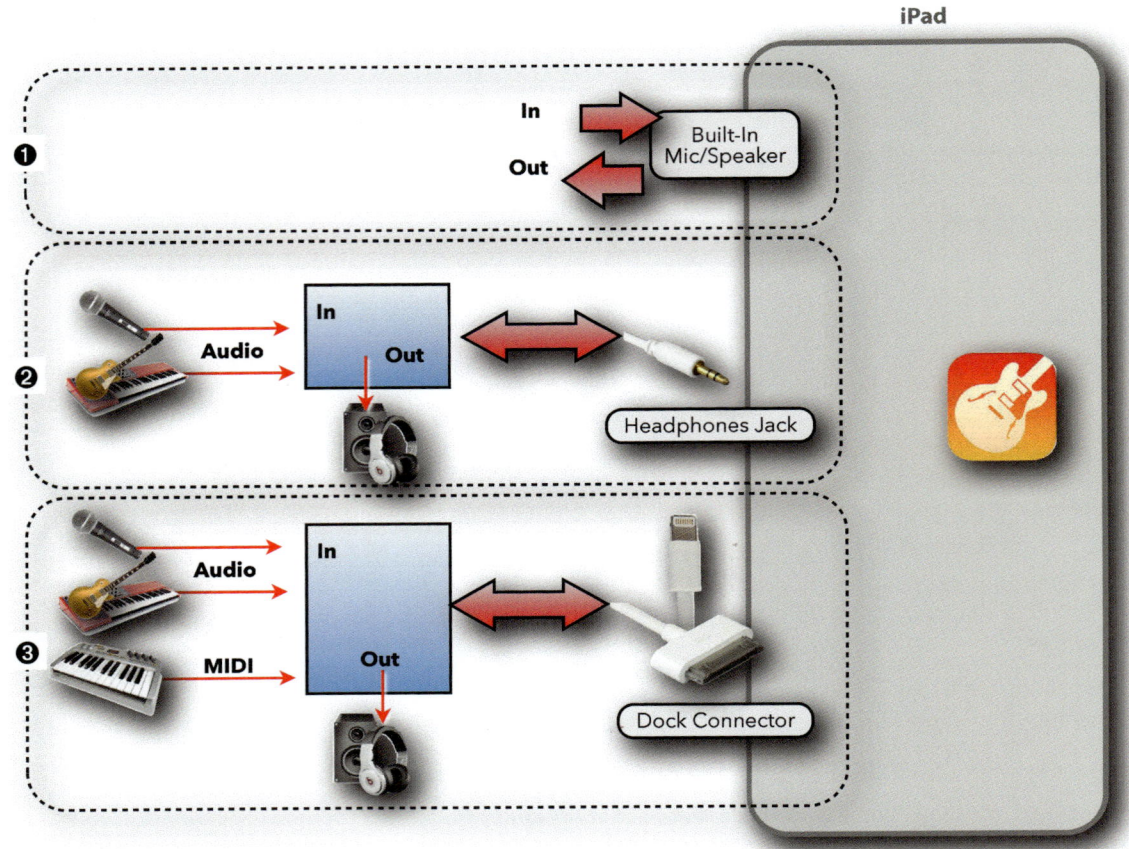

Built-in Microphone/Speaker ❶

The first option is to connect nothing to your iPad. You can listen to your Song in GarageBand on the built-in iPad Speakers without the need for any additional device. You can even use the built-in Microphone on your iPad to record any acoustic audio source with GarageBand. However, the built-in speaker and microphone don't deliver such good quality.

Headphones Jack ❷

Connecting an external Device to the Headphones Jack is as simple as plugging in your earbuds (which is technically also a Device). Please note that the Headphones Jack sends <u>and</u> receives audio signals. You can use the earbuds as headphones and as a microphone. Most third party solutions that use the Headphones Jack are just adapter cables that allow you to connect your guitar cable or microphone cable to the iPad to record on it.

Dock Connector ❸

Connecting a Device to the iPad's Dock Connector provides the most options with the best quality. Those Devices from various companies function as external audio interfaces that provide the audio ins and outs (and even MIDI in some cases). This is the same concept as using an external Audio Interfaces on your Mac that uses USB or any other data port instead of the Dock Connection.

Product Overview

Here are a few examples from various companies that provide those external hardware solutions ranging from about $30 to $1,500. There are many more products available in different price ranges from other companies like Tascam, Alesis, Roland, Behringer, Lexicon, etc.

➡ *Headphones Jack*

These are the least expensive solutions to record your electric guitar or microphone in GarageBand. However, there could be some issues with noisy signals (crosstalk). See the last chapter about the GarageBand Settings.

- Earbuds from Apple or other vendors
- iRig (IK Multimedia): 1/4" jack (with additional headphones jack)
- GuitarConnect (Griffin): 1/4" jack (with additional headphones jack)
- MicConnect (Griffin): XLR jack (with 48V phantom power)

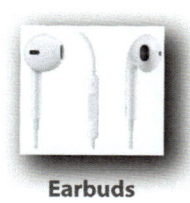 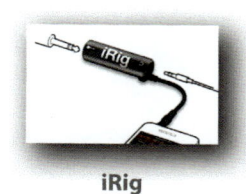  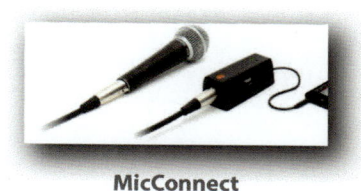

| Earbuds | iRig | GuitarConnect | MicConnect |

➡ *Dock Connector*

Devices connected to the iPad Dock Connector provide the highest quality because the processing (analog - digital conversion) is done in the external box and the data is sent to the iPad's Dock Connector as a data stream.

Please note that older iPads and iPhones use the 30-pin Dock Connector and the newer iDevices use the Lightning Connector. Make sure the external Device provides the proper connection for the iPad or iPhone you are using.

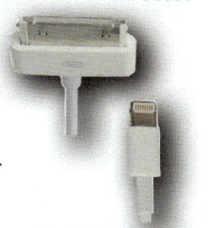

30-pin Dock Connector

Lightning Connector

- MIDIConnect (Griffin): 5pin DIN MIDI (in and out) to 30-pin Dock Connector
- GuitarConnect Pro (Griffin): 1/4" jack to 30-pin or lightning (or USB)
- Jam (Apogee): 1/4" jack to 30-pin or lightning (or USB)
- One for iPad (Apogee) 2 inputs (instrument, mic) to 30-pin or lightning (or USB)
- Duet (Apogee): 2 inputs (1/4" or 1/8" jack) to 30-pin or lightning (or USB)
- Quartet (Apogee): 4 inputs (1/4" and XLR) to 30-pin or lightning (or USB)
- MiC 96 (Apogee): Professional microphone to 30-pin or lightning (or USB)

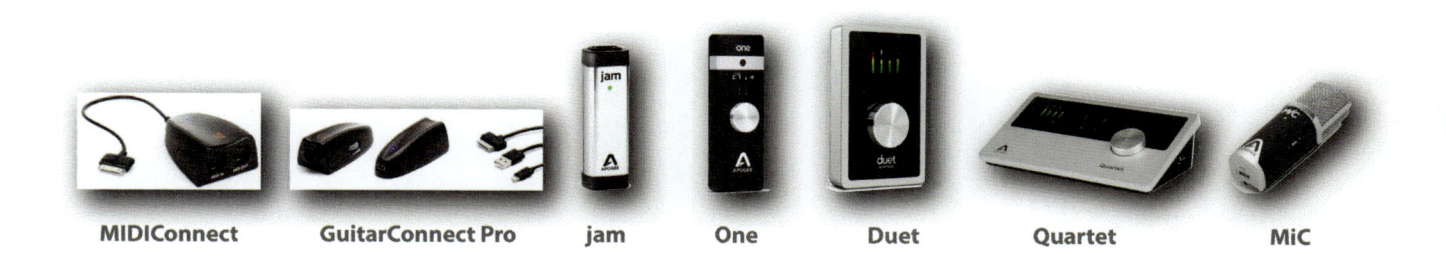

| MIDIConnect | GuitarConnect Pro | jam | One | Duet | Quartet | MiC |

Before getting into any functionality of the GarageBand app and telling you where to tap in order to start your first recording, I will go over the various interface elements first. That way, you'll know how to navigate through the windows and won't get stuck or be surprised where you land.

Windows Overview

GarageBand has a very simple and elegant interface with only five main windows. It is important to understand this hierarchy and know how to navigate between those windows. First, here is an overview:

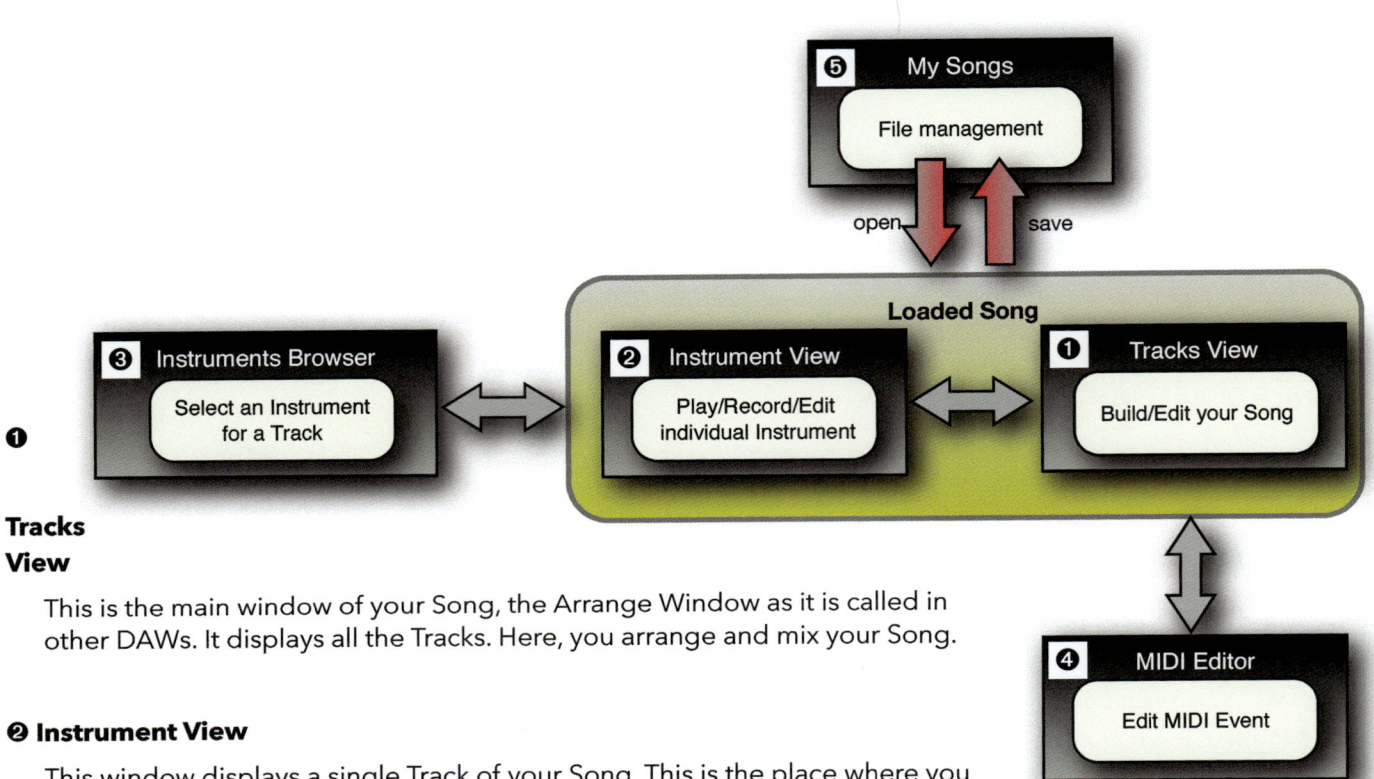

Tracks View

This is the main window of your Song, the Arrange Window as it is called in other DAWs. It displays all the Tracks. Here, you arrange and mix your Song.

❷ Instrument View

This window displays a single Track of your Song. This is the place where you edit the Instrument assigned to that Track similar to the Editor Window in GarageBand X. As we will see later, the recording on a Track can only be done in this window.

❸ Instrument Browser

This is the window that opens up when you launch GarageBand for the first time. When creating new Tracks for your Song, you will go to this window to assign an Instrument to that new Track.

❹ MIDI Editor

This window lets you edit the MIDI Events inside a MIDI Region.

❺ My Songs Browser

This is the file management window that includes everything to get stuff in an out of your GarageBand app.

Window Navigation

Now let's look at how to switch between those windows. iOS apps don't have a Main Menu or Key Commands to switch to various windows nor can you have multiple windows open at the same time. You are always in one (full screen) window view and you have to understand the underlying hierarchy how to get from one window to the other.

🟡 Hierarchy

First, think of the *Tracks View* ❶ and the *Instrument View* ❷ as the representation of your currently loaded Song. They provide the two different *Views* that you use when working on your Song. The Tracks View displays all the Tracks in your Song and the Instrument View displays only one Track with more details about the Instrument that is assigned to that Track.

Those two main windows have in common a Control Bar at the top, which contains the window navigation buttons to switch to a different window.

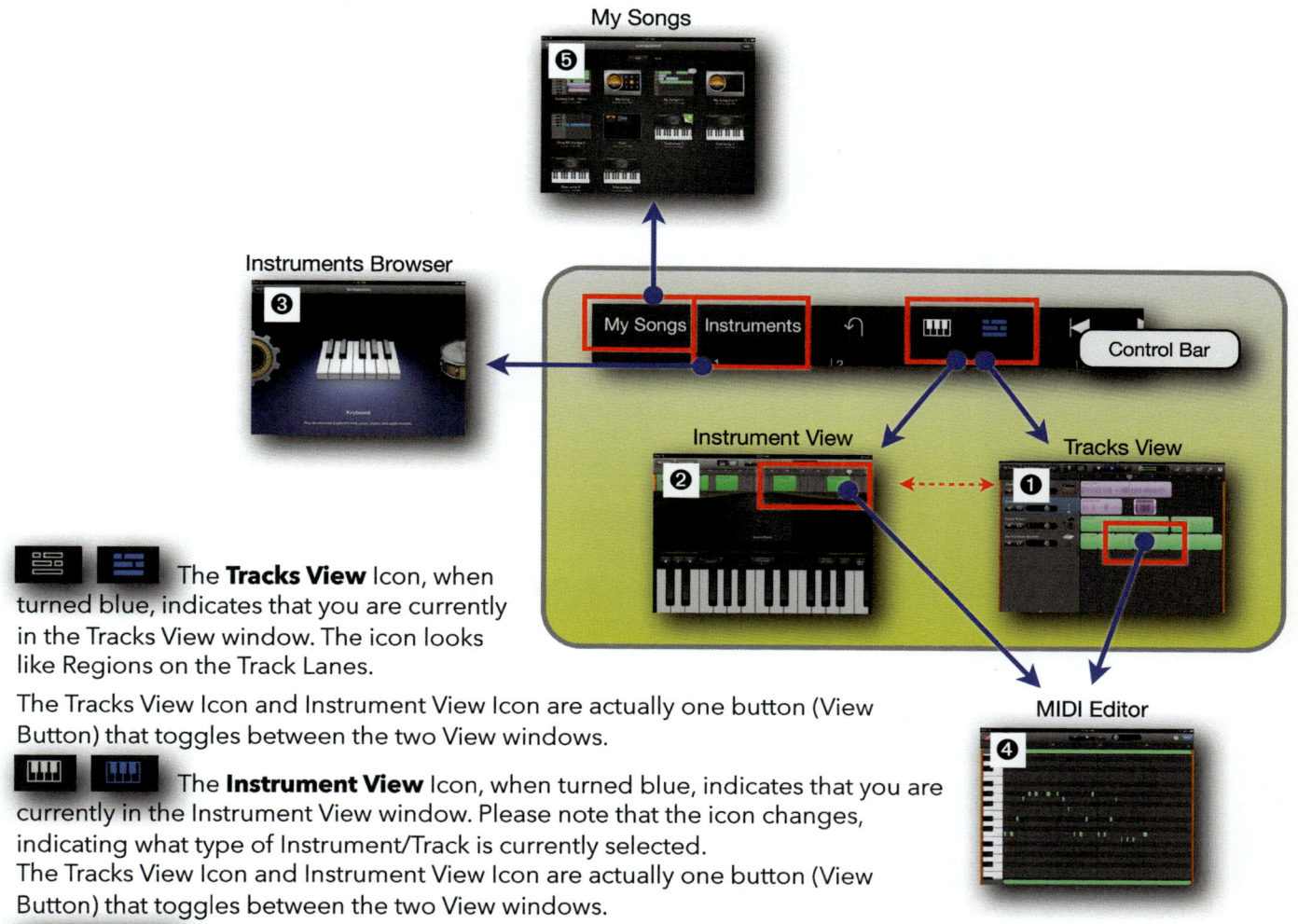

The **Tracks View** Icon, when turned blue, indicates that you are currently in the Tracks View window. The icon looks like Regions on the Track Lanes.

The Tracks View Icon and Instrument View Icon are actually one button (View Button) that toggles between the two View windows.

The **Instrument View** Icon, when turned blue, indicates that you are currently in the Instrument View window. Please note that the icon changes, indicating what type of Instrument/Track is currently selected.

The Tracks View Icon and Instrument View Icon are actually one button (View Button) that toggles between the two View windows.

Instruments The **Instruments** Button switches to the Instrument Browser ❸ window that lets you select a new Instrument. You can go back to the Tracks or Instrument View from where you came from or make an Instrument selection (by *tapping* on an Instrument), which switches always to the Instrument View.

My Songs The **My Songs** Button switches to the My Songs Browser ❺. However, there is more going on with this button. It functions as a Save button. Whenever you *tap* that button to go to the My Songs Browser, the current Song will be saved (and technically closed). You only get back to the main window by selecting a Song (the same or a different one), which is actually an "Open" command that loads that Song.

There is "*no button*" for the fifth full screen window, the MIDI Editor Window ❹. It can be accessed from the Tracks View or Instrument View when *double-tapping* on a MIDI Region.

Additional Windows

Besides these five main windows, GarageBand has two kinds of pop windows to interact with the application. They are standard iOS windows and behave the same way.

These smaller windows pop up as an overlay when you tap on a specific icon or an object on the screens that functions as a button. The open window has a little triangle that points to the icon or object from where they pop up. You close the window by *tapping* on the icon again or somewhere outside that window. If the window contains a command, then executing it will often automatically close the window too.

➡ *Popup Windows*

These windows range from small windows for making a quick selection or switch a function on or off, up to more elaborate windows with different window panes and even more windows to browse inside this popup menu.

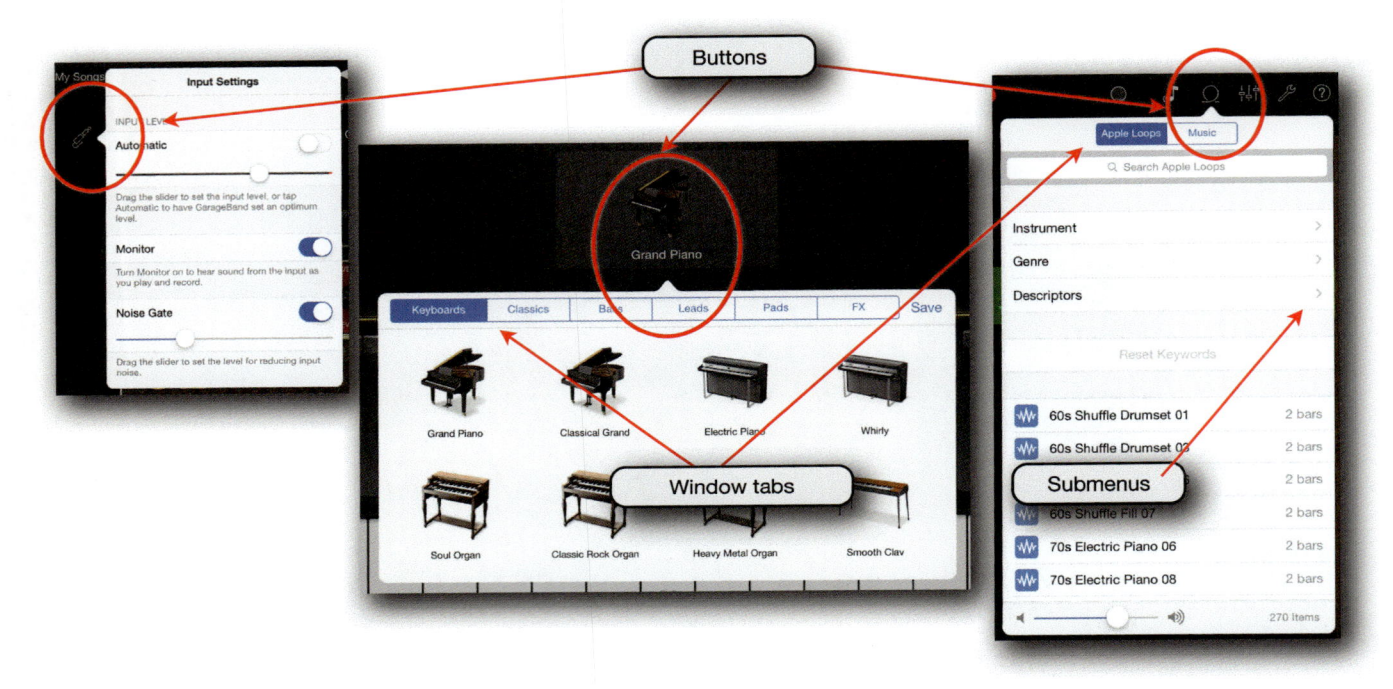

➡ *Control Strip*

Some popup windows contain only a row of commands that get executed when you tap on it. As we will see later, one of the commands is even used to get to one of the five main windows, the MIDI Editor Window.

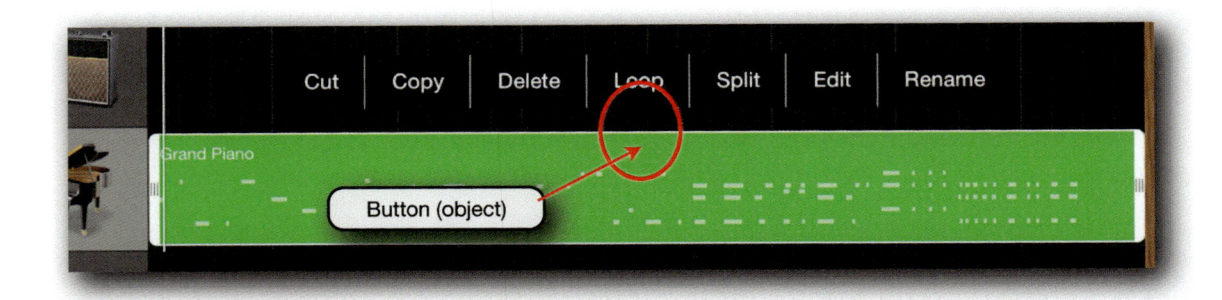

Touch and Gestures

As with any other iOS application, instead of using the mouse and key commands, GarageBand relies on Touch and Gestures to interact with the application. These are the main commands:

- ▶ **Tap**: Tap (and release) with one finger on an item (button, object, or a specific area on the screen). This behaves like the single mouse click.
- ▶ **Double-tap**: Tap twice with one finger on an item. This is similar to a double click with the mouse.
- ▶ **Tap-hold**: Tap on an item without lifting your finger. This is like clicking and holding the mouse.
- ▶ **Swipe** (move): Tap-hold on an object and move your finger to one direction (left, right, up, down, depending on the command). The object will move along with your finger.
- ▶ **Swipe** (flick): Tap-hold on an area and move your finger quickly to one direction and release it like quickly flipping a page.
- ▶ **Pinch/Spread**: Tap-hold with two fingers (thumb and index finger) and move them closer together (pinch) or apart (spread) from each other.
- ▶ **Others**: There a few special gestures like tapping with two fingers or tap-hold one finger and tap with a second finger. These gestures are used, for example, in the Drums Instrument for various playing techniques.

Finally, we are diving into GarageBand to start our first Song. Because this is an iOS app, which behaves differently than a usual desktop app, the procedures are not necessarily as expected. You are not greeted by the Project Chooser window like in GarageBand X to start a new GarageBand Project. GarageBand on the iPad doesn't even use the term "Project", common in GarageBand X and other DAWs. I'll discuss that in the File Management chapter.

The Instrument Browser is the window that opens up when you launch GarageBand for the first time on your iPad. It is a very simple window with 10 different Instrument Types to choose from. There is an additional Instrument when you have "Inter-App Audio " apps (IAA) installed on your iPad. More on that topic in the last chapter.

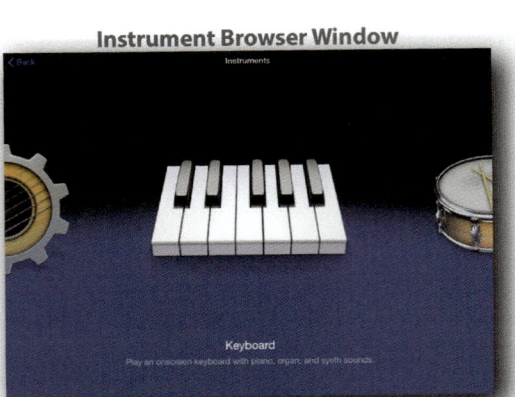

Instrument Browser Window

You see the icon of one Instrument at a time in the center of the screen with its name and a short description below it. On the left and right edge of the window you see the next Instrument.

 Swipe left or right to scroll to the next Instrument Type (like on a carousel).

 Tap the Instrument in the middle to select it. This will close the window and open the Instrument View window.

 Tap the "Back" button at the top control bar to close the Instrument Browser (like a Cancel Button) and return to the window from where you tapped the Instrument Button, the Tracks View or Instrument View.

Here you can see the importance of the relationship between Instruments and Tracks. In real life, you have to gather a Band (or any ensemble) to play your music (your Song). In GarageBand you "gather" your Band by choosing the Instrument Types in the Instrument Browser. GarageBand then creates a Track with that Instrument assigned to it. Every time you want to add a new Instrument to your "Band", you go back to the Instrument Browser, select another Instrument, and GarageBand adds a new Track with that Instrument assignment to your Song. You can have up to 32 Band members (Tracks) in one Song.

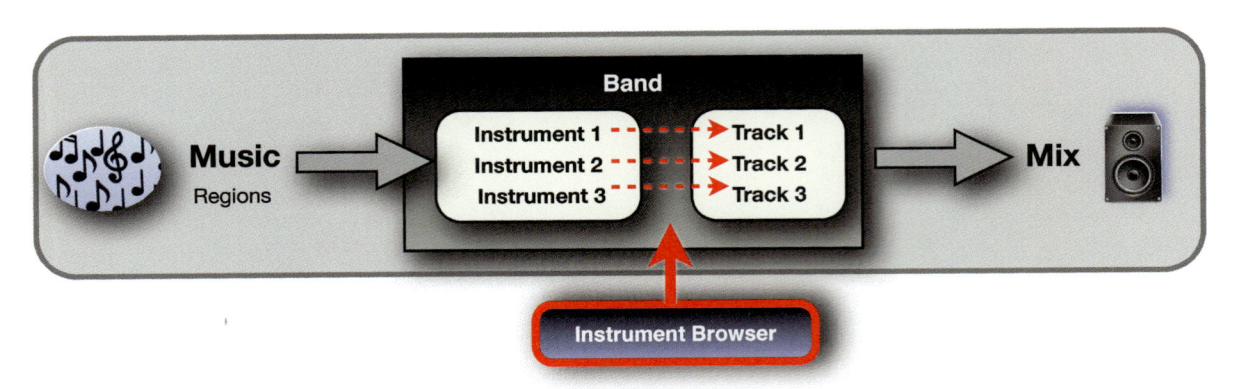

Please note, you are not choosing from 10 different "**Instruments**", you choose "**Instrument Types**".

Now the question is, what is the difference between *Instruments* and *Instrument Types*. When you scroll through the Instrument Browser, you may recognize familiar instrument names like Keyboards, Drums, and Sampler. But you may also wonder how "Guitar Amp" or "Audio Recorder" is an instrument. Remember, GarageBand 11 specified an Audio Track as a "Real Instrument". This is a similar confusion with the terminology because GarageBand tries to avoid using the technical term "Track" altogether and uses "Instrument" instead. You have to stretch your imagination a bit and consider a "Guitar Amp" an Instrument (thinking about the actual guitar that is connected to the amp) and also think of an Audio Recorder, which is a microphone input, as an Instrument (representing the instrument it is recording, including vocals as the most versatile instruments of all).

Here is the list of the 10 Instrument Types, grouped in a way I will explain in a minute:

10 Instrument Types

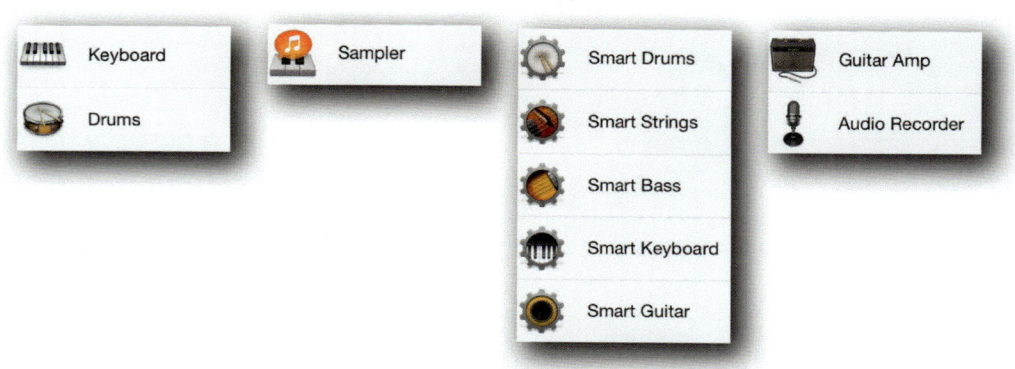

By selecting a specific Instrument Type, GarageBand creates a Track/Instrument with specific configurations:

 **User Interface**

The first characteristic of a specific Instrument Type is its distinct user interface. Every Instrument Type provides a different user interface with different controls and settings that are suitable for that type of Instrument. Remember, the iPad is a touch device that uses the touch interface (your fingers) to "play" an instrument and Apple has come up with some amazing and innovative new ways on how to "play" those Instruments. More about that a little later.

Patch

Once you select a specific Instrument Type, you can choose sound variations for that specific Type (Patches). For example, when selecting Keyboard, it offers a variety of keyboards (organ, synth, piano). When selecting Drums, it offers a variety of drums (acoustic drum sets, electric drum sets, beat boxes). When selecting Guitar Amp, it offers a variety of different amps, etc.

Track Type

This aspect is the least obvious one but the most important. As I mentioned before, GarageBand tries to avoid the terminology of *Tracks* and focuses on *Instruments* instead. That means the GarageBand user interface ignores the existence of different Track Types and won't indicate which Instrument Type creates which of those fundamentally different Tracks. This could lead to some confusion later on.

The following page might seem to be a little bit too technical for the casual user. However, it is important to understand this concept and it is not that complicated once you wrap your head around it.

> Selecting an <u>Instrument</u> Type creates one of three <u>Track</u> Types

So there are three types of Tracks (two types of Audio Tracks and one MIDI Track), similar to GarageBand X (which has a fourth Track Type, the Drummer Track).

Here is a diagram of the simplified signal flow that demonstrates the differences between the three Track Types and the containing components that make them different. This shows the anatomy of a Track, representing the third stage, the Channel Strip, in the 3-part relationship "Instrument-Track-Channel" that I explained earlier:

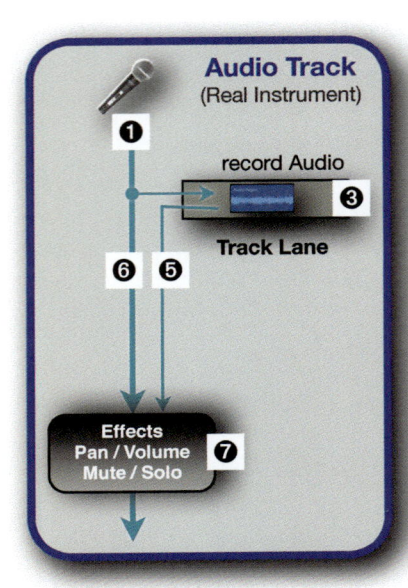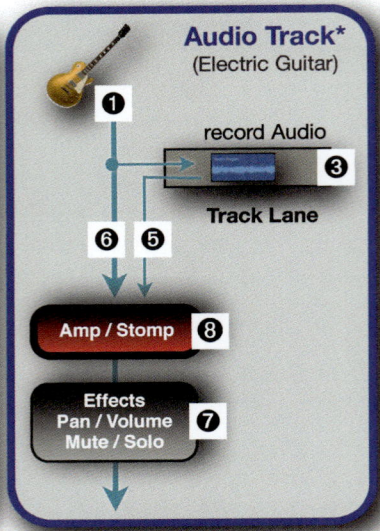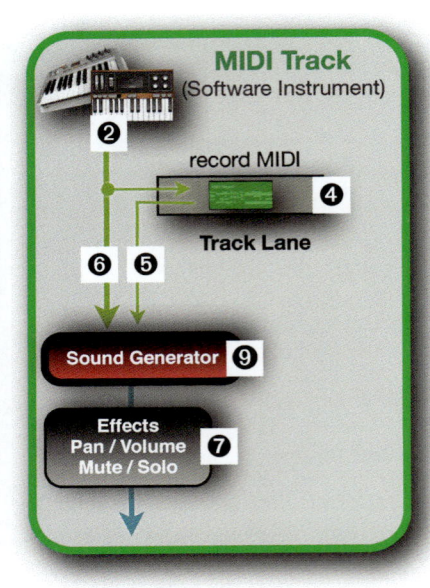

- 🔘 **Input**: The first question is, what type of input signal is the Track expecting. As we know from the earlier chapter, there are two kinds of signals:
    - ▶ Audio Signal ❶: from the iPad microphone (low quality!) or the audio signal from an external device.
    - ▶ MIDI Signal ❷: from the instrument's touch interface when playing it or a MIDI signal from an external MIDI Keyboard.
- 🔘 **Recording**: Recording a signal in your Song will create a Region on the Track Lane. An Audio signal will be recorded as a blue Audio Region ❸ and a MIDI signal will be recorded as a green MIDI Region ❹.
- 🔘 **Playing**: The signal you hear on the Track is either the recorded Region ❺ (when GarageBand is playing back your Song), or the input signal ❻ of the selected Instrument that you are currently playing (when GarageBand is not in Play Mode).
- 🔘 **Signal Processing**: The signal on the Track is then going through various components ❼ that enable you to treat the sound sonically (Effects, Volume, Pan).

However, if you look closely at the signal flow of those three Tracks, you will see an additional component. That component defines the difference of the three Track Types:

- ▶ **Audio Track**: The Track has no additional components, a standard Audio Track.
- ▶ **Audio Track***: The Track has an additional Amp/Stompbox component ❽ that makes the signal sound as if it were played through a guitar amp and stompboxes.
- ▶ **MIDI Track**: The Track has the additional Sound Generator components ❾. The Sound Generator or Sound Module is like a MIDI Synthesizer. It receives the MIDI signal and plays that information as an audio signal with any sound that you select on that module.

Now let's look at the 10 Instrument Types and divide them into groups based on their differences. As I mentioned in the Interface chapter, the Instrument View Button changes its icon to indicate what Instrument Type the currently selected Track is.

➡ **MIDI Instruments - MIDI Tracks**

The following Instruments create a MIDI Track. When you play any of the following instruments, they create MIDI Events, which will be recorded as green MIDI Regions. Those Tracks are also called "Software Instruments" in GarageBand X.

⦿ Standard Instruments

The Keyboard Instrument provides a standard musical keyboard interface that you can play by touching the keys (plus other controls). The Drums Instrument provides an interface with pads or virtual drums that you can tap, similar to a drum machine.

⦿ Smart Instruments

Smart Instruments are also MIDI instruments, but with unique new interfaces. Each one of these five Smart Instruments lets you "play" it in a way that is more intuitive and fun and gets you better, more realistic results than, for example, playing a string instrument with a standard musical keyboard.

⦿ Sampler Instruments

The Sampler Instrument is also a MIDI Instrument that you play with the standard musical keyboard. Its specialty is that you can record an audio signal (sample) with your iPad and trigger it (play it) with the keyboard. You can use that to play your own sound effects.

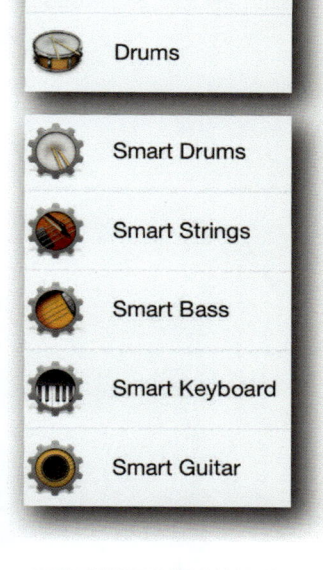

➡ **Audio "Instruments" - Audio Tracks**

The following two Instruments create an Audio Track that records blue Audio Regions.

⦿ Audio Recorder

This is the standard Audio Track that you use to record any audio signal.

⦿ Guitar Amp

This is the other Audio Track that has the additional Amp component in the signal flow. You would use this for recording electric guitars (although you can use it for any audio signal if you want to experiment with it). If you look at the previous diagram again, then you will realize that the audio signal is recorded dry, "before" the amp simulator. That means that you can change the guitar sound any time after you recorded the signal, which would not be possible if you had recorded the actual guitar amp with a microphone.

⦿ (Inter-App Audio)

Although this "Instrument" can also appear in the Instrument Browser (if at least one Inter-App Audio app is installed on your iPad), it is more like a Plugin that is added to an existing Instrument. More about "Inter-App Audio" in the last chapter of the book.

Navigation

Here are the different ways to navigate through the Instruments Browser window:

 The first time you open GarageBand, the Instrument Browser window will be displayed.

Tap the Instruments Button ❶ in the Control Bar of the Tracks View or the Instrument View.

Tap the plus sign ❷ at the bottom of the Track Area in the Tracks View.

Tap-hold on the Instruments Button. This opens a popup menu ❸ with all the 10 available Instrument Types. It works like a shortcut without switching to the Instruments Browser window. Please note that the Inter-App Audio icon will not be displayed in this list because it is technically not an Instrument Type but rather a Plugin.

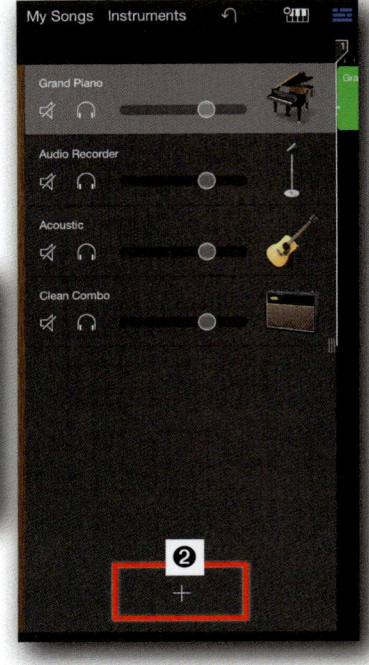
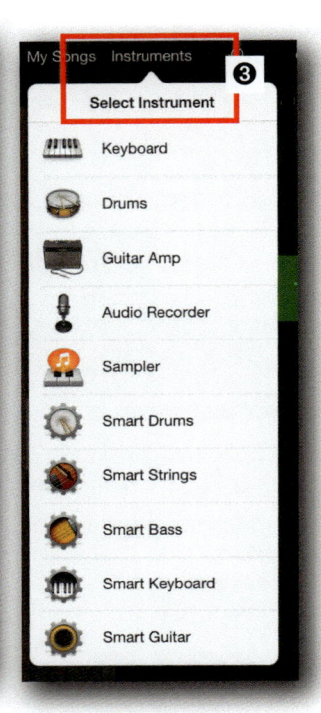

Restrictions

Once you've created a Track with a specific Instrument Type, you can switch to different Instrument Types to change its assignment. For example, if you created a Track with a Keyboard Instrument, you can then change it to a Smart Keyboard or even a Guitar Amp.

However, this is only possible as long as you haven't recorded anything on that Track yet. If there are any Regions on the Track Lane for a Track, then you cannot change the Instrument Type assignment for that Track anymore. GarageBand will instead create a new Track with that Instrument assignment. If you have reached the maximum Track count already in your Song (up to 32, depending on your iDevice), then you will get an error message.

5 - Tracks View (Arrange Window)

After you've selected your first Instrument Type in the Instrument Browser, GarageBand will switch to the *Instrument View* window. But let's explore the *Tracks View* first.

Interface

I've already talked about the Arrange Window as the most common element in all DAWs. This is the place where you arrange, edit, and mix your song. Although the Tracks View has a Record Button, recording is done in the Instrument View. When you press the Record Button, it switches automatically to the Instrument View.

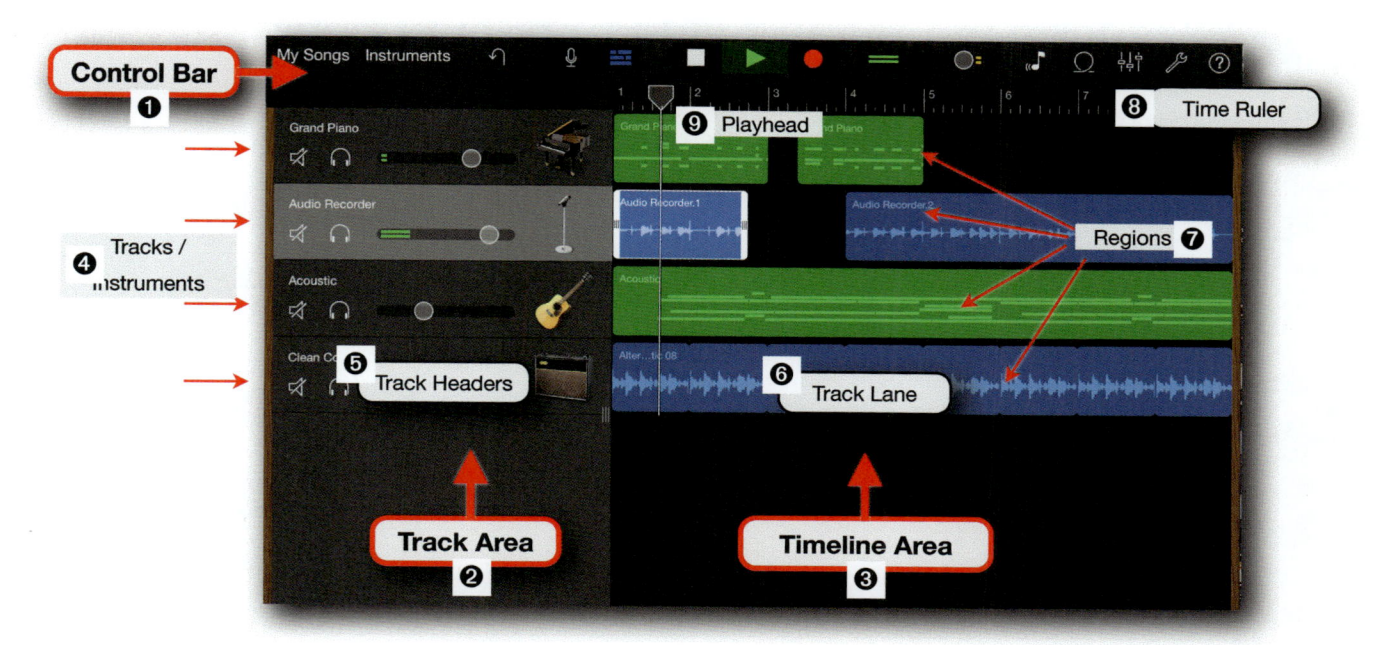

The Tracks View has three window panes (sections):

❶ Control Bar: This horizontal strip on top contains the navigation buttons, the Transport Controls, the Level Meter, and a couple of buttons to access various popup windows. The Volume Slider on top of the Level Meter controls the playback volume for your iPad and, other than that, has no direct affect on your Song.

❷ Track Area: This section on the left lists all the available Tracks as separate rows.

❸ Timeline Area: The section on the right is an extension of those rows. This is your Workspace.

- Each Row represents an individual **Track ❹** with its assigned Instrument.
- The Track Area on the left displays the individual **Track Headers ❺** with their basic mix controls.
- The Timeline Area on the right extends each Track into its **Track Lane ❻** that holds the Regions, the actual music.
- On top of the Timeline Area is the Time Ruler ❽ that is connected to (moves with) the Track Lanes.
- Along the Time Ruler is the Playhead ❾, extending vertically as a thin white line across the Track Lanes to indicate the current position in the Song.
- If the Timeline Area displays the whole Song Section, then the Playhead moves from left to right when playing. If the Timeline Area is zoomed in, then the Playhead switches to "Autoscroll". That means it locks its position when it reaches the center of the Timeline Area and now the Timeline Area moves underneath the stationary Playhead. *Tap* anywhere in the Timeline Area to "unlock" the Playhead while in Play Mode.

Control Bar

The Control Bar, visible in Tracks View and Instrument View, has four sections:

Main Windows Buttons (+Undo)   **Transport Controls**   **Meter / Volume**   **Popup Window Buttons (+Help)**

➡ *Main Window Buttons*

My Songs Button

- ■ *Tap* this button to switch to the *My Songs Browser*. Please note that this will close (after saving) the current Song.

Instruments Button

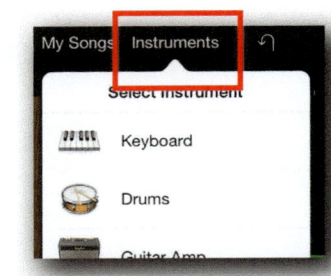

- ■ *Tap* this button to switch to the Instrument Browser window.
- ■ *Tap-hold* this button to open a popup menu that lets you select any of the 10 Instrument Types without leaving the current page.

Undo Button

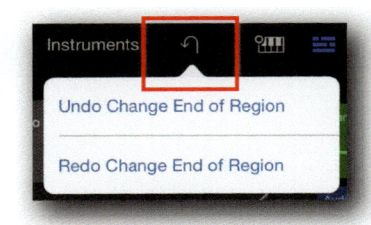

- ■ *Tap* this button to undo the last action.
- ■ *Tap-hold* this button to open a popup menu with two buttons. The upper button is the *Undo* command with a description of what that action was. The button beneath is the *Redo* command with the description of that action.

The Undo Button is only visible if you performed any action that can be undone.

View Button (Instrument View icon - Tracks View Icon)

- ■ *Tap* this button to switch between the Instrument View and the Tracks View.

Please note that this is a linked double button. It doesn't matter where you tap. It always switches to the other View. Remember that the Control Bar remains, only the window view below changes when switching views. The currently active view is indicated by the blue icon. The Instrument Icon changes to indicate what Instrument is currently selected.

➡ *Transport Controls*

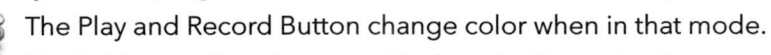

Stop mode

Play mode

Record mode

There are only three transport buttons and no forward or rewind button because you can *tap* right onto the Time Ruler or *slide* the Playhead directly.

- ■ The Play and Record Button change color when in that mode.
- ■ The left button functions as a "Back to the Beginning" transport and changes to a Stop button when in Play or Record mode.

  Please note that "Back to the Beginning" doesn't mean the beginning of the Song. GarageBand uses a feature called *Song Sections* and this button means "Back to the Beginning of the *current Song Section*". More details about that later.

➡ *Meter / Volume*

Please pay attention to the actual functionality of this control because it might be different from what you expect.

⬤ Master Volume Meter

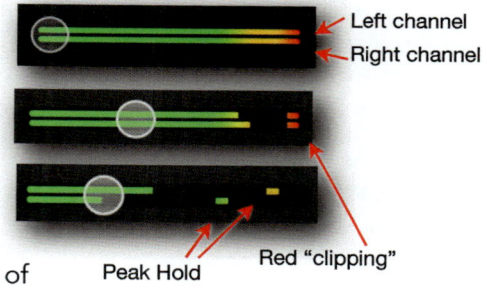

Left channel
Right channel

This stereo colored meter indicates the level of your mix. This is how your Song gets exported so make sure the level is not too low, but also not too high.

- The color segments indicate how strong your signal is, from green to yellow up to the highest level of red.

- The red "clipping" LED on the right is telling you that the mix level of your Song is to high, which could result in distortion (your mix is "clipping"). Once you hit the red light, it stays on even after you stop your Song. It will be reset when you hit the Play Button again or *tap* on the big circle inside, the Playback Volume slider.

- Peak Hold: The LED indicating the highest level always stays on for about two seconds so you can read the meter better if it moves very quickly up and down. This common feature is called Peak Hold.

Peak Hold   Red "clipping"

⬤ Playback Volume Slider

Inside the Level Meter is a big circle (a puck). It is transparent, so you can see the Meter underneath. You can *slide* it left and right like a volume fader. However, it does NOT control the volume of your mix! This is not a Master Fader, common on mixing consoles and virtually every DAW. A Master Fader would control the overall level of your mix. This Volume Slider only sets the playback volume of your iPad and does not affect your Song's mix level.

When you move the slider, the iPad Speaker Control indicator pops up on the screen in the same way as when you change the playback volume with the hardware volume button on the side of your iPad.

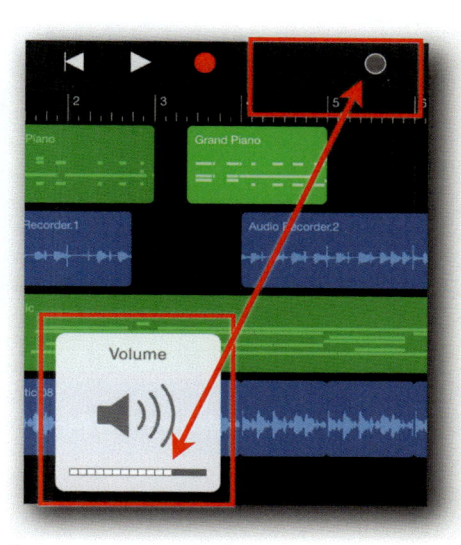

➡ *Popup Window Buttons*

The five icons on the right of the Control Bar function as buttons to open specific popup windows.

Jam Session Configuration Window

 ### Jam Session

The word "to jam" in musical terms means that you play together with other musicians, mostly to improvise instead of practicing a specific tune.

You can also jam with other GarageBand users who run GarageBand on their iDevice by syncing the GarageBand Songs together (as long as they are on the same Wi-Fi or Bluetooth network).

This window lets you configure the setup. I will explain the details in a later chapter.

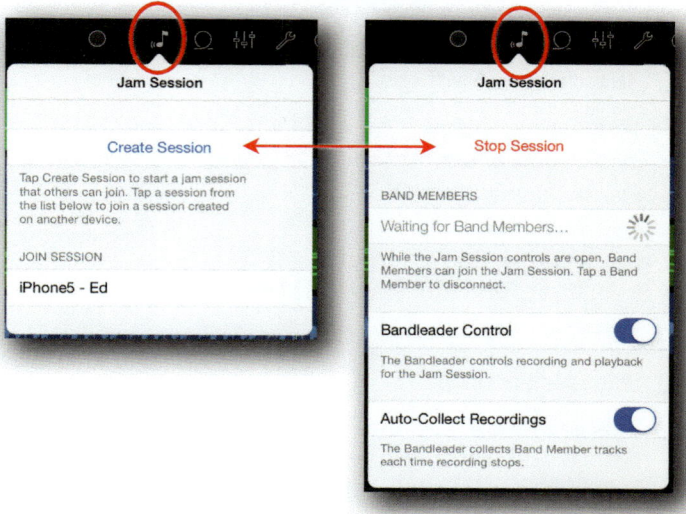

Loop Browser (Media Browser)

Media Browser Window

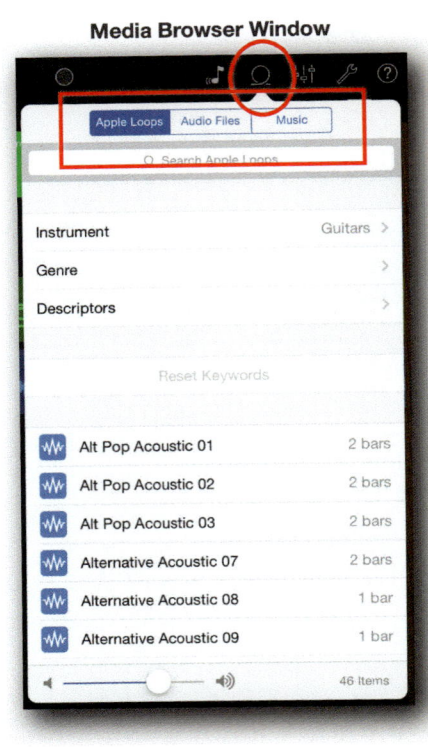

This window functions as a combination of the Loop Browser and the Media Browser. It has a maximum of three tabs at the top to switch to different windows inside the popup window. I will discuss the details in the File Management chapter. Here is just a quick overview:

- **Apple Loops**: This tab is like a mini Loop Browser.
- **Audio Files**: This tab displays the audio files that are currently synchronized via iTunes File Sharing between your iDevice and your desktop computer. The tab is only visible if you have shared files.
- **Music**: This tab switches the view to display the audio files of your iTunes Library on your computer that are currently synced to your iDevice. The tab is only visible if you have files synced to your iDevice.

 Track Settings

This popup window functions as a mini Channel Strip on a Mixing Console with the limitation that you can only see one Channel Strip (one window) at a time.

The window functions as an *Inspector,* which means, "it stays open and changes its content depending on what object you select in a main window". Here, the main window is the current Tracks View and the objects from which you choose are the Tracks that you **tap** on (on the Track Icon). **Tapping** anywhere else outside the window will close the popup window.

Opening this popup window in the Instrument View will display the Settings for the selected Instrument.

The window is divided into the header and two or three sections. Which section and which controls are displayed depends on the selected Track. I will go over the details later.

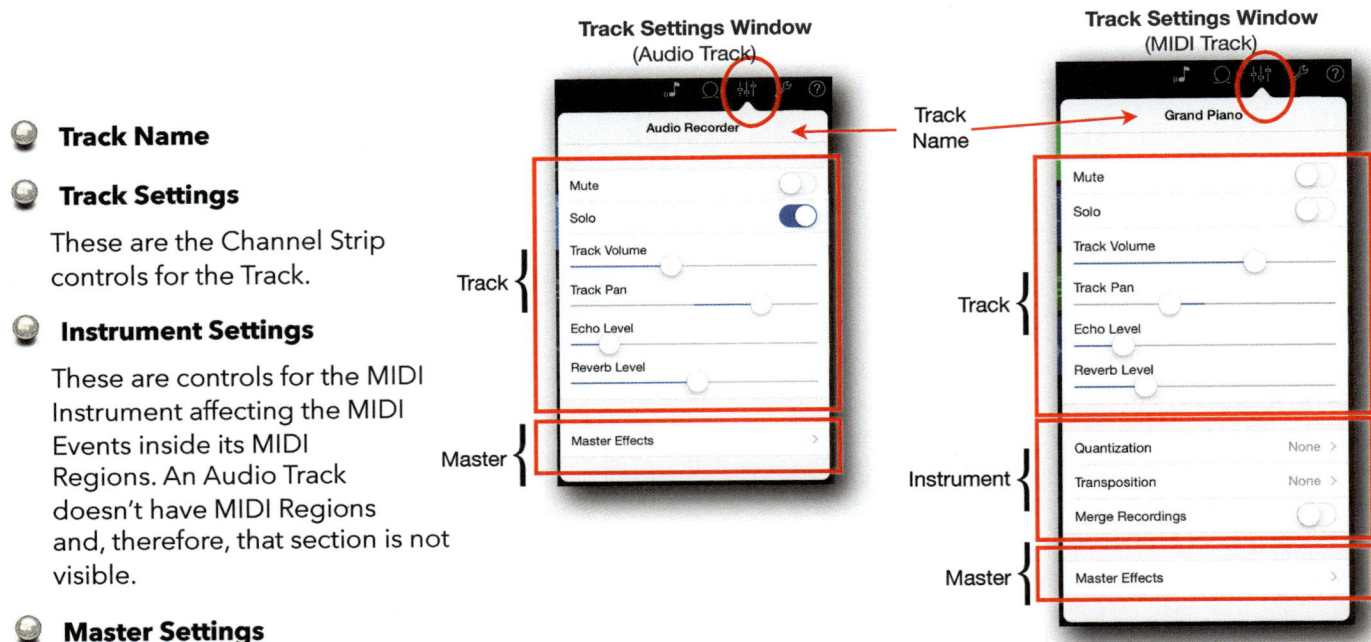

- **Track Name**

- **Track Settings**

  These are the Channel Strip controls for the Track.

- **Instrument Settings**

  These are controls for the MIDI Instrument affecting the MIDI Events inside its MIDI Regions. An Audio Track doesn't have MIDI Regions and, therefore, that section is not visible.

- **Master Settings**

  This is another Channel Strip control, usually referred to as *Aux Sends*. Here, they are called Master Effects and they behave the same as in GarageBand 11. GarageBand X has only limited support for these Master Effects.

Song Settings

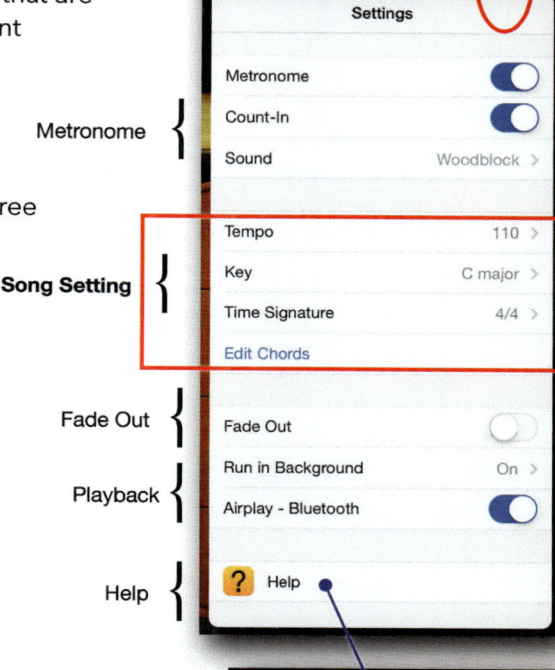

This window has different types of controls. They include settings that are stored with your Song, but also settings that are Song independent (Preferences).

I'll cover them in more details in the "Create your Song" chapter. Here is a quick overview:

☑ Various Settings, including the Song Settings, referred to as "Project Settings" in GarageBand X. These are the three musical characteristics of a Song:
Tempo - Key Signature - Time Signature

☑ Basic Preference Settings that defines how the application behaves (Song independent).

☑ Help Menu. This button opens the integrated online Help Menu window, which gets overlaid on top of the current view (requires an Internet connection!)

Smart Guides

The Info Button is the last button on the Control Bar. Instead of opening a window, it will activate various Helper Tags that get overlaid on top of the current window to explain the functionality of some of the controls and buttons.

The Info Button turns yellow when activated . It stays activated even when switching between windows. This is especially helpful when switching to various Instruments with their different user interfaces. *Tap* the button again to deactivate it.

If a Helper Tag has an arrow, then you can *tap* on it to switch to the built-in Help Menu explaining that functionality in more details.

This button is extremely helpful with the Touch Instruments, especially the Drums, where it indicates where to tap and with what gestures.

Smart Guides activated

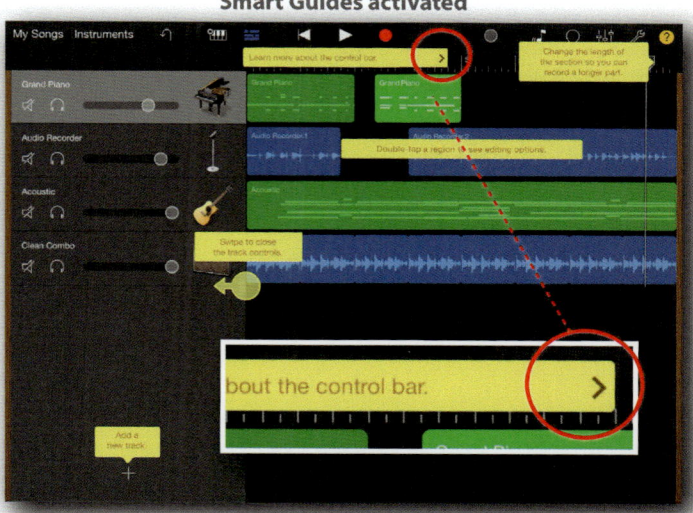

When going through the various controls of the Tracks View window, always keep in mind the three functions of a standard music production process that are all combined in GarageBand's Tracks.

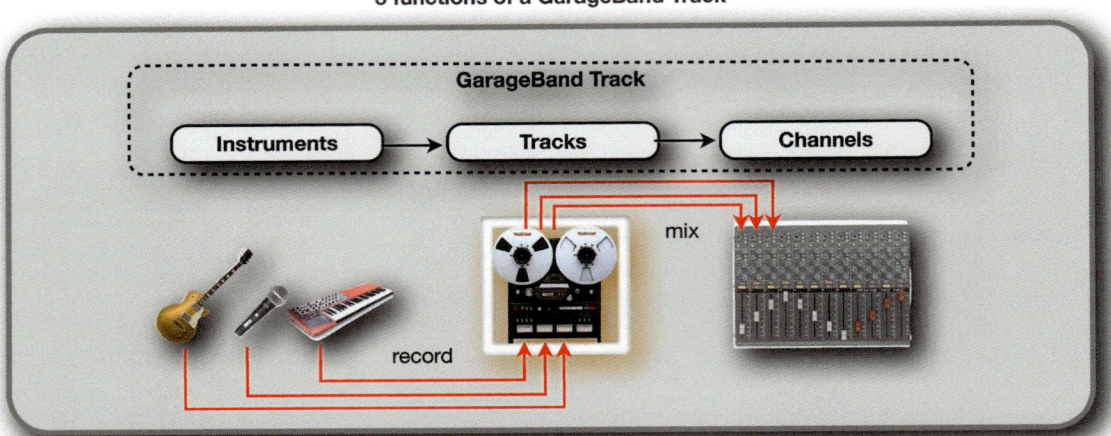

3 functions of a GarageBand Track

- By choosing an Instrument Type in the Instrument Browser, we define the type of Track that represents that **Instrument**. From now on, the Instrument and the Track are referring to the same component in GarageBand.
- The next section, the Tape Machine, is represented by the Timeline Area where you record the Instruments on those **Tracks**.
- The next section, the **Channels**, are represented by the Track Area with the controls of a virtual Mixing Console that the Track is connected to (GarageBand doesn't have a separate Mixer Window). With this third function, Instrument, Track, and Channel are now merged into one unit represented as one row in the Tracks View.

The Track Area on the left side of the Tracks View displays all the available Tracks (aka Instruments, aka Channels).

➡ *Track Area Display Mode*

The Track Area has two display modes, open or close. The divider line between the Track Area and the Timeline Area has a handle in the middle that can switch between them.

- **Close**: *Swipe* the handle (or any Track Icon) to the left to close the Track Area so only the Track Icons are visible.
- **Open**: *Swipe* the handle (or any Track Icon) to the right to open it again and reveal all the controls on the Track Header.

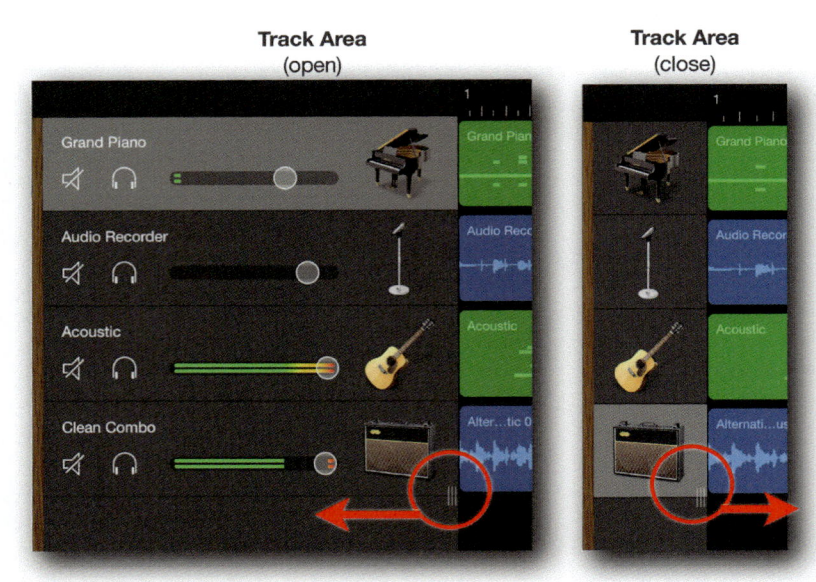

Track Area
(open)

Track Area
(close)

➡ *Track Header*

The Track Area represents a mini-Mixing Console with the Track Header as the very "limited" Channel Strips. To access more controls of that virtual Channel Strip you have to open the Track Settings Window as we have just seen in the Control Bar section.

Track Header

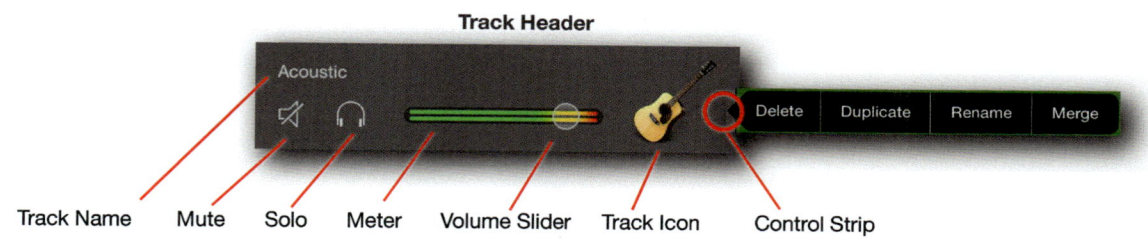

Track Name   Mute   Solo   Meter   Volume Slider   Track Icon   Control Strip

🟡 Track Name

The Track inherits its name from the selected Patch of the current Instrument. However, you can overwrite the Track Name and give it your own name with the "Rename" command from the Control Strip.

🟡 Mute

Tap the Mute Button to silence this Track. The button will turn blue when active (muted). This button is available on all common Mixing Consoles which lets you quickly mute a specific Track in the mix. *Tap-hold* on a button and *slide* across multiple Tracks to change the Mute Button for all those Tracks.

🟡 Solo

Tap the Solo Button to mute all other Tracks. You can enable Solo Mode on more than one Track. *Tap* again to disable Solo Mode. This button is also available on all common Mixing Consoles and lets you listen very quickly to a single Track in isolation. *Tap-hold* on a button and *slide* across multiple Tracks to change the Solo Button for all those Tracks.

🟡 Meter

This LED Meter displays the level of that Track (left channel is the upper LED, right is the lower LED). The color segments indicate how strong your signal is, from green to yellow up to the highest level of red.

- The red "clipping" LED is telling you that the level on that Track is too high. Once you hit the red light, it stays on even after you stop your Song. It will be reset when you hit the Play Button again or *tap* on the big circle inside, the Volume Slider.

Left channel
Right channel

Peak Hold   Red "clipping"

🟡 Volume Slider

The Volume Slider represents the Fader on a Channel Strip. Here it is a transparent circle (on top of the Meter) that you can *swipe* left and right on the Meter to raise or lower the volume of that Track. *Double-tap* to reset the level to 0dB (WIKI-Moment: dB, Decibel). Please note that the Meter displays the signal after the Volume Slider, which means the lower the Volume Slider, the lower the resulting level on that Track.

🟡 Track Icon

The Track Icon has multiple functions. It displays the type of Instrument that is assigned to the Track. *Tap* to select the Track. Also, when you *double-tap* on the icon, it switches the window to display the Instrument View for that Track.

🟡 Control Strip

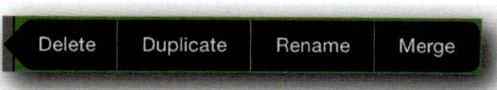

If you *tap* on the selected Track Header right next to the Track Icon, a Control Strip with four buttons pops up. *Tap* on one of them to delete, duplicate, or rename the current Track. I explain the Merge feature in the next section.

➡ **Manage Tracks**

🌑 Add Tracks

Use the plus button at the bottom of the Track Area to add a new Track. The selected Instrument defines which one of the three Track types is created:

- Audio Track
- Audio Track (with amp simulator)
- MIDI Track

🌑 Select a Track

Selected Track (highlighted)

Tap the Track Icon of a Track to select that Track. The Track Header will be highlighted.

🌑 Duplicate Tracks

Tap on the area next to the Track Icon you want to duplicate. This pops up the Control Strip where you can *tap* on the Duplicate Button.

🌑 Delete Tracks

Tap on the area next to the Track Icon you want to delete. This pops up the Control Strip where you can *tap* on the Delete Button.

🌑 Rename Tracks

Tap on the area next to the Track Icon to display the Control Strip and *tap* on the Rename Button. The keyboard slides up where you can enter a new name.

🌑 Re-order Tracks

Reorder Tracks

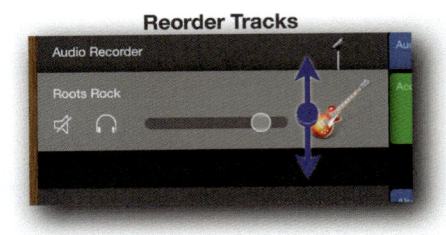

You can *drag* the Track Icon up or down to change the Track order in the Track Area. This is just a visual thing and has no effect on the mix.

🌑 Re-assign Tracks

You can select a different Instrument Type for an existing Track only if there are no Regions on its Track Lane yet. Open the Instrument Browser or *tap-hold* on the Instruments button in the Control Bar to make a new selection.

🌑 Track Limitation

The maximum amount of Tracks you can create in your Song depends on how powerful the chip is in your iDevice. The iPhone 5s with the A7 chip can manage up to 32 Tracks. Use the *Merge* feature if you reach the limit.

🌑 Merge Tracks

Merge Tracks

After *tapping* the Merge command from the Control Strip, the Tracks View window changes.

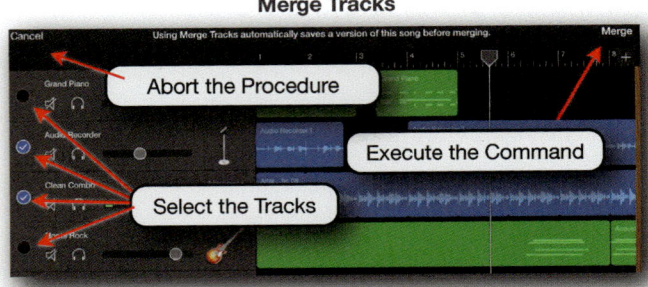

- Each Track Header now displays a circle on the left that lets you select which Track you want to merge.
- The "Merge" Button in the upper right corner executes the Merge command.
- The Cancel Button in the upper left corner aborts the procedure.

Please note that this is a "mixdown procedure". GarageBand mixes all the selected Audio <u>and</u> MIDI Tracks together to a new Audio File. It puts this Audio File as an Audio Region on a newly created Audio Track. The original Tracks are deleted. However, before GarageBand deletes them, it creates a duplicate Song so you can go back to the original "pre-merged" version of your Song.

Timeline Area

- The Timeline Area is the place where you record and edit your Music to create and arrange your Song.
- The Timeline Area (called Workspace in GarageBand X) contains the Track Lanes. These are the extensions of the individual Track Headers. Think of it as the roll of tape on a tape machine or a cassette where you record music on (if you are old enough to have seen one of those "ancient" devices).
- Unlike the Track Area, which is a fixed window area (besides its wide and narrow view mode), the Timeline Area can be scrolled horizontally by *swiping* left and right.
- The *Pinch* or *Spread* gesture lets you zoom in and out horizontally.

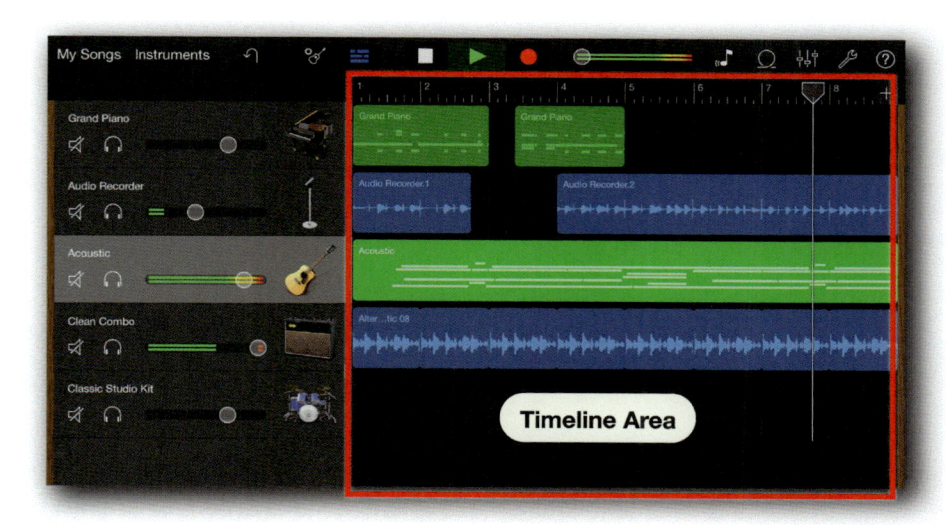

Timeline Ruler

At the top of the Timeline area is the Time Ruler (or Timeline) that divides the Timeline Area vertically into time units. GarageBand can only display Musical Time as bars and beats and not Absolute Time as minutes and seconds.

Playhead

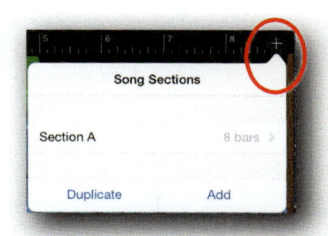

Along the Ruler is the Playhead, the triangle that extends vertically as a white line across the Timeline Area. It indicates the position that the song is currently parked at, or moves across while in Play Mode.

- *Slide* the Playhead left or right to place it at a new position. The Playhead can only be moved by 8th note steps as the finest resolution. Zooming in the Timeline Area will increase that Grid and you can position the Playhead as fine as 64th notes. Zooming in all the way will turn Snap to Grid off. A little tag appears above the Playhead to indicate its bar.beat position while moving it.
- *Tap* on the Ruler to position (jump) the Playhead there. The same zoom related Grid applies.
- *Tap* the "Back to the Beginning" button to position the Playhead at the beginning of your Song Section.
- The Playhead switches to "Autoscroll" if the Timeline is zoomed in. It becomes stationary while the Timeline scrolls underneath. *Tap* on the Timeline while playing to disable Autoscroll.

Song Sections

On the far right of the Time Ruler is a plus button. This opens the *"Song Sections"* window to extend your Song longer than the default 8 bars. I cover that in the "Record your Song" chapter.

Regions

The Regions are the building blocks of your Song that are created or placed on the Track Lanes. More about that also in the "Record your Song" chapter.

6 - Instrument View

While in Tracks View, you can see your whole Band (all the Tracks) playing (all their Regions). In the Instrument View, you look at only one Track at a time, or to be precise, at that one Instrument that is assigned to that Track. There is one special thing about the Instrument View:

➡ Switching to the Instrument View

🔘 **Tap** on the View Button in the Control Bar when in Tracks Views.

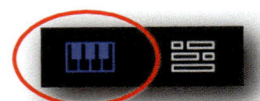

🔘 **Double-tap** on the Track Icon in the Tracks View.

🔘 When you start recording in the Tracks Views, GarageBand switches automatically to the Instrument View.

➡ Window Elements

🌑 Control Bar

The buttons on the Control Bar and their functionality are identical to the Control Bar in the Tracks View. The only exception is the missing Loop Browser Icon on the right

You can switch to a different Instrument in the Instrument View without going back to the Tracks View. **Tap-hold** the View Button. This opens the *Select Track* menu listing all the current Instruments (Tracks) in your Song. **Tap** on one to switch the Instrument View to that Track.

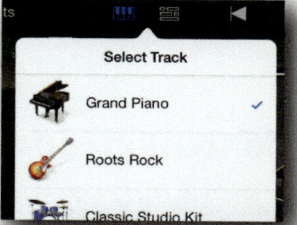

🌑 Time Ruler

The functionality of the Ruler is slightly different:

- Any Regions on the Instrument's Track Lane are now displayed as colored areas directly on the Ruler, indicating where the Regions are located.
- You can zoom in-out with the **Pinch** and **Spread** gesture on the Time Ruler.
- You can move the Playhead along the Time Ruler as usual.

🌑 Control Area

This is the area in the middle where you control the sound of the Instrument. Choose from different Patches and do everything related to the Instrument, the sound source for that Track. Of course, every Instrument Type has a different user interface specific for that type. I will cover that in the separate Instruments chapter.

🌑 Play Area

The lower portion of the window provides the touch interface to play that instrument. That could be a conventional musical keyboard, drum pads, or some exciting new interface choices that GarageBand provides with their Smart Instruments.

Please note that the two "Instruments" that create Audio Tracks (Audio Recorder and Guitar Amp) are not really instruments that you can "play" with a touch interface on your iPad. Therefore, they don't have a Play Area on their Instrument View.

➡ *Single Track Lane View*

**Instrument View
(Single Track Quick Edit)**

As you can see on the Time Ruler, the Regions on that Track are only displayed as areas and you cannot edit them. If you want to do some Region edits, but don't want to switch back to the Tracks View, you can display the full Track Lane view.

- **Swipe** down from the Ruler to open the single Track Lane for that Instrument.
- **Swipe** up from the Control Area or **tap** the View Button to close the Track Lane and return to the default Instrument View.

In Single Track Lane view, you can use the same commands for editing Regions as in the Tracks View. The Control Area and Play Area are dimmed and cannot be used while in this mode.

Now with a basic understanding of the user interface, I want to cover file management next before we learn how to create and edit a Song. This topic is often neglected in manuals, but I think it is worth a full chapter because:

> **GarageBand for the iPad faces a dilemma regarding File Management**

Content-creation Application

GarageBand is a type of app that is referred to as a *"content-creation application"*. These apps create something new from scratch, i.e. a letter in Pages, a spreadsheet in Numbers, or a song in GarageBand. Those "new creations" are then stored as files or documents. Very often, you even import other files (existing content) in the process of creating your new content.

So the important question is, where is all that stuff (those files) stored and how do we get that stuff in and out of our application? The answer is:

❶ Files are stored on drives (hard drives or flash drives) of your device (Mac, iDevice).

❷ You access the files through a "File Management" application, the Finder.

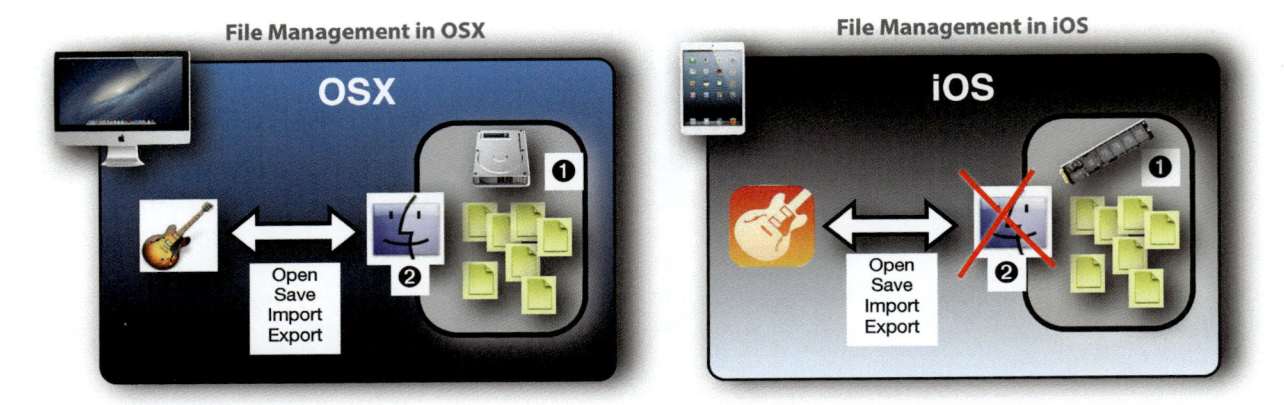

But here is the dilemma:

> **iOS doesn't have a Finder**

◉ No File Management System

There is no file management system available to the user on iDevices like the *Finder* on OSX. This is ok when playing Angry Birds or browsing the web. However, if you use content-creation applications like GarageBand, that content is most likely represented by a file that has to be stored and accessed. iOS uses different (unfamiliar) procedures when dealing with files and you have to be aware and get familiar with those procedures before you start your Song.

◉ iCloud

One way to circumvent a local file system is to store files "in the cloud", which means somewhere on a remote server via the Internet. Apple's cloud solution is called, *iCloud*. This is a fairly new procedure and I will cover that too, so you'll fully understand where and how your GarageBand Songs are stored.

Before diving into the details about File Management, we have to be sure about the meaning of specific terms that are used in that context.

● Project

This term is widely used in content-<u>creation</u> applications that create something new (a song, a movie, or just a text document or spreadsheet that is stored as a new file). iPhoto and iTunes, on the other hand, are content-<u>management</u> applications, apps that manage existing content. You don't usually shoot pictures in iPhoto or record music in iTunes, you just collect and manage pictures and songs in those apps. If the content you are creating in a content-creation app is more complex than just a letter or a spreadsheet, then it is referred to not just a *Document,* but as a *Project,* which is saved as a *Project File*. Remember, these are just names to better describe what's inside a file.

GarageBand in OSX uses the term Project. When you launch the app, it opens up the *Project Chooser* where you create a new Project or choose an existing Project.

● Song

GarageBand on the iPad seems to avoid the term Project altogether. Instead, it uses the friendlier term *Song*. This makes sense because you are working on a song. GarageBand X also lets you create Movie soundtracks besides Songs, so the more generic term Project in that app makes sense. In the end, "Song" or "Project" are just two different words that describe what you are creating.

● Project File (Song File)

Saving a Project in GarageBand X creates a "Project File" with the file extension <u>band</u>. This marks it as a *"GarageBand Project File"*. Project Files can usually be opened only by the application that created them (i.e. GarageBand) or applications that are compatible with it (i.e. Logic). GarageBand on the iPad also saves its Song as a Project File with the extension *band* (even if it doesn't mention it). This makes it upwards-compatible with GarageBand X and Logic. Although a saved Song is technically a "Project File", I refer to it in this manual as a *"Song File"*.

.band
(Project File)

● Audio File

When you want to play the Song that you've created in GarageBand (or any other DAW) in iTunes or upload it to YouTube, SoundCloud, or any other service, you have to "export" it. This process is also called *mix, bounce,* or *share,* which creates an Audio File from the Project that can be played on virtually any audio applications. An Audio File can be in different audio *formats* like mp3 or aiff (*WIKI-Moment: Audio File Format*).

.mp3
(Audio File)

● Open - Save

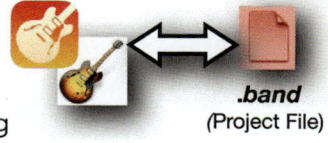

These two commands refer to the Song File. You <u>open</u> a Song File in GarageBand to continue to work on that Song, or you <u>save</u> a Song with the new changes to a Song File to continue to work on it later.

.band
(Project File)

● Share (Export)

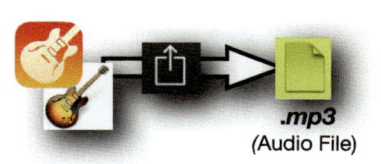

Share is a term that is now commonly used by Apple in most of its content-creation apps. Those apps often have a dedicated Share Menu (or the *Share Button* ⬆️) that includes all the commands to export a Project to a file format that can be shared with (played by) other apps.

.mp3
(Audio File)

Here is a comparison diagram with a (simplified) version of the file management in GarageBand X and GarageBand for the iPad. By just glancing over it, you might get the idea that file management on the iPad is a bit more complex (maybe due to the fact that there is no easy file management in place for the user).

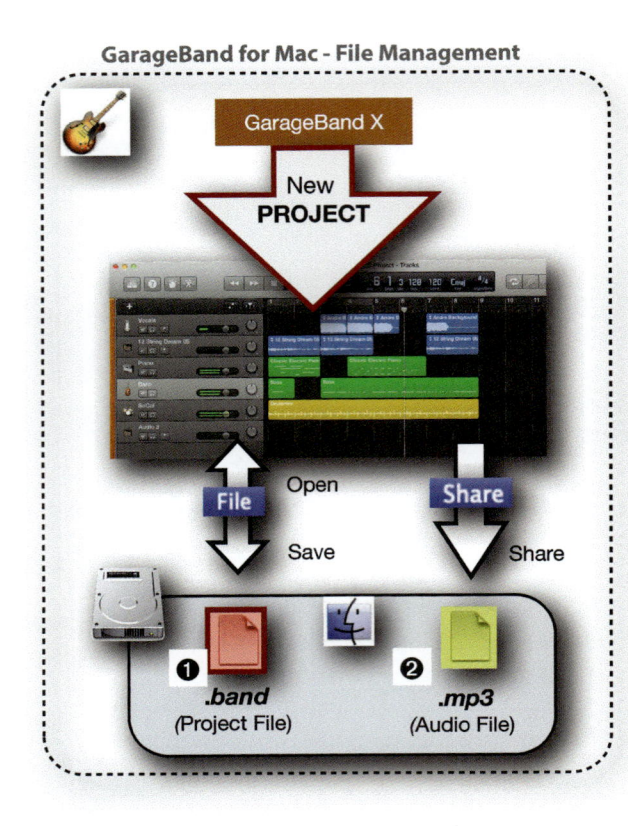
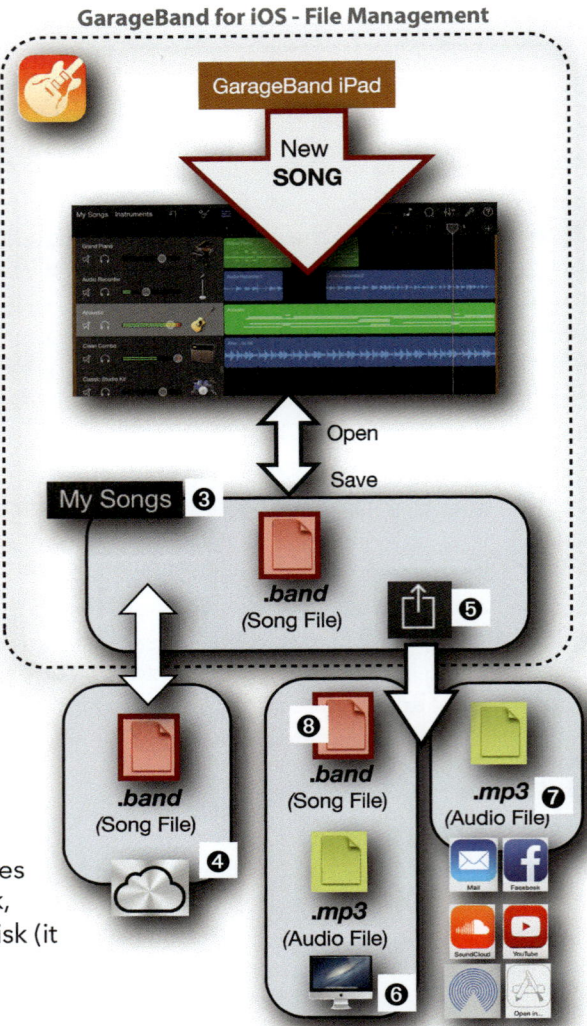

➡ GarageBand for Mac

In GarageBand X, the Project Files ❶ and the exported Audio Files ❷ are located on the same system (Mac). You open from the disk, save to the disk, and also share the exported audio files to the disk (it is called "Export Song to ...) through a Finder window.

➡ GarageBand for iOS

In GarageBand on the iPad, the Song Files are managed in the My Songs Browser ❸. This window functions as the quasi Finder for GarageBand Song Files. The iCloud location ❹ functions as an extension of the My Songs Browser.

The Share ⬆ command ❺, which creates the Audio File of the Song File, is also initiated from the My Songs Browser ❸. This is a different convention if you think about it. You mix (share) a song not from an open Song like in GarageBand X (or any other DAW), you initiate the mix from a Song File. Imaging you click on a GarageBand file in the Finder to mix it.

The Share destinations, however, are all "outside". Instead of sharing to the (non existing) local disk, you can send the Audio File to your desktop computer ❻ (via iTunes File Sharing), attach it directly to an email message and send it off, or post it to any of the popular social media sites ❼.

You may notice in the diagram that this Share command can also share a Song File ❽ to the desktop computer. This is part of the "File Sharing" procedure via iTunes sync that lets applications on iDevices exchange files with the desktop computer. I will explain that procedure later in this chapter.

Although the iPad version of GarageBand is supposed to be simple and very easy to use, this diagram demonstrates that at least the file management part is not that intuitive and requires some explanations. That's why I dedicated a whole chapter to it.

Because the iPad doesn't provide a central file management system like the Finder on OSX, GarageBand has its own built-in file management system. It is the My Songs Browser.

My Songs Browser = GarageBand's Finder

Every content-creation application on the Mac relies on the standard Open, Save, and Share procedure and you pretty much know how they work even with a new application. The procedures in GarageBand on the iPad, however, are different.

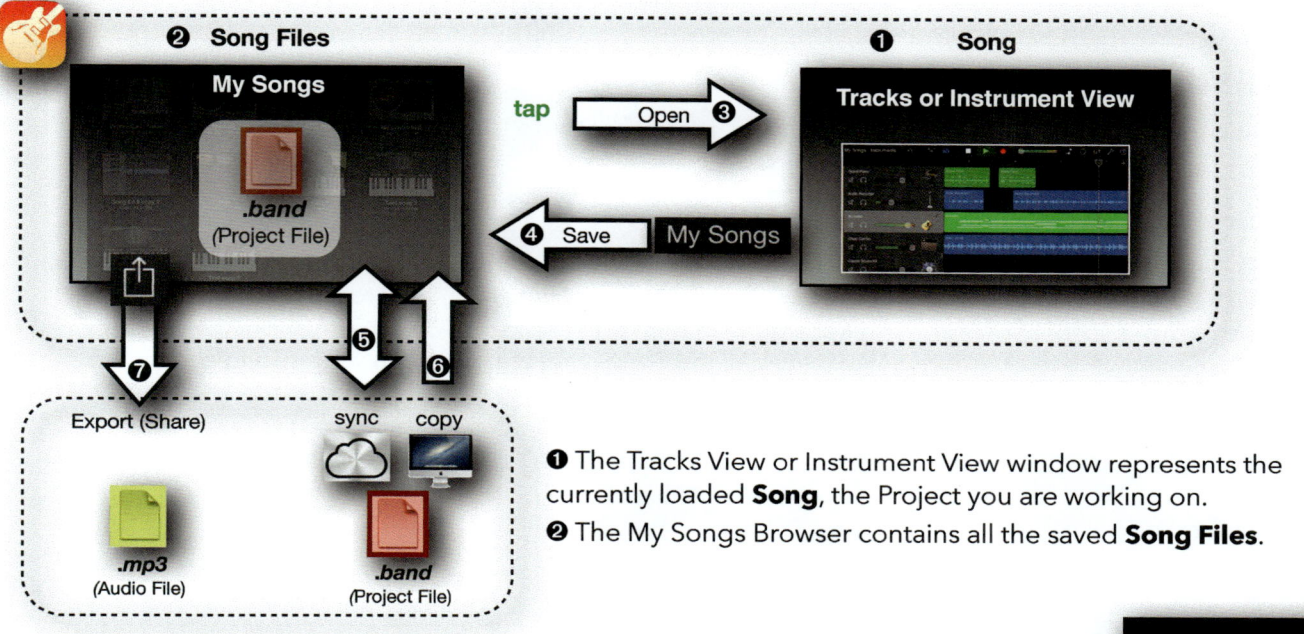

❶ The Tracks View or Instrument View window represents the currently loaded **Song**, the Project you are working on.

❷ The My Songs Browser contains all the saved **Song Files**.

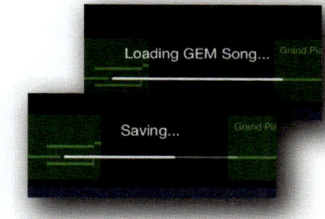

Internal File Management

❸ *Tap* on any Song File in the My Songs Browser to open it and make it the currently loaded Song. The window will automatically switch to the Tracks View or Instrument View depending on what was last open when the Song was saved. Once a Song is loaded, you have no indication what the name of that Song is. There is no Title Bar.

❹ There is NO SAVE BUTTON. *Tapping* the My Songs Button in the Control Bar will automatically close and save the currently loaded Song. Closing the GarageBand app or switching to a different app will also save the Song first. You will see a red colored bar on top of the iPad screen that says "GarageBand (Recording)" ❽.

When you tap on the My Songs Button (and, therefore, save the Song), GarageBand takes a screenshot of the current window (Tracks View or Instrument View) and uses it as the file icon for the Song File. This icon is also used when you export it to your computer (to continue with GarageBand X or Logic).

External File Management

❺ You can sync Song Files with Song Files stored on iCloud.

❻ You can import Song Files from your desktop computer via iTunes File Sharing (sync).

❼ You can export the Song File to an Audio File and send it to various destinations in the same process.

My Songs Browser

Now let's go through all those options step-by-step to better learn these new concepts regarding file management. First, a look at the My Songs Browser.

The My Songs Browser ❶ is like a single Finder Window. It displays ❷ all the GarageBand Song Files that are stored locally on the iPad ❸. This is similar to the Mac where the Finder displays all the files that are stored on the local hard drive.

Those GarageBand Songs you see can get onto the local iPad storage in three ways:

🌐 Create Song ❹

You can create a new GarageBand Song that will be added as a new GarageBand Song File to the local iPad storage ❸, which then will be visible as a new Song in the My Songs Browser ❶.

🌐 Import Song ❺

You can import an existing GarageBand Song File from your Mac to the local iPad storage ❸, which then will be visible as a Song in the My Songs Browser ❶.

🌐 Sync Song ❻

You can sync existing GarageBand Song Files from your iCloud storage ❼ to the local iPad storage ❸ which then will be visible as Songs in the My Songs Browser ❶. Please note that this procedure is different from importing a Song. Instead of importing individual Songs, you enable the iCloud sync mode ("Use iCloud"), which then displays in the My Songs Browser ❶ all the Songs that are stored on your iCloud account ❼.

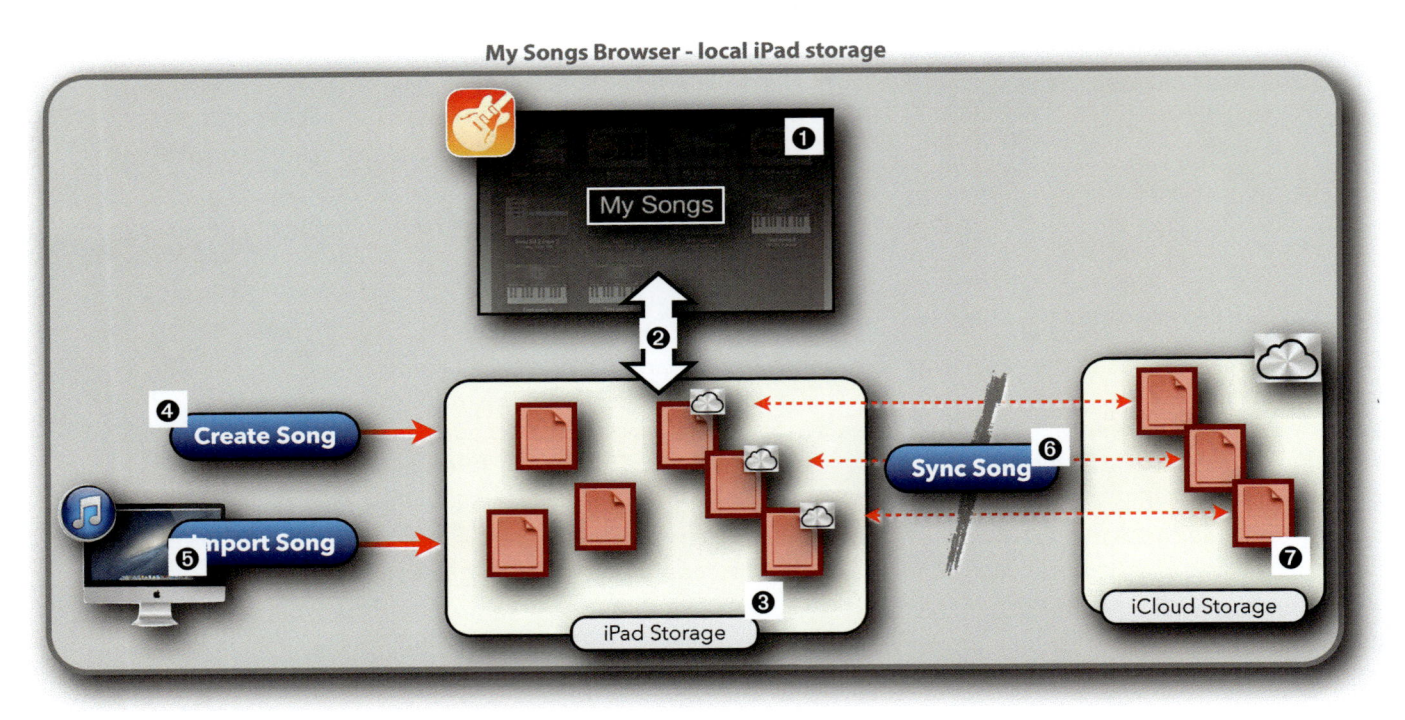

My Songs Browser - local iPad storage

Be careful, you lose all the Songs stored on your iPad when you delete the GarageBand app from your iPad, unless ...

- ☑ The Songs are synced to iCloud
- ☑ You have exported the Songs to your Mac

Now let's look at those three options on how to get Songs onto the My Songs Browser.

1 - Create a Song

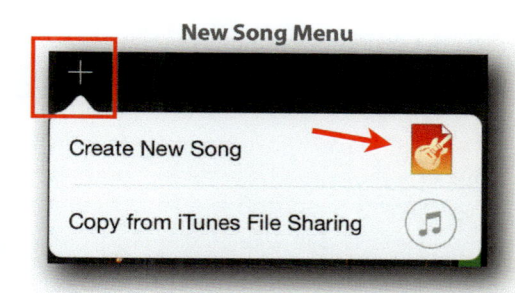

New Song Menu

Create New Song

Copy from iTunes File Sharing

Tap the plus icon, which is the Add Song Button ✚, in the upper left corner of the My Songs Browser

This opens a menu with two choices. Please note that this menu appears only if you have at least one Song already copied to iTunes. Otherwise, the menu will not appear and the Add Song Button functions as the "Create New Song" command.

Two possible options :

 Tap the Add Song Button ✚ (Menu doesn't pop up)

 Tap the Add Song Button ✚ (Menu pops up) and then *tap* the "Create New Song" Button 🎸 from the menu.

➡ *Create New Song Procedures*

Tapping this button will not yet create a new Song. There are three possibilities and only the third one will actually create a new Song File:

❶ *Tapping* on the Create New Song Button will open the Instrument Browser. *Tapping* the *My Songs* Button in the upper left corner of the window will return to the My Songs Browser without a new Song. Nothing has been created or saved.

nothing saved

❷ *Tapping* on the Create New Song Button will open the Instrument Browser. *Tapping* on an Instrument will create a Song and that Song will be opened in the Instrument View window. *Tapping* the *My Songs* Button, however, will return to the My Songs Browser without saving that Song.

nothing saved

❸ *Tapping* on the Create New Song Button will open the Instrument Browser. *Tapping* on an Instrument will create a Song and that Song will be opened in the Instrument View window. So far so good. Now only if you record something in that Song and then *tap* the *My Songs* Button will the Song be saved as a new Song File, visible as a new Song in the My Songs Browser.

New Song File saved

The new Song File will be named "My Song", but you can rename it in the My Songs Browser.

2 - Import a Song

You can also import an existing Song File from your Computer to your iPad. This is useful when someone sent you a GarageBand Song File (per email or on a USB stick). You have to make sure that the file was created with GarageBand for iOS and not GarageBand for OSX (both files have the same file extension).

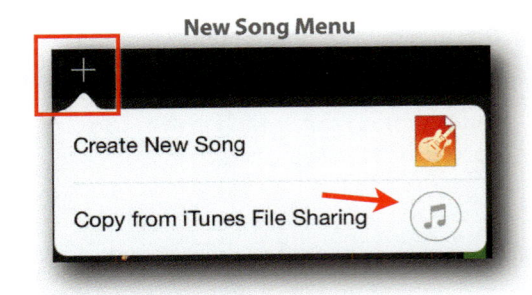

New Song Menu

Before using this button, you have to understand how to exchange files between your iDevices (iPad, iPhone, etc.) and your desktop computer.

This is easier said than done. You cannot just mount your iPad on your desktop computer and drag files from one Finder window to another like on a mounted drive. Remember, iOS doesn't have a Finder. Instead, you have to use the very clumsy method of syncing files via *iTunes File Sharing*. This is not very intuitive, you have to learn it. So here we go. The following diagram shows the basic concept:

To exchange files between OSX and iOS, you have to use the iTunes app as the middleman, the "messenger". The service is called *iTunes File Sharing,* which lets you exchange files between your desktop computer (OSX) and your iDevice (iOS).

iTunes File Sharing

If you've ever synced your iDevice to iTunes in the past, then you know that you can choose which of your purchased apps you want to put on your iDevice. You make this selection under the Apps tab. This Apps tab has a section at the bottom, the File Sharing section. It lists all your apps that use the File Sharing mechanism. This is the important "Exchange Place".

- ☑ Any files you place in this area will be synced (transferred) to your iDevice.
- ☑ Any file that you send to iTunes from your iDevice will show up in that iTunes File Sharing "Exchange Place" (will be synced). This is the procedure for sending a file from an iDevice app to iTunes. Once the file "arrives" in iTunes, you can grab it there and put it anywhere (save to) on your desktop computer.

Please note that there is not one single central "File Exchange Place" in iTunes. Each app has its own section for exchanging files. On top of that, each iDevice (in case you have multiple iDevices synced to your iTunes) has its own list of files that it synchronizes with its own apps. Still sounds easy?

🌐 OSX to iOS

These are the steps to send files from your desktop computer to an app on your iDevice running iOS:

- ☑ Launch iTunes on your computer and select from the Devices section in the sidebar the iDevice ❶ you want to send files to.
- ☑ Select the *Apps* tab ❷ from the top.
- ☑ From the File Sharing area at the bottom, select the app you want to send files to, in our case GarageBand ❸.
- ☑ The section to the right displays all the files that are synced (exchanged) between iTunes and GarageBand ❹.
- ☑ Add files to this list by *dragging* them from the Finder onto this area or use the *Add...* button ❺ to select from an Open Dialog window. This will initiate an automatic sync to your iDevice so it is available right away without performing a manual sync (as long as the iDevice is "mounted" in iTunes).
- ☑ To use any file from that list (that has been sent from the iDevice) on your computer, you have to copy it to the Finder either by *dragging* it onto a Finder window or use the *Save to...* button ❻.

This is just the general transfer process. I'll show later where we can grab those files on the iPad in GarageBand.

OSX - iOS File Sharing

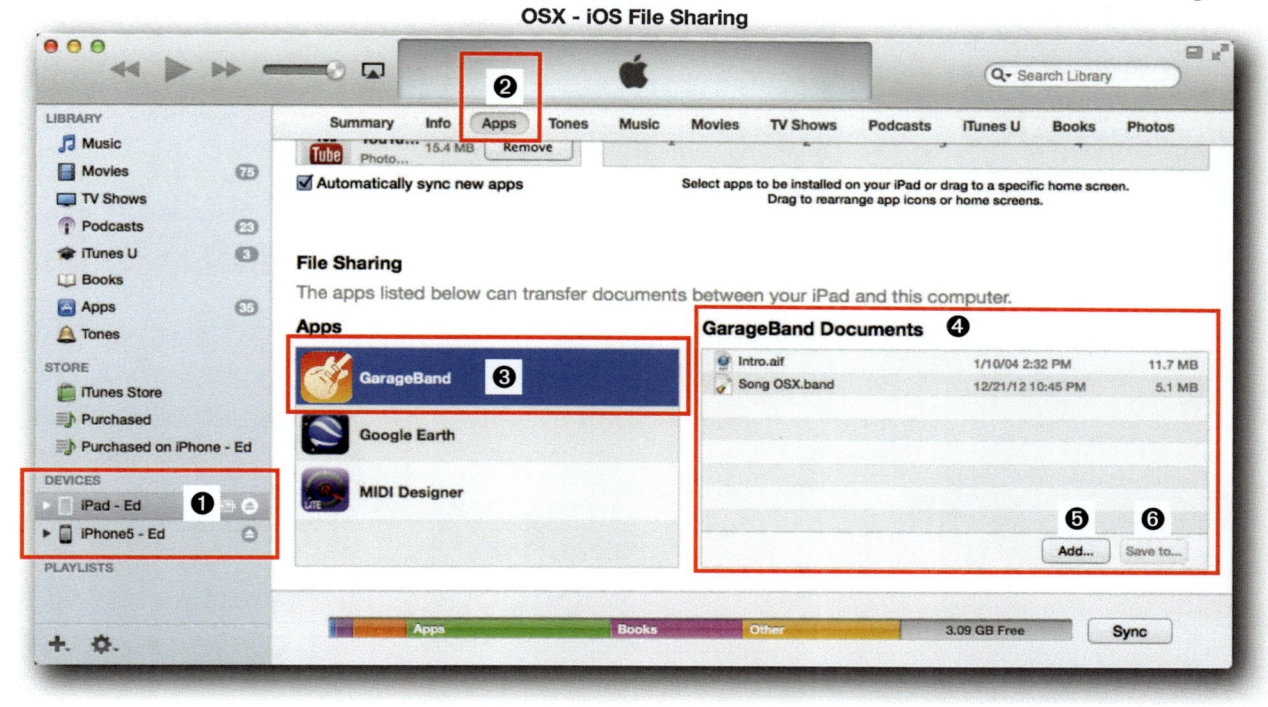

🌐 iOS to OSX

The term in GarageBand to send a file to your desktop computer is **Send "NameOfYourSong" to iTunes**. This is very important to understand and not to be confused with the term used in GarageBand X. When you send something to iTunes in GarageBand X, you create an audio file that will be added automatically to the iTunes **Library** so you can play that Song in iTunes. In GarageBand for the iPad, you send a file to the special <u>File Sharing area</u> ❹ in iTunes.

- ☑ From the My Songs Browser in GarageBand, select the command to Share a Song via iTunes (explained a little later).
- ☑ Any time you send a file via the Share command to iTunes, it will automatically sync to iTunes. If your iDevice is listed in the iTunes sidebar, then the files that you Share from GarageBand will be transferred (automatic sync) to iTunes and show up moments later in the GarageBand Documents list ❹.
- ☑ Now you can grab the file from that list and save it ❻ to the Finder.

Delete Files from iTunes File Sharing

You can delete any file in iTunes from the File Sharing Documents list by selecting the file and hitting the **_delete_** key. iTunes pops up an Alert Window telling you that the file will no longer be available on your iDevice.

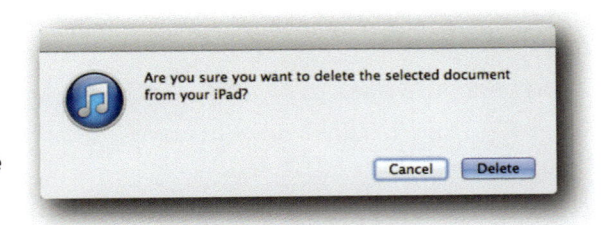

➡ *Open Song from iTunes*

Now, after this little detour of iTunes File Sharing, let's go back to our original task of opening a Song in the My Songs Browser. The second option on the popup menu is "Copy from iTunes File Sharing".

Here are the steps to take and the things to pay attention to:

☑ **_Tap_** the Add Song Button ➕ in the My Songs Browser ❶.

☑ **_Tap_** the iTunes Button 🎵 on the popup menu ❷.

☑ A new window opens up with the header "Import Song" ❸. It lists all the GarageBand Songs ❹ that are available from the File Sharing area on iTunes ❺.

☑ **_Tapping_** on any of the listed Songs in the Import Song Window will copy that Song to the My Songs Browser. Please note that the button uses the term "Copy from iTunes" ❷ and the window title uses "Import Song" ❸. Although a little inconsistent, both terms describe the same action. The iTunes File Sharing procedure only makes the files available for GarageBand. You have to do the extra step and copy (import) them to the My Songs Browser in GarageBand. After they are visible in the My Songs Browser, you could remove the Song from the File Sharing list. Once the Song is listed in the My Songs Browser, you can open it in GarageBand.

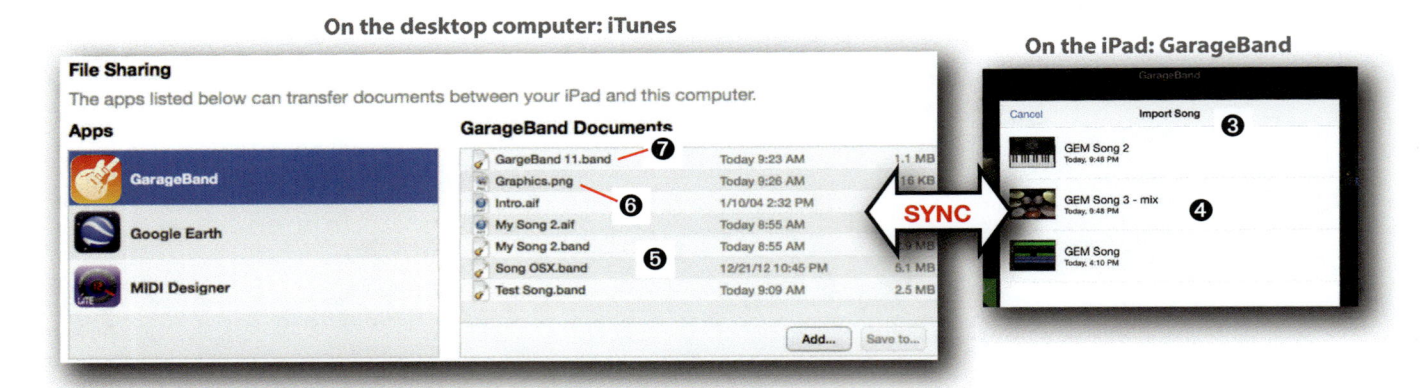

Attention:

Technically, you can place any file in the iTunes File Sharing list. However, only Audio Files (i.e. aiff, mp3) and Song Files (extension .band) are synchronized. Other file types are ignored (i.e. png ❻). But there is one more catch. The screenshot shows a Song File named "GarageBand 11.band" ❼. It has the correct file extension but doesn't show up in GarageBand. The reason is that GarageBand 11 and GarageBand iPad use the same file extension but they are only upwards compatible. This means you can open a GarageBand iPad file in GarageBand 11 (or GarageBand X), but not a GarageBand 11 file in GarageBand iPad. The extension is the same and the only indication is the file icon, which uses a screenshot of the Song. However, the file icon in the File Sharing list uses a generic file icon and you can't see that this file "GarageBand 11.band" is a GarageBand 11 Project File.

There are more procedures in GarageBand that rely on iTunes File Sharing that I discuss later.

3 - Sync a Song

The third type of Song Files that are displayed in the My Songs Browser (besides newly created Songs and importing Songs) are Songs that are located on your iCloud account.

I will go into much greater detail about iCloud syncing in the next chapter. Here is a quick overview.

iCloud is the name for Apple's own cloud system. A service you can sign up for free to use 5GB of storage that you can access over the Internet from any of your devices (computer or iDevices).

GarageBand Settings

- You have to enable that feature in the GarageBand Settings. Open the Settings app ❶ on your iPad, select the GarageBand tab ❷ in the Sidebar to display the GarageBand Settings on the right, and enable "Use iCloud" ❸ .
- When "Use iCloud" is enabled, you can save a Song File to the iCloud storage.
- Every time you then save the Song in GarageBand, the actual file (located on the iCloud server) will be updated (synced).
- You can access Song Files stored on iCloud from any iDevice that has access to your iCloud account.
- You can still work on (and save) the Song even if you are offline (not connected to the Internet). As soon as you are online again and connected to iCloud, GarageBand will automatically sync (update) the Songs.

As you can see in this diagram, the "Use iCloud" switch is an online/offline switch to access the iCloud storage:

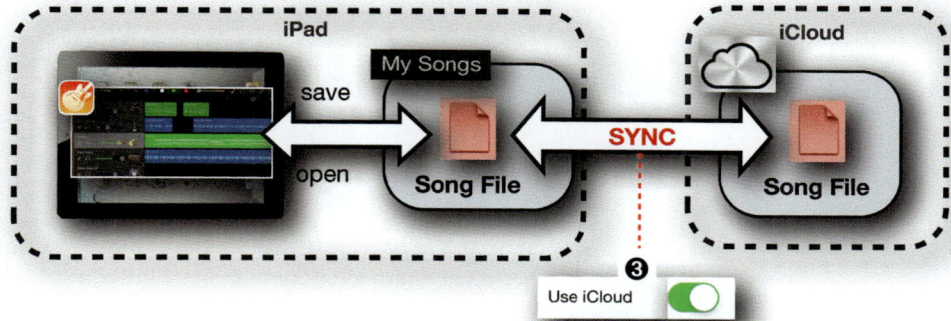

iCloud Badges

A GarageBand Song that is stored on iCloud can have three stages, which are indicated by a little badge on the Song icon in the My Songs Browser.

❹ **Ready for download**: The green download arrow badge indicates that this Song File is located on iCloud, but hasn't been downloaded (synced) to your GarageBand app yet. *Tap* on it to start the download.

❺ **Synced to iCloud**: The cloud badge indicates that this Song is located on iCloud and currently synced to your GarageBand app. *Tap* on it to open the Song.

❻ **Out of Sync Song**: The gray upload arrow indicates that this Song is located on iCloud but it wasn't synced last time you made changes to it in GarageBand. Once you connect to iCloud, the Song will automatically sync and change to the cloud ❺ badge again.

Once you have activated iCloud and used Songs that are synced with iCloud, you can use them (open, save) just as the other Songs that are stored locally on your iDevice.

File Management

So far we learned that the My Songs Browser displays all the GarageBand Songs that are stored locally on your iPad. And we also understand that the displayed Songs get there by creating new Songs, importing existing Songs, or syncing existing Songs with your iCloud account. However, the My Songs Browser provides much more features.

➡ Two Views

The My Songs Browser has two views. You switch between them with the button in the upper right corner. *Tap* the **Select** Button ❶ to switch to the "Select a Song" View and the **Done** Button ❷ to switch back to the Default View:

🔘 Default View

This view contains the Add Song ➕ Button ❸ we just discussed, plus a few display commands.

🔘 Select a Song View

This view contains the additional file management commands ❹:

▸ 📤 **Share** the selected Song

▸ 📑 **Duplicate** the selected Song(s)

▸ 🗑 **Delete** the selected Song(s)

▸ ☁ **iCloud** Songs Management

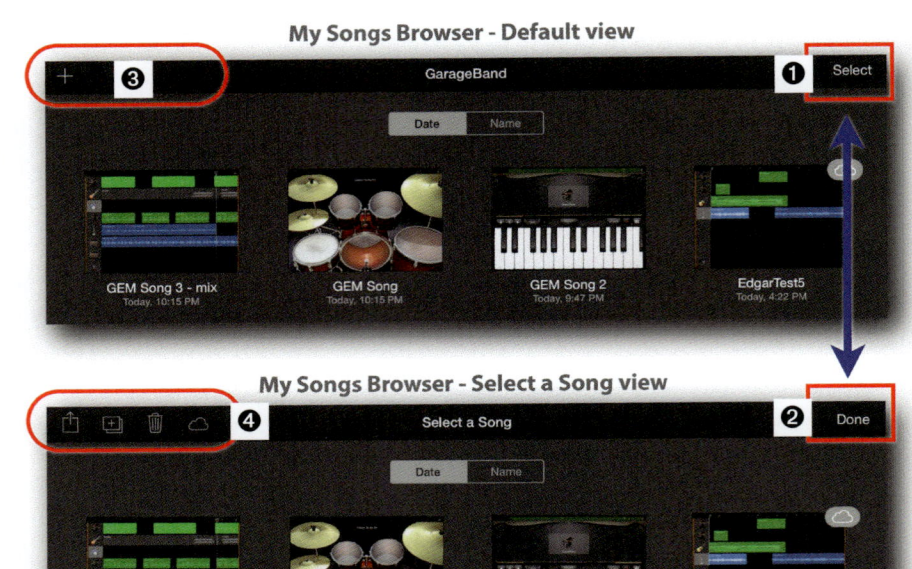

Default View

The basic file handling is pretty straightforward in standard iOS fashion:

🔘 **Display**: Each Song is displayed with its Song File Icon (the last window view when it was saved), the Song Name, and the time it was saved.

🔘 **Scroll**: If there are too many Songs listed, then you can scroll through the My Songs Browser by *swiping* up and down.

🔘 **Sort**: You can sort the list by Date or Name by selecting the appropriate Date/Name button at the top. Date is the default sorting order.

🔘 **Folder**: You can create folders in the same way you create folders for apps on your iPad's home screen. Just *drag* one Song over another Song to create a new folder or drag a Song onto an existing folder. *Tap* on a folder to open its content below.

🔘 **Open**: *Tap* on the Song File Icon to open it.

🔘 **Rename**: *Tap* on a Song Name to open the "Rename Song" window to enter a new name. You can rename Songs and Folders.

Open Song Folder

Select a Song View

The first thing you will notice when switching to the Select a Song View is that the icons are wiggling. The four buttons in the left upper corner are grayed out (inactive) and you have to select one (or more) Song(s) to make the buttons active. Any selected Song will have a blue border so you know which Song is the target for the following command:

Edit Buttons

➡ ***Duplicate***

Select one Song and ***tap*** the Duplicate Button to create a duplicate of that Song. The new song will have the word "copy" added to its name.

➡ ***Delete***

Select one or multiple Songs and ***tap*** the Trash Button. An additional button will appear, telling you how many Songs you are about to delete. ***Tap*** it to execute the command. Be careful, you cannot undo this step!

When deleting iCloud Songs, an additional Dialog window will pop up. See the iCloud chapter for details.

➡ ***iCloud***

Select one or multiple Songs and ***tap*** the iCloud button. An additional button will appear. When you ***tap*** on it three things will happen:

- The Song Icon will get the upload badge.
- The Song starts to upload indicated by a progress bar.
- The upload badge will change to the iCloud badge once the upload is finished. Now that Song is synced to the Song File on iCloud and every change to the Song will be updated to the iCloud File. See the iCloud chapter for details.

➡ ***Share***

Select one Song and ***tap*** the Share Icon to open the Share popup menu. It includes all the destinations you can share a Song to.

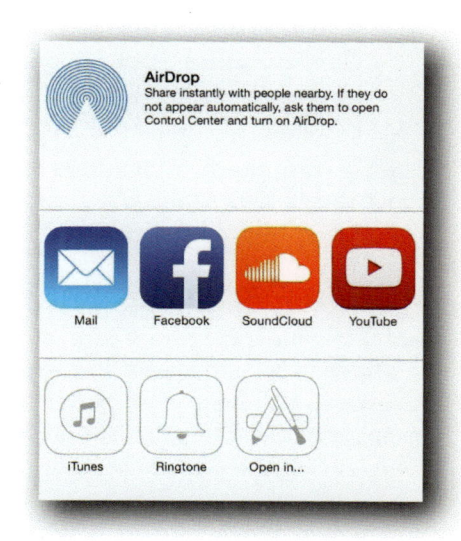

Share (Export)

Before going through the various options on how to share a Song, let's review the three stages of a SONG:

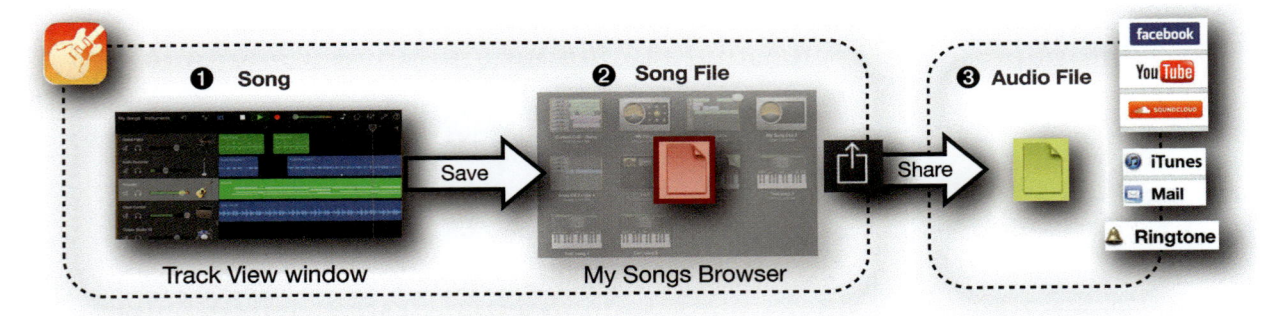

❶ The **Song** that you are currently working on in GarageBand, loaded into the iPad's memory.

❷ The **Song File**, the document that contains the data of the saved GarageBand Song.

❸ The **Audio File**, the document that was created from the Song File by performing a (offline) mix of that Song to a file in a common audio format (i.e. mp3, aiff) so it can be played by any audio player like iTunes or uploaded to an Internet service.

The actual Share (export) process includes three steps:

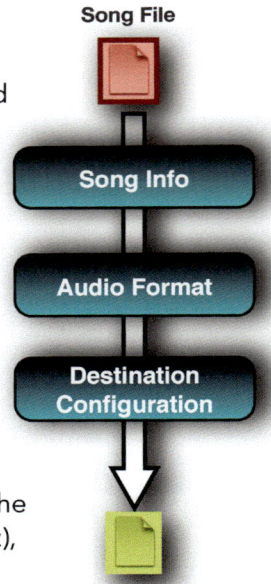

🔘 Song Info

Many audio files can have embedded information about their music. This extra data is called "Metadata" or "ID3 tags". It can be the name of the artist, composer, style, album title, and more. iTunes can display and also edit most of that metadata. Instead of adding that info later in iTunes, you can enter some of it in GarageBand while creating the Audio File.

🔘 Audio Format

When you create a new audio file, you have to make two decisions:

- **File Type**: There are a wide variety of different audio file types available, used for different purposes. The File Type is indicated by the file extension. For example, a *MyFile.aif* is an uncompressed file type with a good quality but a big file size. A *MyFile.mp3* is a compressed audio file type that is usually smaller but also has a lower sound quality.

- **Configuration**: Each file type (audio format) has specific parameters that determine the final quality of the audio file. For example, mono-stereo, Sample Rate (44.1kHz, 48kHz), Resolution (16bit, 24bit), and Transfer Rate (128kbps, 192kbps).

Often, a user interface provides only basic configuration choices, i.e. high, medium, low quality and hides all the details about the chosen parameters to make it easier for the casual user.

🔘 Destination Configuration

With a plain export procedure, an app usually creates just the audio file that is saved to the Finder. From there, you have to take the extra steps to get the audio file to where you want it (i.e. post on Facebook, YouTube, or attach it to an email). GarageBand lets you do all the configuration steps as part of the export process, saving you a lot of extra steps. Just one or two additional configuration windows and everything is taken care of without even leaving the GarageBand app.

Export Destinations

I will explain now each export destination, but choose a different order than on the popup menu.

➡ *Share Song via iTunes*

There are two important things you have to be aware of with the iTunes share feature:

- ◯ Although it looks like the exported file will be sent to the iTunes *Library* like in GarageBand X, this is NOT the case. The iTunes logo refers to the *iTunes File Sharing* feature, so the exported file will end up in the "iTunes ➤ iPad ➤ Apps ➤ File Sharing ➤ GarageBand ➤ GarageBand Documents" section ❹. This is the same area I discussed earlier.

- ◯ I explained in this chapter that the Share process creates an Audio File from the GarageBand Song File. The iTunes export feature, however, includes also the option to export the actual GarageBand Song File. Because there is no visible file system on the iPad, as discussed already, GarageBand uses the Share feature (which relies on iTunes File Sharing) to send a Song File to the desktop computer.

Tapping on the iTunes Button ❶ will open a window with two big file icons:

Tap on the GarageBand icon ❷ to send the GarageBand Song File to iTunes via iTunes File Sharing. A progress bar "Sending to iTunes File Sharing..." ❸ will indicate the transfer process. If your iPad is connected to iTunes on your desktop computer (USB or Wi-Fi), then the Song File will show up right away under the GarageBand apps in the iTunes File Sharing section ❹. Otherwise you have to initiate a manual sync later. Technically this is rather a "save" command than an "export" command because it is sending the file as it is without converting it.

Tap the iTunes Icon ❺ to initiate the actual export process, which creates an Audio File from your Song. It will open a "Share Song" configuration window with two sections.

❻ **My Info**: Here you can enter the additional metadata that will be embedded with the audio file. This info will be displayed in iTunes when you import it later into your iTunes Library.

❼ **Audio Quality**: You can choose from four quality levels of compressed audio files. This creates an audio file with the extension *m4a*, which is an AAC (Advanced Audio Coding) audio format (similar to mp3). The fifth option creates an uncompressed aiff (Audio Interchange File Format) audio file.

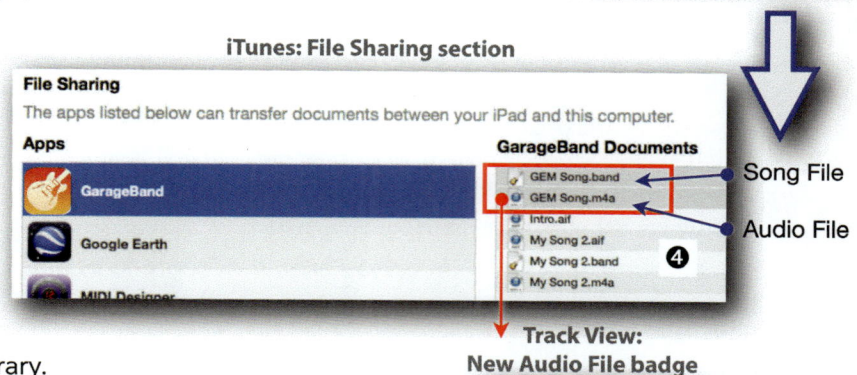

Every newly created audio file in the iTunes File Sharing section will be indicated with a notification badge ❽ on the Track View's Loop Browser Icon. You can import that audio file via the Loop Browser now into any GarageBand song. I cover that topic in a later chapter.

➡ *Export Song as Ringtone*

The reason I choose Ringtone next is because it also uses the iTunes File Sharing procedure. It might look a little bit complex at first, but once you understand the exact meaning of the various buttons, then the sequence is very logical and easy to do.

🟤 Prepare the Ringtone

- ☑ *Tap* on the Ringtone Button ❶ to open the "Export Ringtone" window.
- ☑ *Tap* on the Name if you want to rename it.
- ☑ *Tap* on the "Your Ringtones" Button ❷ to open a window that displays all the Ringtones that you have exported previously. You can delete Ringtones from the list with the *Edit* Button in the upper right corner. Please note that all those Ringtones are available as choices in the Settings app ❸ to assign them as the Standard *Ringtone* and Standard *Text Tone* on your iDevice.

🟤 Create the Ringtone

- ☑ *Tap* the Export Button ❹ to start the mix-down of your Song File to an Audio File with the .m4r extension (m4r files are placed in iTunes in the *Tones* section when imported into iTunes).
  - GarageBand creates the Audio File and places it into the iTunes File Sharing area ❻ on your computer. If your Song is longer than 30s, then it will be shortened.
- ☑ You will get another Alert window ❺ after the Ringtone has been successfully created. *Tap* OK to finish the procedure or *tap* "Use sound as..." for more options to assign the Ringtone you just created on your iDevice.

🟤 Assign the Ringtone

Once you've created the Ringtone, it will be available in your *Sounds* Settings on your iPad. Now you can assign it to use as an alert sound for specific actions. However, you can do that assignment as part of the actual export procedure. *Tap* the "*Use sound as...*" Button ❺ to open another window with three options:

❼ *Standard Ringtone*: *Tap* this button to assign the Ringtone as the default tone when your iDevice is getting a phone call.

❽ *Standard Text Tone*: *Tap* this button to assign the Ringtone as the default tone when your iDevice gets a text message.

❾ *Assign to contact*: *Tapping* this button will open yet another window that displays all your contacts on your iPad. Selecting a contact will pop up two buttons where you can choose to use the new Ringtone if that contact ...

- ... calls you (*Assign as Ring Tone*)
- ... sends you a text message (*Assign as Text Tone*)

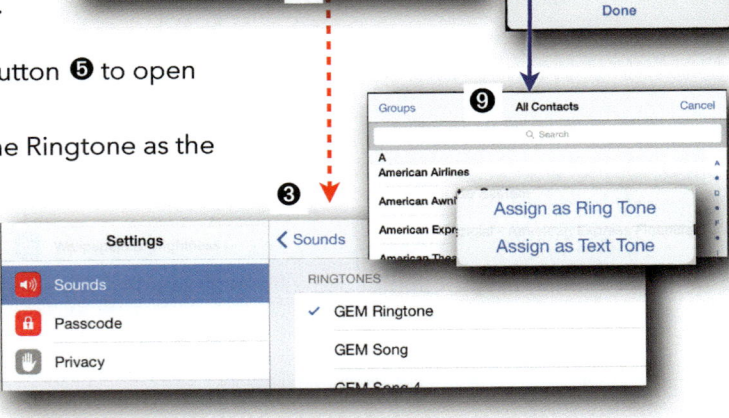

➡ **Open Song in other iPad Apps**

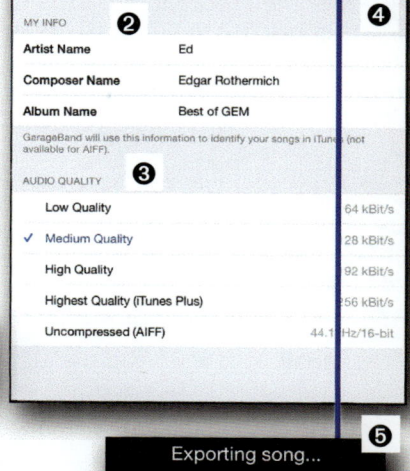

I mentioned already the problem of having no direct file management system on the iPad. For example, if you created a Song in GarageBand on the iPad and want to use it in iMovie on the iPad, you cannot just save the Song from GarageBand on the iPad disk and then open it in iMovie. Instead, GarageBand has the option to send the mixed Audio File of your Song directly to any app on your iPad that is able to receive such a file.

☑️ *Tap* on the "Open in..." Button ❶.

☑️ The Share Song window pops up with the following selections:

- **My Info** ❷: Here you can enter the additional metadata that will be embedded with the audio file.

- **Audio Quality** ❸: You can choose from five quality levels for the Audio File. These are the same options as with the iTunes export.

☑️ *Tap* the Share ❹ Button to start the process.

☑️ A progress bar ❺ indicates the export procedure.

☑️ When finished, a popup window ❻ opens underneath the Share Icon 📤 displaying all the apps on your iPad that can "receive" the audio file.

☑️ *Tap* on an app ❼ to send the Audio File to it. The iPad switches to that app where you follow the instructions on what to do with it.

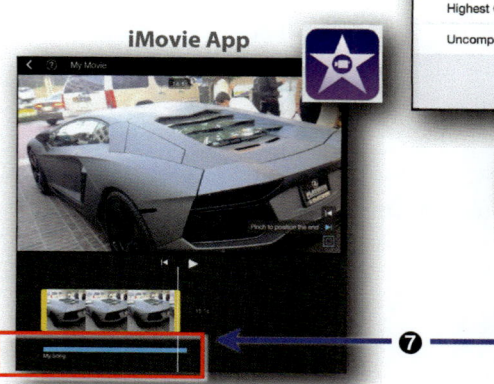

iMovie App

Exporting song...

➡ **AirDrop to a different iDevice**

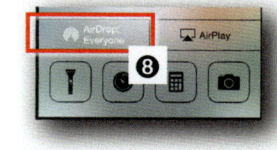

This feature allows you to send a Song File wirelessly to any iDevice nearby. It is only available for newer iDevices with a Lightning connector. First of all, the sending and receiving device has to have AirDrop enabled ❽ in their Control Center (*slide* up from the bottom).

🌐 On the sending Device ❾

☑️ *Tap* on the AirDrop icon. It changes to display all Devices nearby that can receive files via AirDrop.

☑️ *Tap* on the Device Icon you want to send the Audio File to.

🌐 On the receiving Device ❿

☑️ On the receiving Device, an AirDrop window pops up with the information that you want to send a GarageBand item.

☑️ Once you select "Accept" on that receiving Device, another window pops up that list all the apps on that device the incoming file can be sent to. If you select "GarageBand", then the GarageBand app will open with the receiving Song File.

sending

receiving

➡ *Share Song via Mail*

Sending a mix of your Song via email is easy with less steps and options.

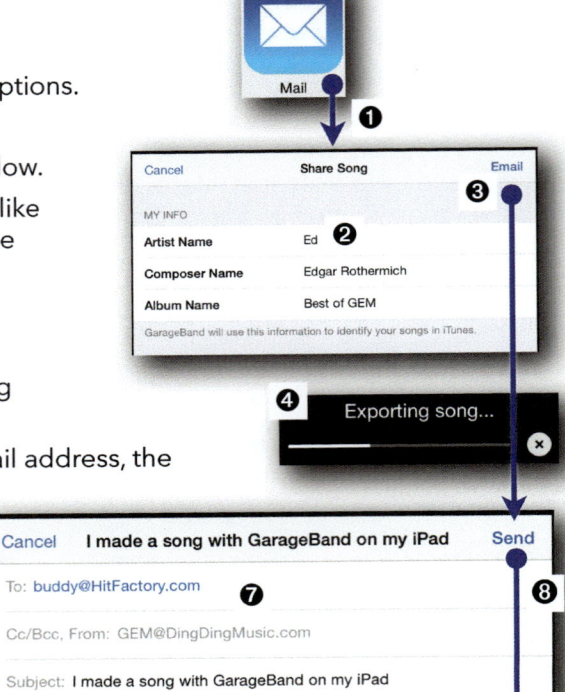

☑ **Tap** on the Mail Button ❶, which opens the "Share Song" window.

☑ Enter the metadata for the Audio File in the three fields ❷. Unlike GarageBand X where the Song info can be (pre-)entered in the Preferences window, here on the iPad version, GarageBand remembers the info you entered during your last file export.

☑ **Tap** the *Email* Button ❸, which starts the following process:

- An Audio File will be created from the mix-down of the Song displayed by a progress bar ❹.

- A window opens up with a new email message ❺. Your email address, the Subject, and a basic text will automatically be filled in.

- The newly created Audio File ❻ will be attached to that email. This will be in the AAC format with the extension .m4a encoded at 128kbps.

☑ Enter the email address(es) ❼ to whom you want to send the file.

☑ **Tap** the *Send* Button ❽ to send the email. It will be sent in the background (if you have an Internet connection) and no further window will appear.

Email sent in the background

Social Media Sites

The next three share options are for posting the mix of your Song to those popular social media sites:

These procedures are convenient and extremely time saving.

- You don't have to leave the GarageBand app.
- You can log into the various accounts from inside GarageBand.
- You don't have to remember the individual upload procedure, which is different on each site.
- You can do basic configurations before uploading.

➡ *Share Song to Facebook*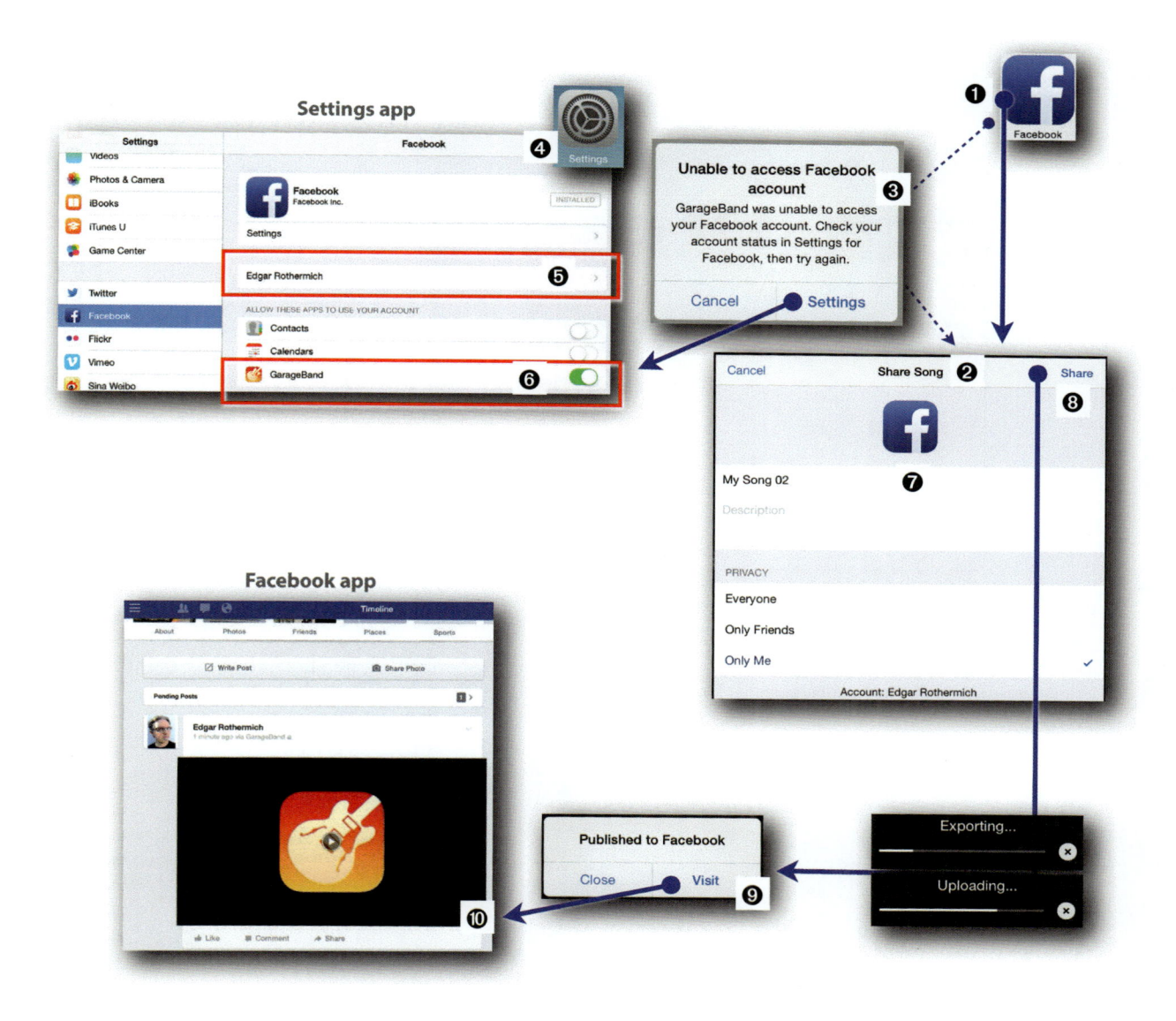

☑ **Tap** on the Facebook Icon ❶, which opens the "Share Song" ❷ window.

☑ If you haven't logged into your Facebook account, a window ❸ pops up that lets you switch to the Settings app displaying the Facebook Settings ❹. Here you can login to your Facebook account ❺ and allow GarageBand access ❻.

☑ In the Share Song window you can change the song name, add a Description, and choose the Facebook Privacy setting ❼.

☑ **Tap** on the Share Button ❽ to start the process. A progress bar displays the "Export" and "Upload" process.

☑ **Tap** on the Visit Button ❾ on the confirmation window to switch to the Facebook app ❿ and view your new posting.

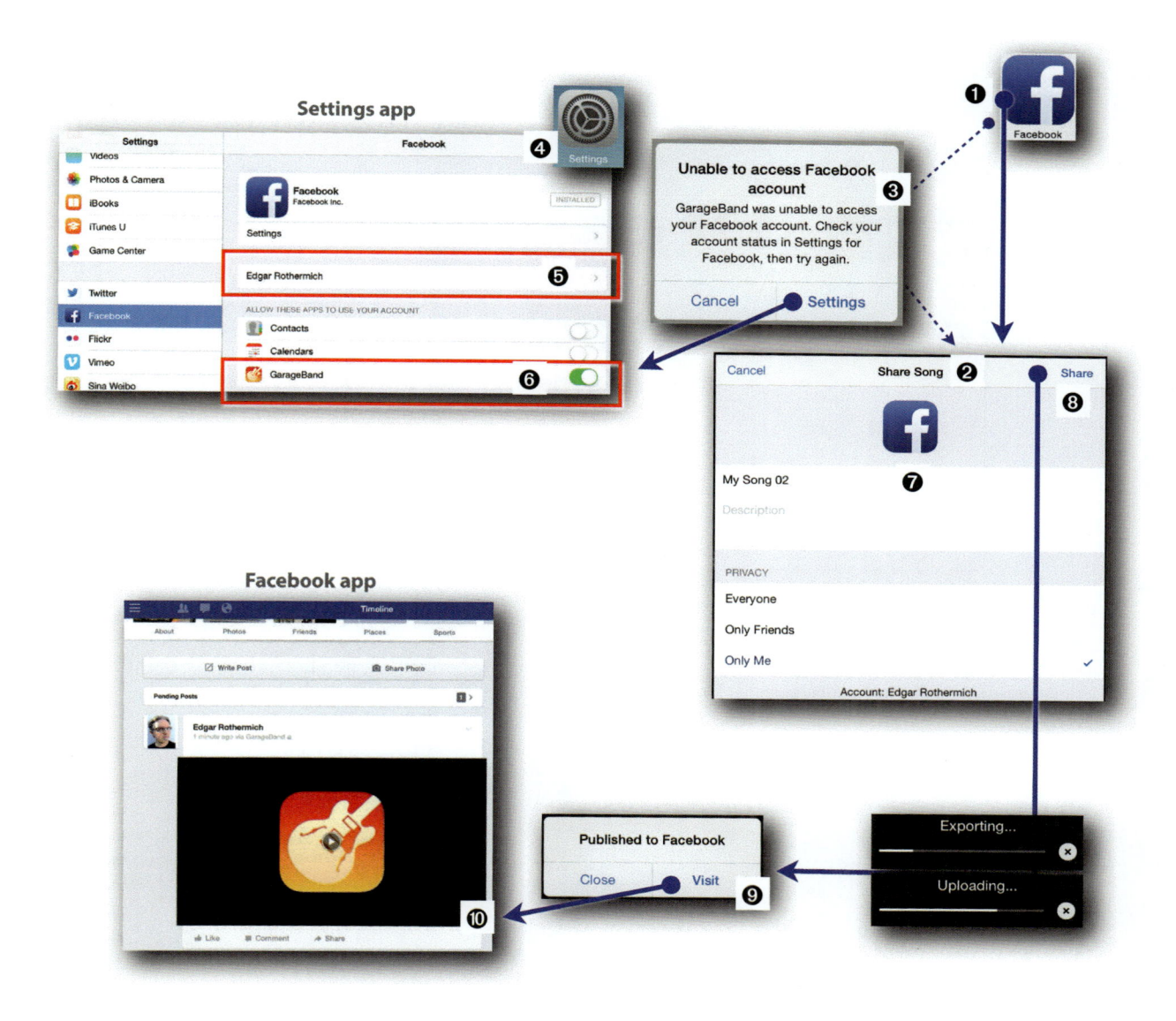

➡ *Share Song to SoundCloud*

☑ *Tap* on the SoundCloud Icon ❶, which opens the "Share Song" window.

☑ If you haven't logged in to your SoundCloud account, an additional window pops up ❷ where you can login with your email and password.

☑ In the Share Song window, you have four sections ❸ to configure your uploaded song:

- Change the Song name
- Set the Visibility
- Set the Permission
- Set the Quality of your exported audio file. These are the same five options as in the iTunes export.

☑ *Tap* on the Share Button ❹ to start the process.

☑ A progress bar ❺ displays the "Export" and "Upload" process.

☑ A little window ❻ confirms the successful upload to SoundCloud.

☑ Go to your SoundCloud page to view your song ❼.

➡ *Share Song to YouTube*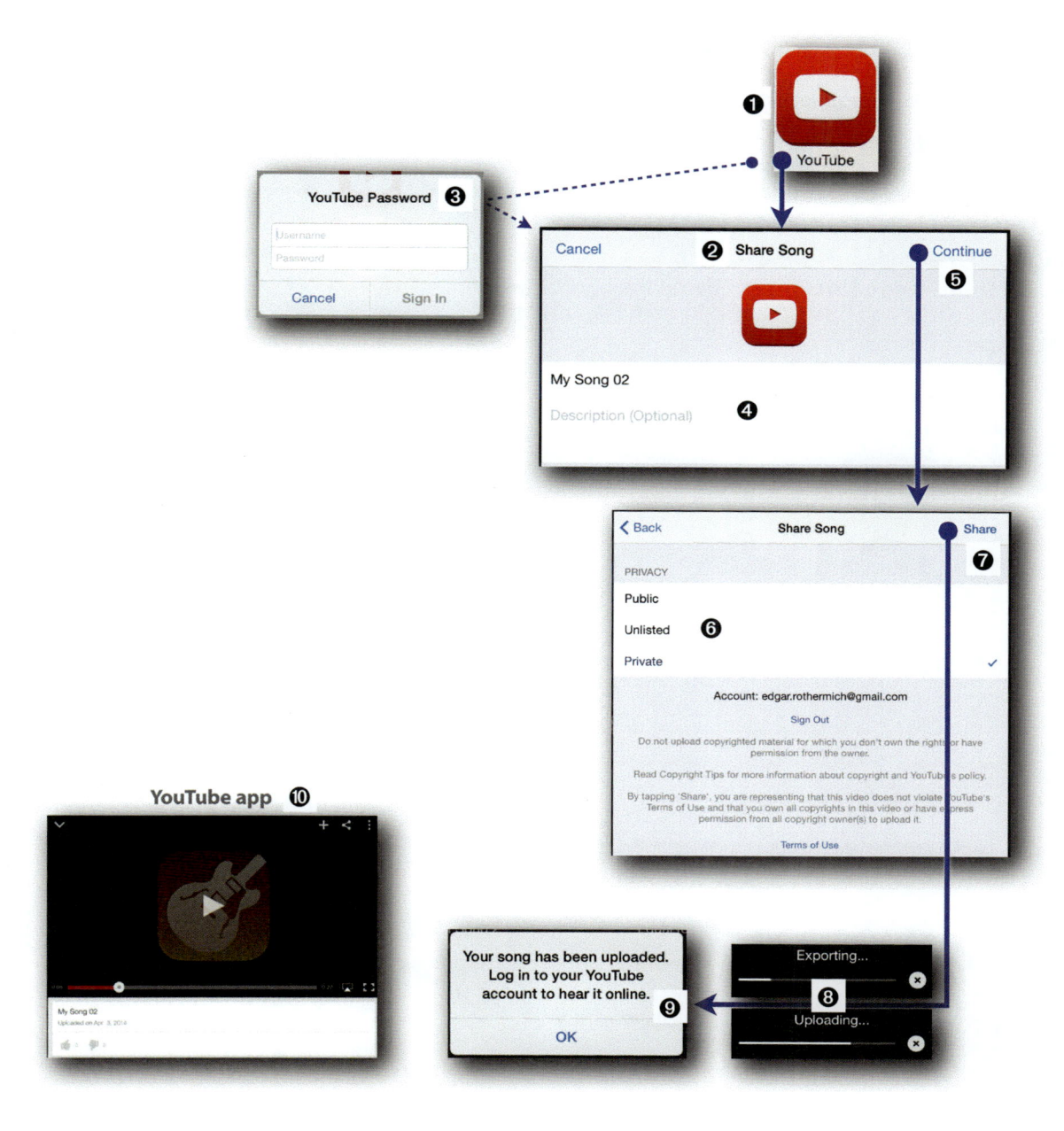

Although GarageBand only exports an Audio File without any video, you still can upload it to YouTube like a "single picture slide show".

- ☑ **Tap** on the YouTube Icon ❶, which opens the "Share Song" ❷ window.
- ☑ If you haven't logged into your YouTube account, a little window pops up ❸ where you can login with your username and password.
- ☑ You can change the song name and add a description in the Share Song window ❹.
- ☑ **Tap** *Continue* ❺ to open the next window to enter the Privacy settings ❻.
- ☑ **Tap** on the Share Button ❼ to start the process. A progress bar displays the "Export" and "Upload" process ❽.
- ☑ A little window confirms the successful upload ❾.
- ☑ The uploaded "video" of your song is displayed with the GarageBand picture on your YouTube channel ❿.

This is a little bonus chapter that explains how iCloud works. It goes a bit beyond the coverage of GarageBand, but if you are using the app for more serious recording then you might want to know exactly where your GarageBand Songs are located and how to manage them in the cloud. Besides that, iCloud is getting more and more important on your computer with other apps too, so it might be a good idea to understand that concept a little bit better.

> **iCloud functions as a virtual Hard Drive, connected via the internet**

This is the easiest explanation of the concept. Just think of iCloud as a hard drive that you can store data on. You can access that storage, located somewhere on Apple's server, over the Internet.

Actually, iCloud is a bit more, a whole system that provides various services beyond storing data. You can sign up for an iCloud account that provides 5GB of storage for the free account (minimum requirement OSX 10.7.2 or iOS 5, iPhone 4, iPod touch 4th generation, any iPad).

Document vs. Document File

Before explaining how iCloud works, let's look at the following basic principles:

When you create a new Document in an app (a content-creation app), the Document that you work on and see on your computer screen is stored temporarily in the computer's memory, the so-called RAM (Random Access Memory). If you were to close the app, turn off the computer, or lose power, then that Document would be erased, lost.

In order to keep the Document, you have to save it to a hard drive. This process takes the **Document** data from the RAM and stores it as a **Document File** on the hard drive. Now you can close the app or shut down the computer. Later, when you open that Document File from the hard drive, it will be loaded into the RAM again and you can continue to work on it.

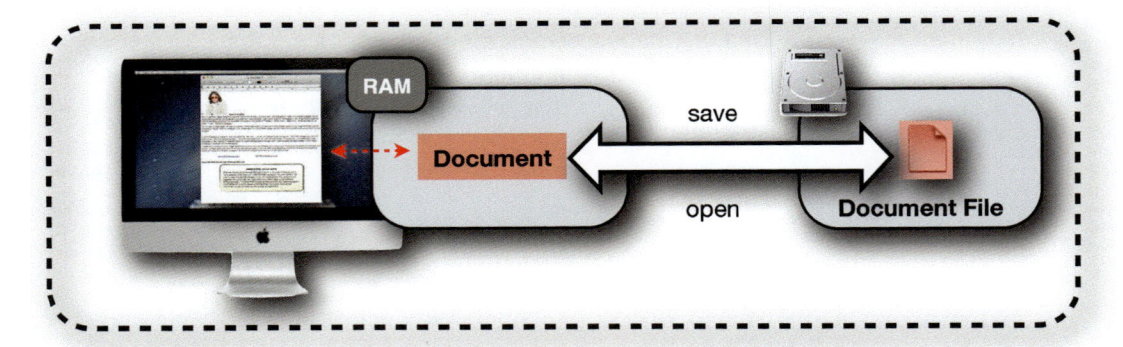

The concept with iCloud is technically the same. The two main differences are:

- The hard drive is located somewhere on a server, managed by Apple.
- You access that drive over the Internet.

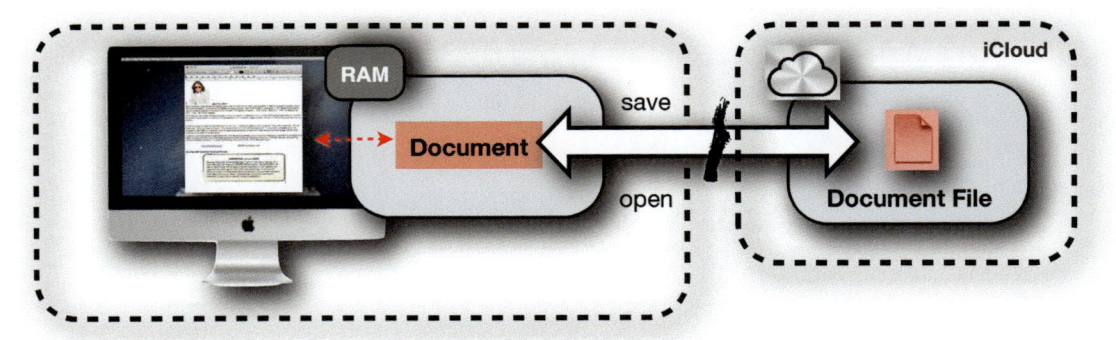

Most of the time, basic understanding is enough to work with iCloud. However, there are a few more things going on behind the scene. Once you understand those procedures, then it is easier to work with it and avoid any frustration if potential problems require some troubleshooting. After all, it is not that complicated, just slightly different.

➡ *The synchronized local Document File*

Hidden in the whole "save that Document to iCloud" process is a "middleman", an <u>additional</u> Document File on your local drive. Even if you think you are saving a Document File directly to the iCloud, there are a few more steps involved.

Here is the actual procedure:

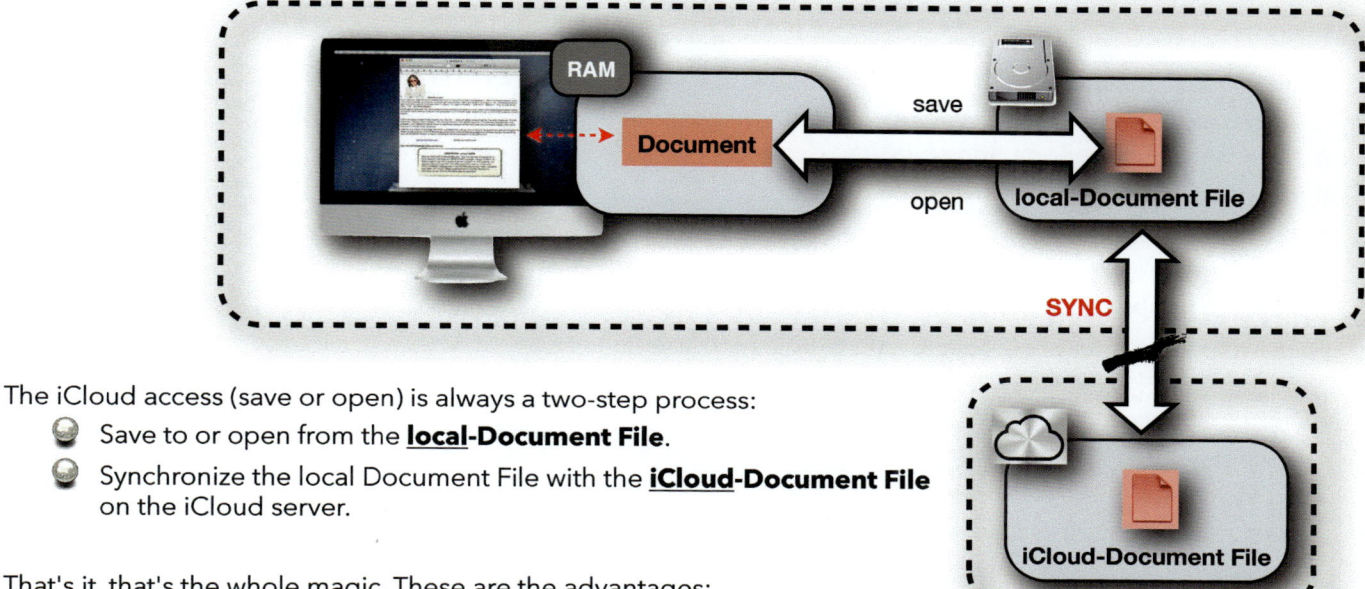

The iCloud access (save or open) is always a two-step process:

- ⚪ Save to or open from the **local-Document File**.
- ⚪ Synchronize the local Document File with the **iCloud-Document File** on the iCloud server.

That's it, that's the whole magic. These are the advantages:

- ☑ The iCloud-Document File is stored offsite on a different computer that provides you with data safety if your local drive and/or computer dies or gets lost.
- ☑ You can access the iCloud-Document File from anywhere via the Internet, even from different computers as long as they have access to the same iCloud account.
- ☑ You can also work offline (no Internet connection). The Document will be opened from the local-Document File and saved to it. The next time you have Internet connection, that local-Document File will update the iCloud-Document File on the iCloud server.

🔘 Where is it hidden?

If you are curious and wonder where the local-Document Files are stored, here it is. Inside the User Library is a folder named "Mobile Documents". That folder contains a sub-folder for each application that uses iCloud storage. If you look inside, you will find the folder for the GarageBand app. It contains all the Songs that are stored on your iCloud account. You can see the actual Project File (extension .band) and its screenshot file (extension .png).

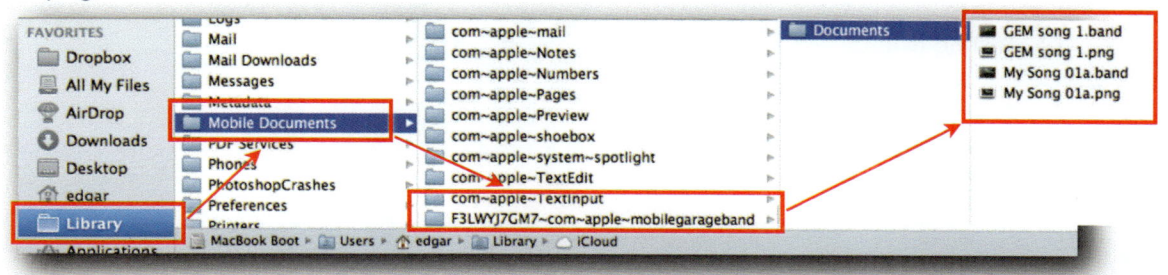

➡ *iCloud in GarageBand*

Now let's look at how the iCloud syncing procedure works in GarageBand:

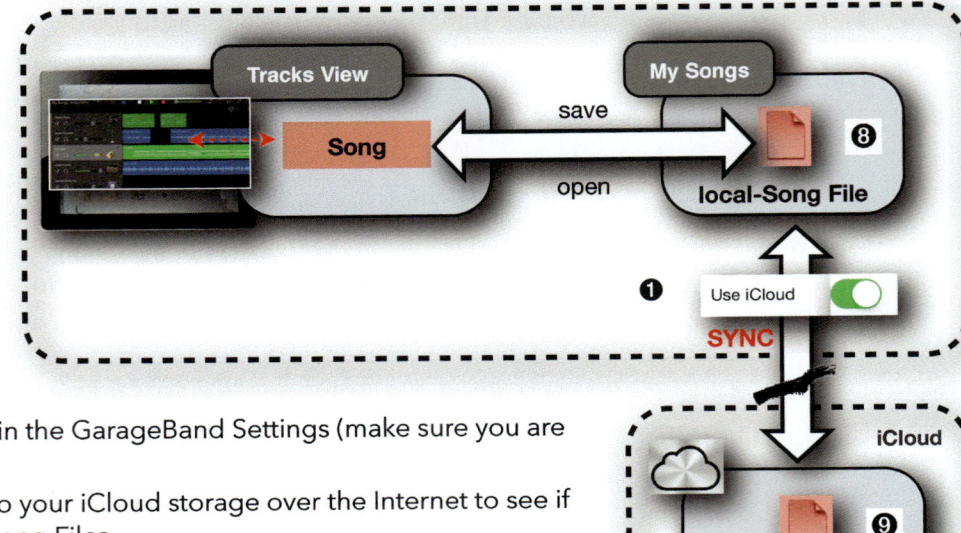

- You turn on "Use iCloud" ❶ in the GarageBand Settings (make sure you are connected to the Internet).
- GarageBand is connecting to your iCloud storage over the Internet to see if there are any GarageBand Song Files.
- If it finds a GarageBand Song File:
  - It will download the image file (not the Song File yet!)
  - It will display the Song Icon with a green download badge ❷ in the My Songs Browser.
- To download the Song File from iCloud to your iPad, *tap* on the Song Icon.
- Now the iCloud-Song File will be downloaded to the iPad as a local-Song File. You will see a white progress bar ❸ that indicates the duration of the download.
- Once the download is finished, the Song icon in the My Songs Browser gets an iCloud badge ❹ to indicate that this Song is located (and synced) on iCloud.
- As we know by now, the file exists in two places:
  - The local-Song File ❽ on your iPad.
  - The iCloud-Song File ❾ on your iCloud account.

What happens when we work on an "iCloud" Song?

- *Tap* the Song icon in the My Songs Browser to open it in GarageBand. This loads the local-Song File ❽ into the iPad memory and you can work on the Song in the Tracks View, record more in the Instrument View, etc.
- When you *tap* the *My Songs* Button, the Song will be closed and any changes will be saved to the local-Song File ❽.
- But because this is an iCloud Song, an additional step happens. GarageBand recognizes that the local-Song File (the one it just saved) is newer than the last time it saved (or opened) the iCloud-Song File ❾. The two files are "out of sync" and the local-Song File needs to be uploaded. It indicates that by changing the badge to the up-arrow badge ❺.
- If you still have Internet connection, the synchronization process starts automatically. The local-Song File ❽ will be uploaded to the iCloud and updates the existing (out of date) iCloud-Song File ❾. You will see a progress bar ❻, which indicates the duration of the upload.
- Once the upload is finished, the Song icon displays the iCloud badge again ❼ to indicate that the local-Song File ❽ and the iCloud-Song File ❾ are in sync again.

Now let's look at what happens to the synced relationship between the local-Song File and the iCloud-Song File under various circumstances:

🌐 Disable iCloud

What happens when you have iCloud Songs on your iPad and you are disabling iCloud in the GarageBand Settings?

▶ **Turn "Use iCloud" off** [Use iCloud ⚪]

In previous GarageBand versions you had the option to keep or delete those Songs. Now, they are just removed from the My Songs Browser. The Song Files, however, remain on the iPad storage

▶ **Turn "Use iCloud" back on** [Use iCloud 🟢]

When you turn iCloud syncing back on, GarageBand looks them up on the local iPad storage and makes them visible again in the My Songs Browser. Any Songs that are outdated (have been updated on iCloud through a different GarageBand iDevice) will be updated.

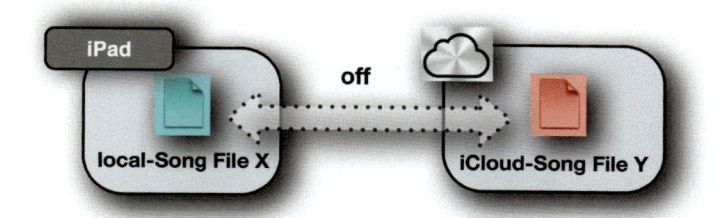

🌐 Sync Conflicts

One of the advantages of iCloud storage is that you can access the files from different Devices/Computers as long as they are on the same iCloud account.

▶ As long as you have the same Song loaded (open) only in one Device at a time, then any update will be pushed to the other iDevice to keep the iCloud-Song File in sync to all local-Song Files.

▶ If you have the same (iCloud) Song loaded on two devices at the same time and made changes (or made changes while offline) then GarageBand will notice that the files are out of sync. A "Resolve Conflict" window will pop up that lets you choose:

☑ Select one of the Songs in the window to make it the new iCloud-Song File and update the other local-Song Files.

☑ Selecting more than one file in the conflict window will create individual iCloud-Song Files for all the selected Songs on the list. All those Songs are then placed on all the other devices as iCloud synced Songs.

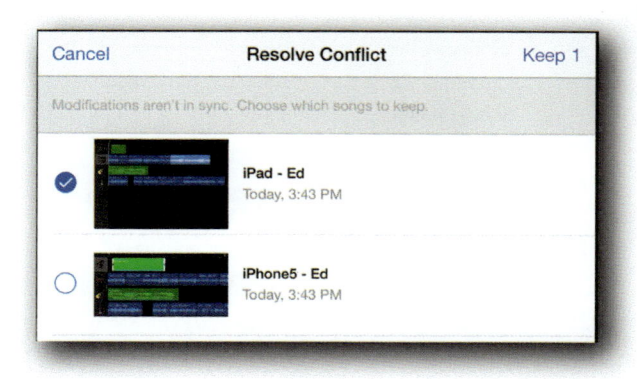

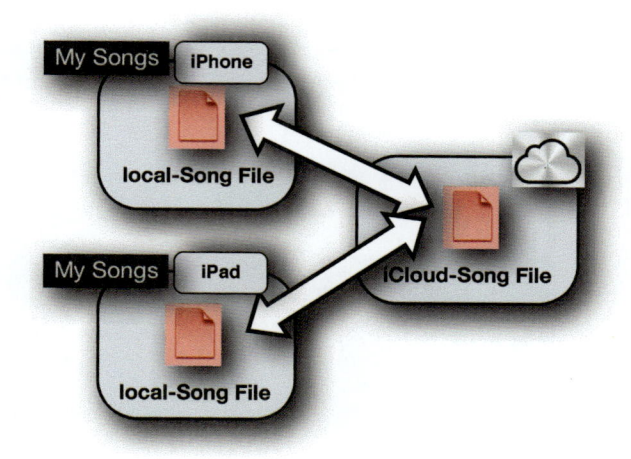

Now let's look at the basic file management commands again with the understanding of iCloud syncing:

● Upload Song to iCloud

The local-Song File of the selected Song will be copied to the iCloud as the iCloud-Song File and synced from now on. The Song Icon in the My Songs Browser gets the iCloud badge.

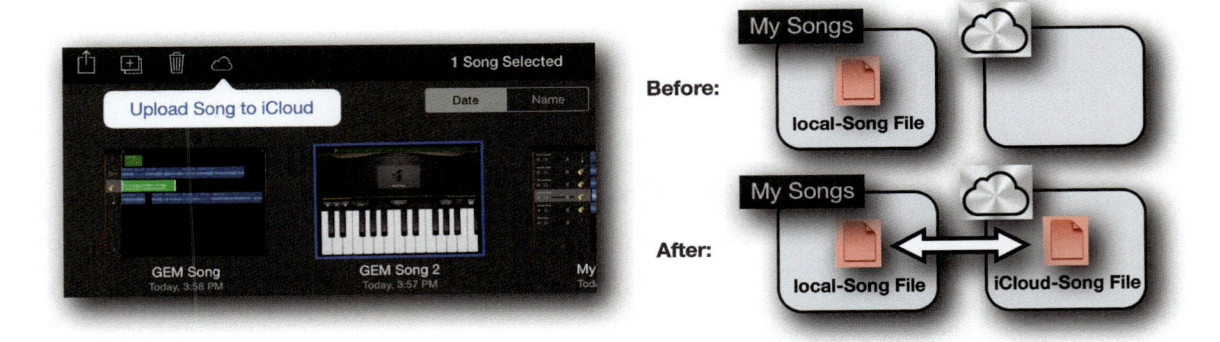

● Remove Song from iCloud

The iCloud-Song File on the iCloud will be deleted. The local-Song File stays on the iPad and in the My Songs Browser, now without the iCloud Badge.

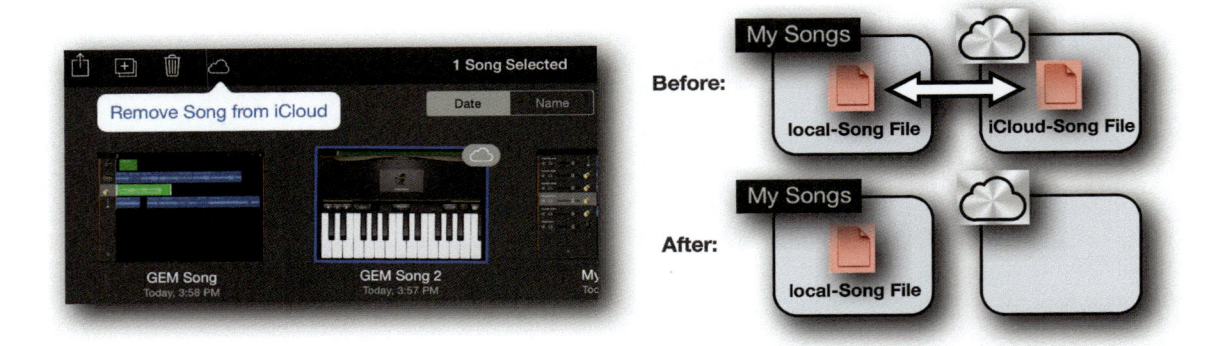

● Delete Song

If the selected Song is an iCloud Song, then the delete command will delete both files, the iCloud-Song File and the local-Song File. The Song Icon will disappear from the My Songs Browser and also from the My Songs Browser on other iDevices on the same iCloud account that have iCloud syncing activated in GarageBand.

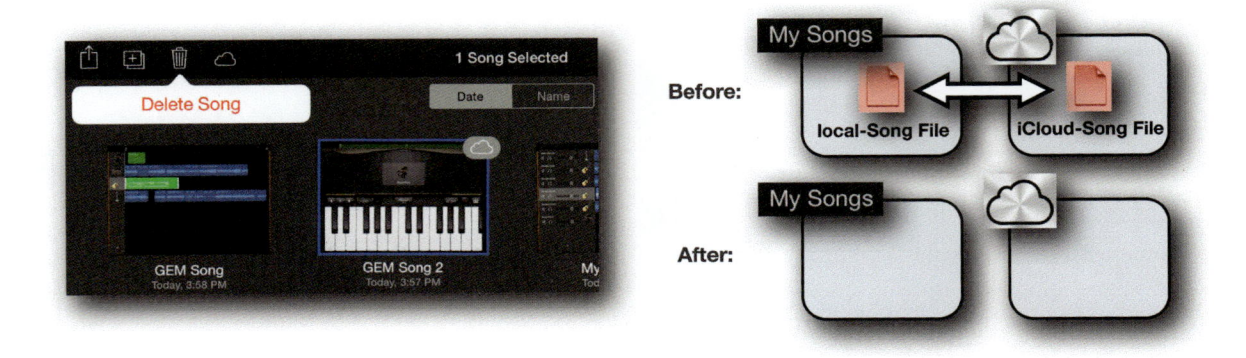

Managing iCloud Documents

As we have just seen, GarageBand provides the command in the *My Songs* Browser to remove a specific File from iCloud storage. There is another option to remove document files stored on iCloud. This works, by the way, for any application that uses iCloud as a storage option, not just GarageBand.

I already showed that the Finder stores those local iCloud Files in the Library folder. They are hidden because the user shouldn't mess with them. (You could copy those files if you want to retrieve a file). However, if you want to manage your Document Files on iCloud (i.e. delete) you cannot do that through the Finder because you cannot just mount the iCloud storage volume.

However, Apple lets you access those iCloud files on your computer and also on your iDevices. As you will see, you have to dig deep through many layers of windows to get to those files.

Manage iCloud files on iOS

These are the screenshots for iOS 7.1:

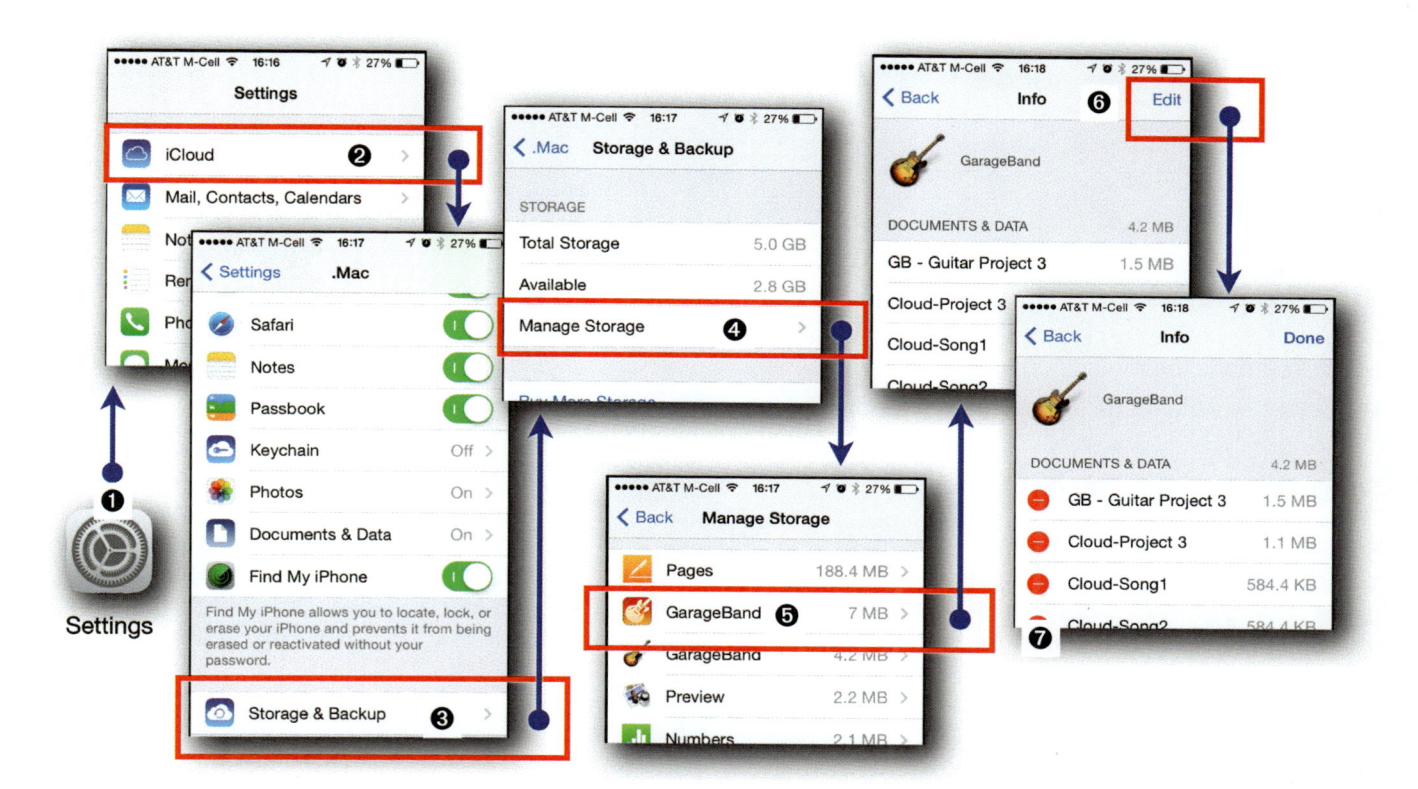

❶ Open the Settings app.

❷ *Tap* the iCloud Button.

❸ *Tap* the "Storage & Backup" Button.

❹ *Tap* the "Manage Storage" Button.

❺ This page shows you all the apps that use iCloud for storing data. *Tap* the GarageBand for iOS Button.

❻ This is the Document folder with all the GarageBand for iPad files that are stored on iCloud. *Tap* the Edit Button.

❼ The window adds the Delete Button next to each file and the "Delete All" button at the bottom. Deleting any file will remove it from iCloud.

Manage iCloud files on OSX

These are the screenshots for OSX 10.9:

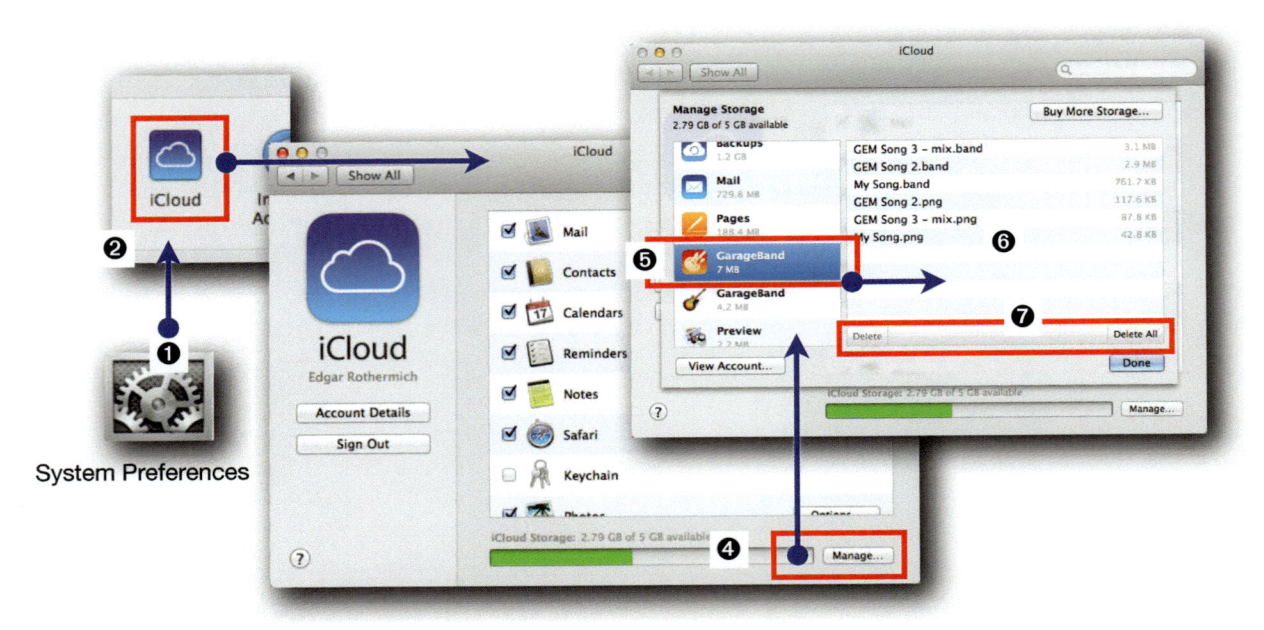

❶ Open the System Preferences.

❷ **Click** on the iCloud Icon.

❹ **Click** on the "Manage…" Button at the bottom of the screen.

❺ The sidebar on the left of this page shows you all the apps that use iCloud for storing data. **Click** on GarageBand to select it.

❻ The window pane on the right displays the content of the Document folder with all the GarageBand files that are stored on iCloud.

❼ **Click** on any file in the list and then **click** the Delete Button at the bottom to delete it.

Song File Transfer (the backdoor)

We learned that when a GarageBand Song on your iPad is synced to iCloud, it is placed on every computer that is logged into that same iCloud account. This enables you to use the following "backdoor file transfer" procedure. On your computer, you can just copy that GarageBand Project File (the local-Documents file) from the "Mobile Documents" folder in your Library directory to anywhere in the Finder. This might be an easier alternative to the somewhat complex *iTunes File Sharing* procedure.

➡ How about Windows?

If you don't have an iCloud account yet, you can sign up with an Apple ID in either the System Preferences on your Mac computer or the Settings app on your iDevice. This is also where you sign into iCloud with your Apple ID.

Even on Windows you can use iCloud with the iCloud Control Panel to sign up and sign in.

The file transfer with iTunes on Windows also works, although, there is not much use for the .band file because GarageBand X runs only on Mac and not Windows. However, there are some third party solutions that can extend the usability on Windows.

iCloud Control Panel for Windows

In this chapter, I will go over the basic configurations of a Song, the settings that are necessary and need to be understood.

Song Settings

 Tap on the Wrench Icon in the Control Bar to open the Song Settings popup window. This button is available in the Tracks View and Instrument View.

The Song Settings provide ten (plus one) parameters that are always visible. However, not all the parameters configure the current Song. In the screenshot, I grouped them together to point out their different functionality:

❶ The first seven parameters configure the current Song and those settings are stored with the Song File.

❷ The next two settings are global GarageBand Preferences and are not stored with the Song File. These parameters would be listed in a Preference window. GarageBand doesn't have one (except the one in the iOS Settings app), so they ended up in the Song Settings window.

❸ The last parameter is not even a parameter. It is a button, which opens a popup window with the online Help manual.

I highlighted the three most important parameters that determine your Song.

❹ Tempo - Key Signature - Time Signature

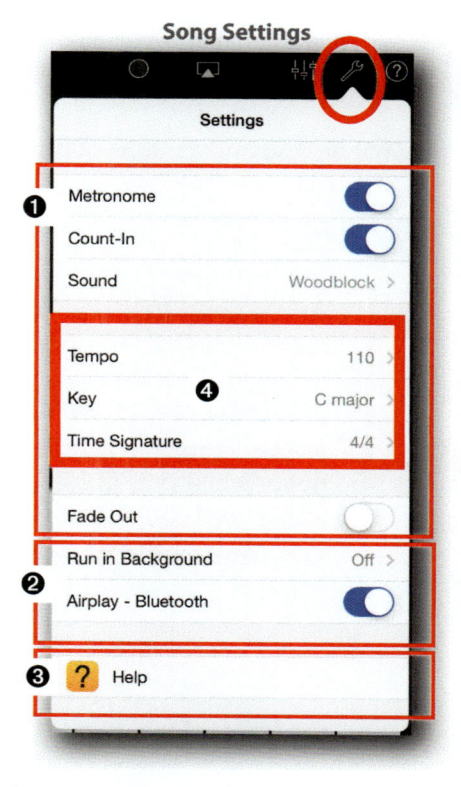

Without the proper understanding of their function and consequences of those parameters, you could get unpleasant surprises when trying to change them later in your Song.

Song Parameter

We already learned that when creating a new Song, GarageBand makes you select an Instrument first from the Instrument Browser window. Now, even before you start recording your first note on that Instrument, you should open the Song Settings and set these three important parameters:

➡ *Time Signature*

The Time Signature Parameter displays the time signature of your Song. **Tap** on the arrow to open the Time Signature Window to change it.

This parameter is the "least dangerous" one. Chances are, 99.9% of all GarageBand songs are created in 4/4 anyway. In case you fancy a waltz, just select the 3/4 or 6/8. You will see the Time Ruler change accordingly. Even changing that parameter after you have recorded some Regions already will only shift the downbeat and the bar numbers in the Time Ruler without affecting the relative position or pitch of your Regions.

One little side effect with 3/4 and 6/8 Time Signature:

 If you use any of those settings and want to select Apple Loops for your waltz, you will get an error message saying *"Loops are not available for this time signature"*. The reason is that Apple Loops have a time signature embedded and GarageBand limits the search results to those Loops that have the time signature that is selected in your Song Settings. All the Apple Loops on your iPad are only in 4/4 time signature, therefore, - nothing found.

➡ *Tempo*

The Tempo Parameter displays the Tempo of your Song. *Tap* on the arrow to open the Tempo Window. You can set the tempo in two ways:

 Tap the up and down arrow on the right to change the Tempo value up or down by increments or *slide* the number up or down.

 Tap a constant beat on the left button and GarageBand detects your tempo and sets its value automatically.

So what are the implications of the tempo setting?

 First of all, for a GarageBand Song on the iPad, you can choose only one constant Tempo value.

🔘 What happens when you change the Tempo after you recorded (or placed) Regions in your Song.

- **Apple Loop Regions** (blue) and **MIDI Regions** (green) will follow the new tempo. That means, you can start with a tempo of 120bpm, record some MIDI Regions, and place Apple Loops in your Song. When you decide that the Song sounds better in 130bpm, just change the tempo and the Regions play faster without changing their pitch.
- **Newly recorded Audio Regions** (blue) do NOT follow the tempo. That means if you record your guitar while at 120bpm and then change the tempo to 130, the guitar recording still plays the way it was recorded (120bpm) and, therefore, is too slow in the new tempo.
- **Imported Audio Files** (blue) have their fixed tempo and do NOT follow the tempo of your Song. You could use those files anyway, only in a Song that matches their tempo.

➡ *Key Signature*

The Key Parameter displays the key signature of your Song. *Tap* on the arrow to open the Key Window.
There are three settings:

🔘 **Key**: Select any of the 12 chromatic keys for your song.
  - Apple Loops Region (**blue**): This is the most important setting for Apple Loops because Apple Loop Regions will be transposed to play in the selected key.
  - MIDI Regions (**green**): This setting is only important when you have "Follow Song Key" activated (see below).
  - Audio Region (**blue**): This setting has no effect on Audio Regions.

🔘 **Tonality**: Set the tonality (scale) to major or minor.
  This setting has no influence on any of the Regions and is more important if you plan to print out your Song as a score later (in GarageBand X or Logic Pro).

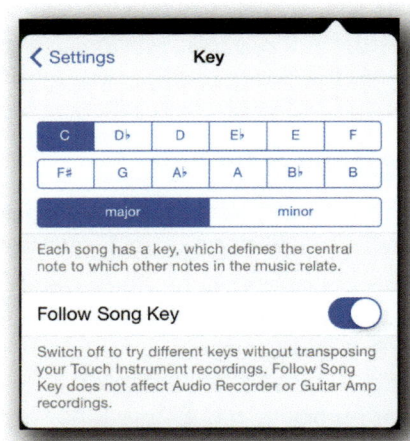

🔘 **Follow Song Key**: This setting will only affect MIDI Regions (Software Instruments). When activated (by default), all the notes in the existing MIDI Regions are transposed when you change the key of your Song; they "follow" the Song's Key Signature.

Understanding Follow Song Key

You have to understand that Apple Loop Regions have a specific Key information embedded in their file. This is the key it was recorded in and was entered by the creator of the Apple Loop (i.e. the key F). If you place this Apple Loop into your Song that is set to G, then GarageBand knows to play the Apple Loop two semitones higher to match the Song's Key. Whatever key you select for your Song, the Apple Loop will follow automatically. You do not have to activate the "Follow Song Key" feature for Apple Loops.

MIDI Regions contain the individual notes you played as single MIDI Events. You can play whatever notes in whatever key and they are not affected by the Key or the Follow Song Key setting. However, once you activate "Follow Song Key", this behavior changes (only for the existing Notes, not the newly recorded notes!). The Key setting doesn't function as an absolute key information as with Apple Loops. With MIDI Regions, they function as a transpose command. There is no key information embedded in a MIDI Region, just the MIDI notes.

> For example, if the Song key is set to C and you activate "Follow Song Key" then changing to the Song Key D will transpose the recorded notes in (all) the MIDI Regions of your Song two semitones higher. Turning the feature off and setting the key to G will do nothing to the MIDI Region. Turning the feature on again and setting the Key to A will transpose the MIDI notes another two semitones. It is just a relative transpose command "if" the Follow Song Key" is activated while you are selecting a different key.

Metronome

The first two settings in the Song Settings window configure the Metronome, your "virtual conductor".

➡ *Metronome*

This switch turns the Metronome on and off, a click that plays on every beat in the selected Tempo. These are the quarter notes in 4/4 and 3/4 and eighth notes when the 6/8 time signature is selected.

➡ *Count-In*

This switch turns the Count-In feature on. It is a recording feature:

- *Off*: When hitting the Record Button, GarageBand start to record at the current position of the Playhead.
- *On*: When hitting the Record Button, GarageBand starts to play on the downbeat of the bar that is before the bar it is parked at right now. For example, if the Playhead is parked at 7.3, then GarageBand starts to play on bar 6.1 with the Metronome sound and switches to Record Mode on bar 7.1.

Please note that the Count-in is independent of the Metronome. If the Metronome is off, then the Click stops after the Count-In.

➡ *Sound*

Tap on the Sound button to open the Sound window where you can choose from four different Metronome sounds.

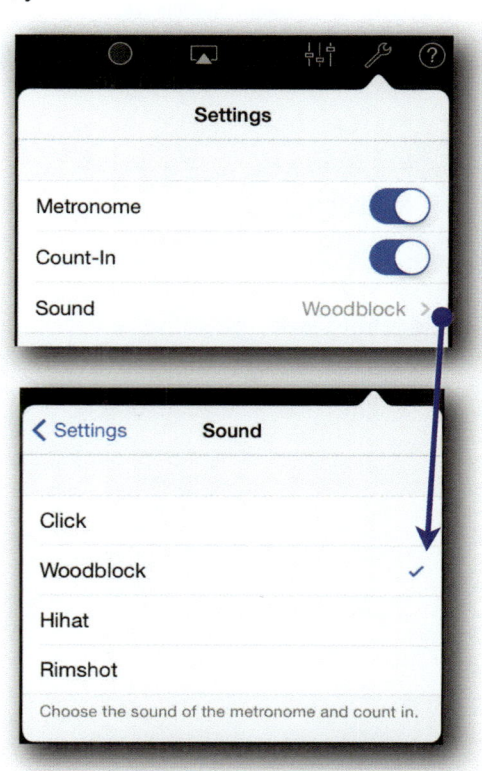

Fade Out

This is a similar feature as in GarageBand X, but here it is even more useful. Because GarageBand on the iPad doesn't have any automation or even a Master Track, this setting lets you create a 10s automatic fade out at the end of your song.

- The end of your Song is always the last Bar of your last Song Section regardless of the Regions.
- The Fade Out is applied during the export of your Song and during playback, but not when recording new Regions.

Edit Chords

If you are in the Instrument View and have a Smart Instrument selected (except Smart Drums), then the Song Settings Menu lists one additional item below the Time Signature, the "Edit Chords" Button. *Tap* it to open the *Custom Chords* configuration window.

🌑 Custom Chords Configuration

The window displays the eight chord strips that are used to play the Smart Instruments. These are the standard major and minor chords for the selected key in the current Song.

However, you can configure any chord strip by selecting it (it turns blue) and setting its parameters by *swiping* the wheels above. The four wheels represent:

- ▶ Root note
- ▶ Third
- ▶ Fifth
- ▶ Bass note

This setting is stored with the current Song.

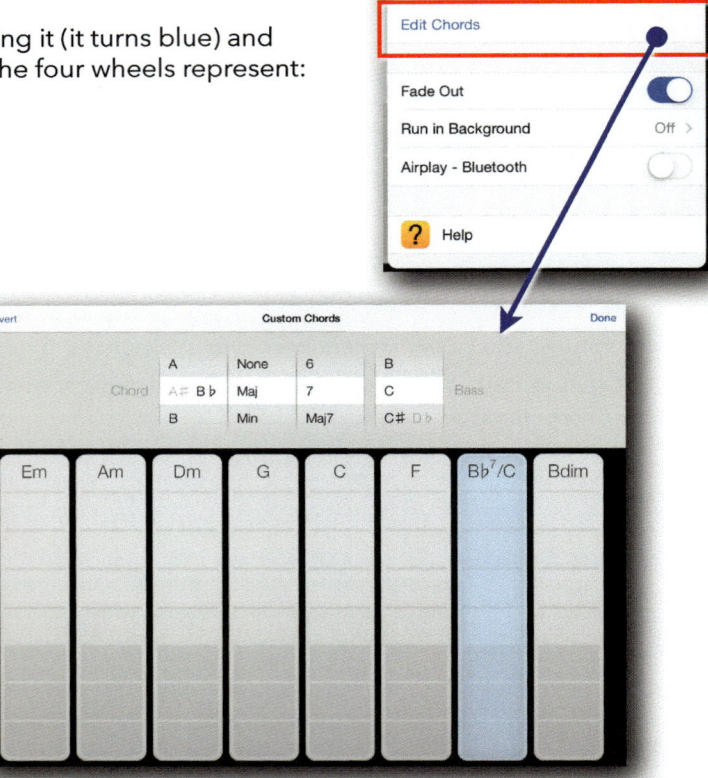

GarageBand Preferences

The next two settings are the ones that are independent from the current Song and apply to the GarageBand app in general.

➡ **Run in Background**

Usually, when you switch to a different app on your iPad, GarageBand will stop playing or recording. Turning this mode on will allow GarageBand to continue to play or record (through external Audio or MIDI input), even when you switch to a different app. The iPad control bar is now red and displays "GarageBand (Recording)".

Tapping on the "Run in Background" feature will popup a window reminding you that by doing so you might experience performance issues. After tapping OK, you'll get to another window where you can turn that feature on and off.

This window has another setting "Use with Music Apps" that improves GarageBand's performance while running with other Music Apps in the background.

➡ **Airplay - Bluetooth - HDMI**

Tap on this button ❶ to turn on "Airplay - Bluetooth - HDMI".

- This enables GarageBand to play back to external output Devices.
- An Alert Window ❷ will warn you about the "side effects" when this feature is enabled. The Audio Input is disabled and the Touch Instruments may have a latency (slow response) when playing.
- When *tapping* OK, you will see that the *Jam Session* Button ❸ in the Control Bar has changed to the *Airplay Button* ❹ (if your iPad detects AirPlay devices).
- Tapping on the Airplay Button opens the Airplay Window ❺ with all the available Airplay devices you can choose from to mirror GarageBand (audio and screen) with those devices (minimum requirement: iOS 5.1 and iPad2).

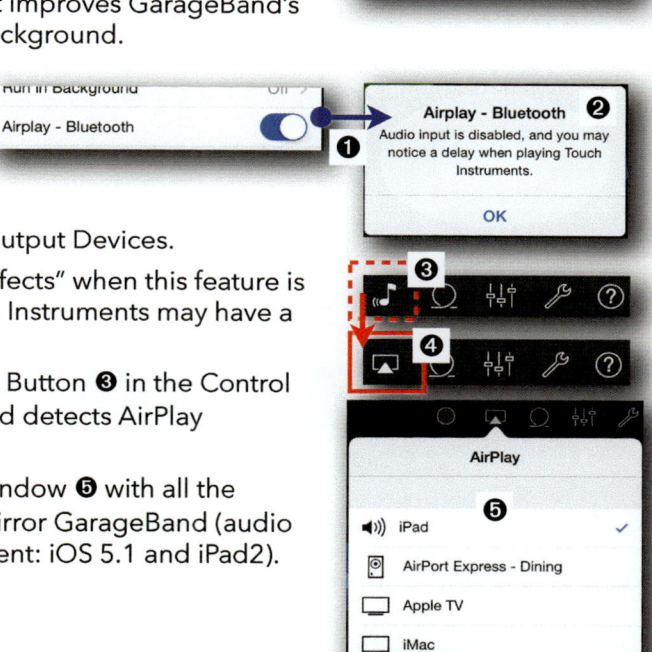

Help Manual

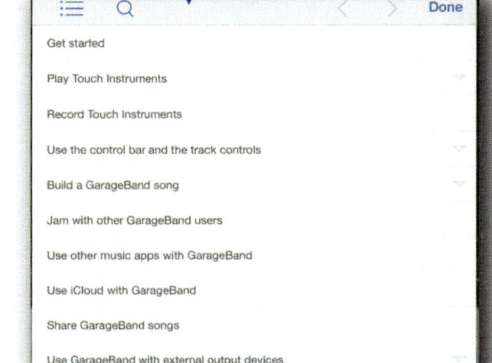

The last button on the Song Settings Window is the Help Button. It opens a big popup window in the center of the screen with a comprehensive online manual.

- *Tap* on a topic to open that chapter.
- *Tap* ☰ to go to the main page (TOC) or *slide* left.
- *Tap* ‹ › to go to the previous or next page.
- *Tap* 🔍 to open the search window.
- *Tap* Done to close the Help window.
- It has hot links that jump to related sections.
- If you close the manual and reopen the next time, it remembers the page you were on.

GarageBand has a unique way of letting you set the length and the structure of your Song.

A GarageBand Song is made up of SECTIONS

This might be a bit different from what you are used to from other DAWs, so let me explain the basic concept first:

Concept

When you create a new Song in GarageBand, it will be 8 bars long. These 8 bars are called a "Section". Because it is the first Section, it is called "Section A".

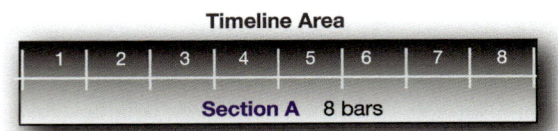

However, the Song you are working on might be longer than 8 bars. In that case you have two different workflow options:

- **Option 1**: Stay with that single Section and extend it to the exact Song length you need.
- **Option 2**: Create multiple Sections that represent the structure of your Song (i.e. Intro, Verse1, Chorus, Verse2, etc.).

Here is a very simple example to demonstrate that principle. The Song you want to create is 16 bars long.

➡ Option 1

You keep **Section A** and extend its length to 16 bars. No structure, just one section.

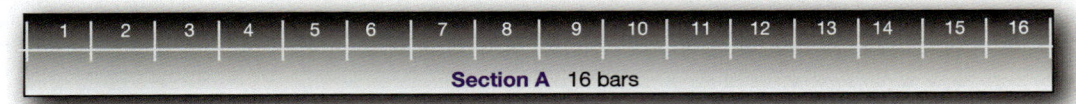

➡ Option 2

You keep **Section A**, but add two more sections. **Section B** with 4 bars and **Section C** also with 4 bars.

If you think about it, option 1 is the standard workflow in many DAWs where the Timeline represents the whole duration of the Song, one long section. If you are familiar with the Arrange Track in GarageBand X, then you find that it is similar to option 2. Regarding the length of the Song, both options are the same. However, when you structure your Song into Sections (these are called "Arrange Markers" in GarageBand X) based on the structure of your Song, then you have some advantages later when it comes to editing.

For example, you've recorded all the rhythm tracks for Verse1. Those will probably be the same in Verse2 and Verse3. So you can just duplicate Verse1, and all the Regions inside the range of that Section (Verse1) will be duplicated in one step instead of copying all the Regions one by one.

Please note: The Track Settings Parameter *Quantization* and *Transposition* can be set differently for individual Song Sections.

Now let's go through the steps on how to create and manage those Sections.

Song Section Controls

At the right end of the Time Ruler is a plus sign ❶, the Song Section Button. *Tap* on it to open the Song Sections Window with the necessary controls for creating and managing Sections.

The Song Sections Window is dynamic; it changes its content, displaying all the Sections in your Song. When you open it for the first time, it has only three buttons ❷:

- **Section Button**: This button displays the name of the Section (the default "Section A") and how many bars it has (the default 8 bars). *Tapping* on the arrow to the right will open the Length Window ❹. Please note that new Sections are named with consecutive letters (Section A, Section B, Section C, etc.). They cannot be renamed (even if you re-order the Sections later).
- **Duplicate**: *Tapping* this button will duplicate the selected Section, creating a new Section with the same length at the end of the last Section. It also duplicates all the Regions inside that Section.
- **Add**: *Tapping* this button will add a new 8 bar Section at the end of the last Section.

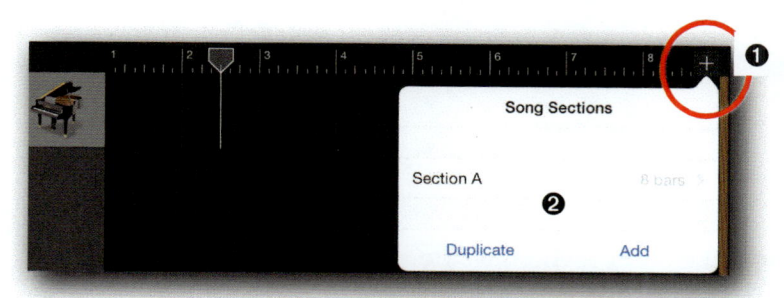

Once you've created at least one more section, the Song Section window will change.

- The top of the window has a new button "All Sections" ❸ that lets you display all the Sections in the Timeline. *Double-tap* the button or select it and *tap* outside the window to close it. Selecting a single Section will display only that Section in the Timeline Area.

- *Tapping* the ⓘ button on a Section Button opens the Length Window ❹.
  - Set the length of the Section manually by *swiping* up or down on the number ❻ or incrementally by *tapping* on the up or down arrow. Please note: Shortening a Section will delete any Region that might be there!
  - Set the length to Automatic ❼ so GarageBand automatically extends the length of the Section instead of returning to the beginning when you reach the end of the Section while recording. The Automatic Button is only available on the last Section. Select *Automatic* when you import Audio Files. Otherwise, the Audio Region will be shortened (not the Audio File) if the current Song Section is shorter than the imported Audio Region.

- *Tap* the Edit button ❺ to open the Edit window.
  - **Delete** a Section by *tapping* the minus button ❽ and then the Delete Button.
  - **Move** a Section by *dragging* the 3-stripe handle ❾ up or down to easily change your Song structure without moving Regions manually.

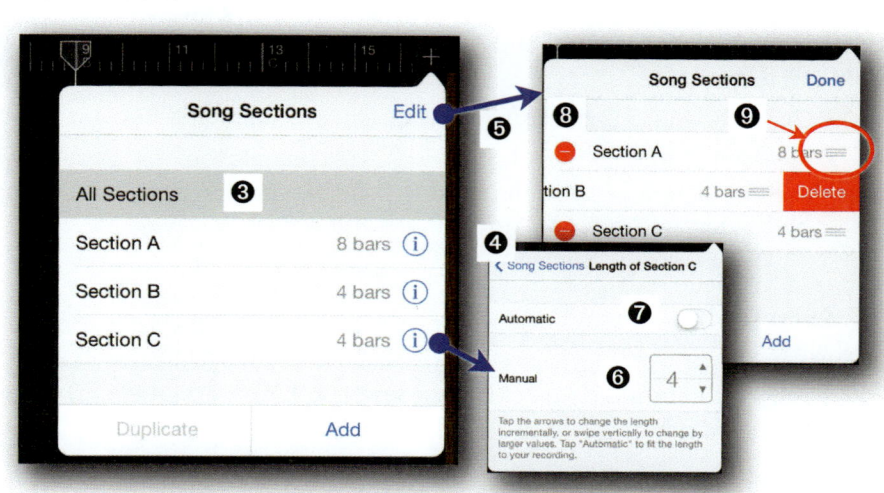

Sections in the Timeline

Once you have more than one Section created in your Song, then you can choose what is displayed in the Timeline Area of your Song (the Workspace).

🔵 All Sections View

If you select the "All Sections" button ❶ in the Song Section window, then the Timeline will display your whole Song with all the Sections. The Ruler will show the letter ❷ of the Section to indicate where each individual Section starts.

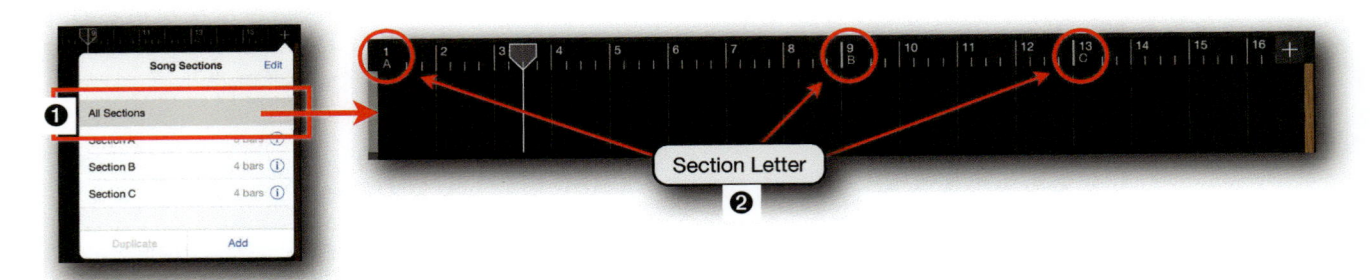

🔵 Single Section View

If you select a single Section in the Song Sections window, then two things will happen:
- The Timeline in the background (behind the Song Sections window) will display the whole Song with the selected Section highlighted ❸.
- When **double-tapping** on the Section (or **tapping** outside the window), the Song Sections window will close and the Timeline will zoom to display only the bars ❹ of the selected Section.

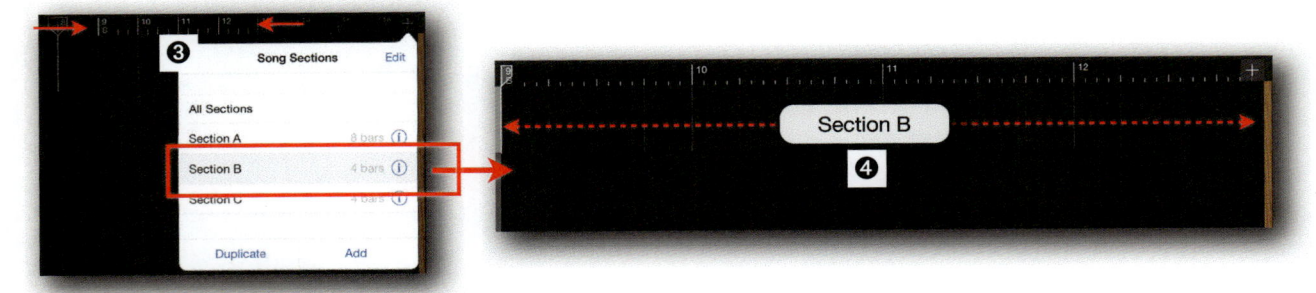

🔵 Go to different Section

Once you are in the Single Section View, GarageBand plays and records in Cycle Mode between the beginning and end of that Section. You can go to a different Section in two different ways:
- Go to the Song Sections window again and select the Section you want.
- **Swipe** the Timeline area left or right. This reveals the next Section with a little arrow marker ❺. Release your finger and the next Section snaps into place. This works also on the Single Track Lane in the Instrument View window.

🔵 Song Limit

The maximum length of a Song in GarageBand can be 320 bars, as one single Section or all Sections combined (max 10 Sections). If you exceed that limit, GarageBand will popup an Alert window.

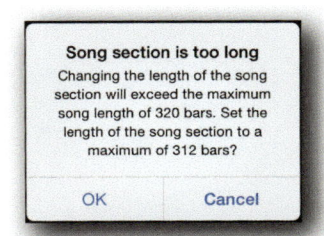

Now we are finally getting to the point where we actually record something in our Song. Especially for a beginner, this can be sometimes overwhelming with all the choices and options, even with an easy app like GarageBand. To avoid any confusion and to always stay on top of what is happening (or why something is not happening), let's start with a simple diagram that demonstrates the concept of recording in GarageBand and a DAW in general.

Recording Basics

Whenever you are about to record, you have to ask yourself two questions:

☑ **Which Source** do you want to record? Or where is the signal coming from?

☑ **What Signal** are you recording, or better, what type of signal is the Source producing?

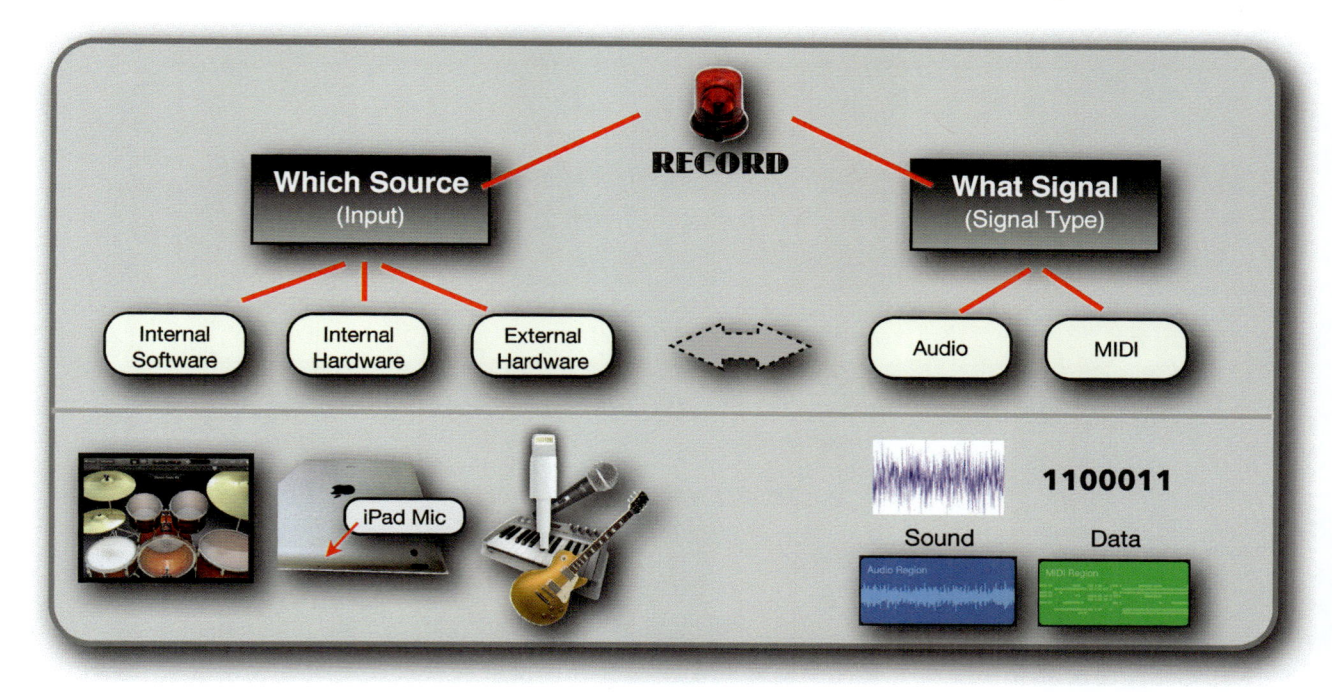

In GarageBand, there are three different Sources:

- **Internal Software**: Use the iPad interface to record music by using GarageBand's Touch Instruments (Software Instruments) or other audio apps on your iPad via Audiobus or the new Inter-App Audio feature.
- **Internal Hardware**: Use the built-in Microphone.
- **External Hardware**: Use the iPad's Headphones Jack or Dock Connector to plug in earbuds, adapter cable, or an external device (audio or MIDI Interface).

The Source you are about to record can produce any one of two types of signals:

- **Audio Signal:** This is a sound signal coming from an acoustic sound source (i.e. microphone, acoustic instrument) or an electric sound source (i.e. electric guitar, synthesizer).
- **MIDI Signal:** This is a data signal, a MIDI data signal to be specific. In this case, you are recording the raw data of the notes (MIDI Events) generated by the source. The sound itself is produced by a Sound Generator that is part of the MIDI Track. It "plays" the MIDI Signal and, therefore, becomes also an audio signal afterwards.

Recording Setup

Once you picked your source that you want to record and are aware of what kind of signal it produces (Audio or MIDI), then you can ask the next question:

Where do I record the Signal to - on a Track

You always record a signal on a Track, onto the Track that is selected. The selected Track is the highlighted one. And here is where it all comes together:

❶ The Source you want to record determines what Instrument Type you chose in the Instrument Browser.
❷ The Instrument Type determines what Track Type is created (Audio Track or MIDI Track).
❸ The Track Type determines what Signal Type you can record on it (Audio Signal or MIDI Signal).
❹ The Signal Type determines what Region Type is recorded on the Track (Audio Region or MIDI Region).

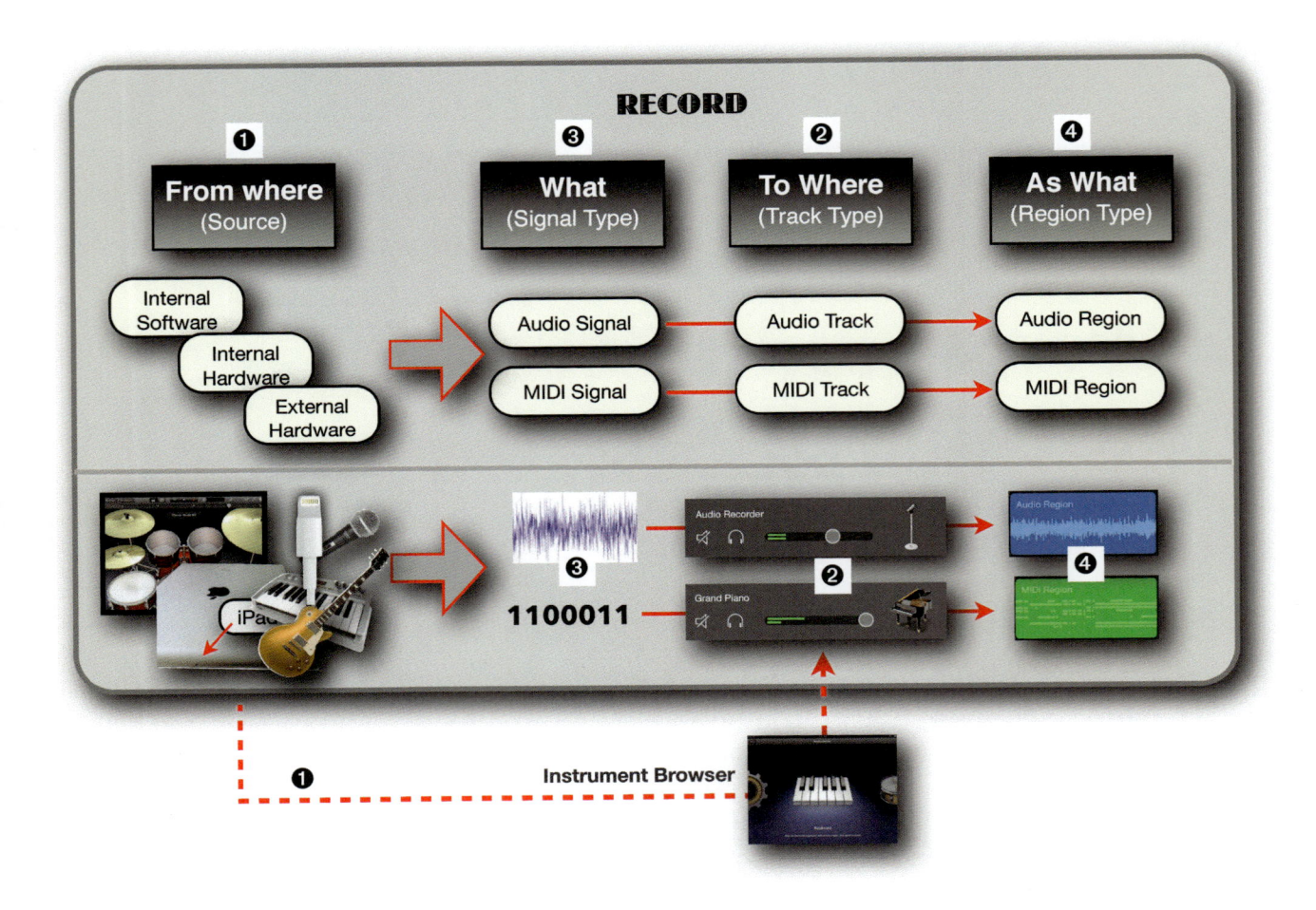

As we can see, everything is related to **Instruments-Tracks-Regions** and the recording procedure in general comes down to the fundamental distinction between Audio and MIDI. Once you are clear about that, then you don't need that "substitute" terminology with "Software Instruments" and "Real Instruments".

Now let's look at how to record a signal, a **MIDI Signal** and an **Audio Signal**.

Recording New MIDI

Source

Standard Instruments
- Keyboard
- Drums

Sampler Instrument
- Sampler

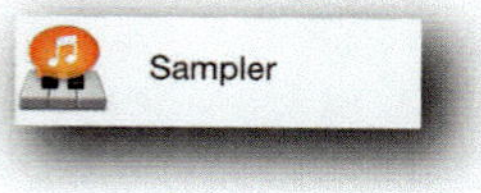

Smart Instruments
- Smart Drums 
- Smart Strings
- Smart Bass
- Smart Keyboard
- Smart Guitar

The Instrument Browser has eight Instrument Types that will create a MIDI Track.

Please remember, as we discussed already in the Instrument Browser chapter, there is no visual indication as to which one of the ten "Instruments" can create a MIDI Track and which one create an Audio Track (only the Audio Recorder and Guitar Amp).

Picking any of those (MIDI) Instruments as the Source will create a MIDI Track that the Instrument is assigned to. Playing the Instrument will produce MIDI data that is recorded as MIDI Regions on that MIDI Track.

Touch Instrument

These eight Instruments are Software Instruments inside the iPad, not a physical hardware musical instrument. We "play" that Software Instrument with Gestures by touching the iPad screen with our finger, therefore the term "Touch Instrument".

➡ *The Big Picture*

Although that instrument, when we play it, produces a sound (an audio signal) it is still a MIDI Instrument and when we record what we are playing with our touch, we are not recording the audio signal we are hearing. We are recording the MIDI data of what we are playing. Here is the signal flow diagram again for a MIDI Track.:

❶ Playing the touch interface on the iPad creates MIDI data of what we are playing. Each note is represented by a MIDI Event.

❷ Those MIDI Events are recorded on the MIDI Track as green MIDI Regions on the MIDI Track's Track Lane.

❸ The Sound Generator (Sound Module) is the component that creates an "audio" sound out of the MIDI data. Changing the Patch on the Sound Module changes the sound of what we are hearing.

The Sound Module's input is coming from two sources:

- ❹ Directly from the Touch Instrument. That's why we can play (hear audio) the instrument even without recording anything.
- ❺ From the MIDI Region when played back on the Track Lane. That's why we can freely change the MIDI recording to any sound, only the played note information (data) is recorded, not the played sound (audio).

❻ It is very convenient to play and record on the virtual keyboard on your iPad or even iPhone anywhere you are without carrying a real musical keyboard with you. However, playing the virtual keys on a touch interface has its limitations compared to real keys. That's why you can connect a MIDI keyboard to your iPad via the Dock connector. The MIDI data from the MIDI keyboard is now treated the same way as the MIDI data created by the Touch Instrument. You actually can play both at the same time.

There are different hardware solutions from various vendors that let you connect MIDI Keyboards to your iPad via the Dock connector. See the chapter at the beginning of the book.

❼ The input of the Sound Module is a MIDI signal, but the output is an audio signal. That means from that point on in the signal flow, the MIDI Track contains the same components as an Audio Track: Audio Effects, Reverb, Volume, etc.

Recording Procedure

In virtually any DAW, including GarageBand X, you will record while in the Tracks Area of the GarageBand Window. In GarageBand for iPad, this would be the Tracks View window. However, GarageBand for iPad won't let you record in the Tracks View window.

> **Recording is done in the Instrument View window**

Although both, the Tracks View and the Instrument View, have the Record Button available, the actual recording is still done in the Instrument View. If you start the recording in the Tracks View, GarageBand will start a 1 bar Count-In (even if Count-In is disabled) and uses that time to switch to the Instrument View before starting the recording there.

➡ Recording (in the Instrument View)

🔘 Select the Track/Instrument

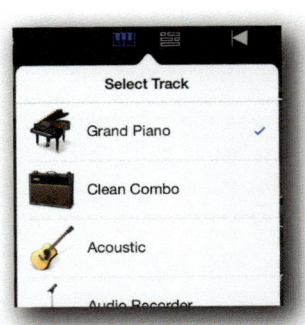

Because an Instrument is always assigned to a Track, by selecting the Track, you automatically select the Instrument and vice versa. As we have already discussed in the Instrument View chapter, you can *tap-hold* the View button (which displays all the available Tracks in your current Song) and switch to a different Track in the Instrument View. *Tap* on a Track to select it.

🔘 Select the Recording Position

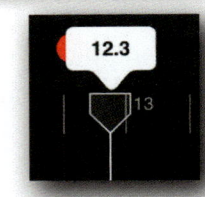

Drag the Playhead along the Time Ruler to the position where you want to start the new recording (bar) or *tap* the "Back to Beginning" Button to set the Playhead to the beginning of the Song Section. Make sure you are in the right Song Section or display all Sections (see the chapter about Song Sections).

🔘 Set Metronome and Count-In (optional)

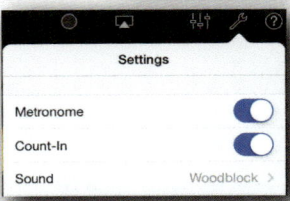

Open the Song Settings window by *tapping* on the Wrench Icon 🔧 in the Control Bar to enable the Metronome and Count-In if needed.

🔘 Start Recording

Tap the Record Button to start the recording

🔘 What will happen next

- ▶ The recording starts at the Playhead position (after the one bar Count-In).
- ▶ The moving Playhead creates a red Region while it is in Recording Mode.
- ▶ Anything played on the Instrument will be recorded as MIDI Events.
- ▶ When you *tap* the Stop or Play Button, GarageBand stops, sets the Playhead back at the position where it started, and a new green MIDI Region appears containing the MIDI Events you just played. The new Region is rounded to start and end at the full bar position. The length of the Region is only as long as from the first to the last recorded note (rounded to the full bar).
- ▶ You can *tap* the Undo ↩ Button to delete the Region you just recorded.
- ▶ If you didn't play anything (didn't generate MIDI data), then no Region will be created.

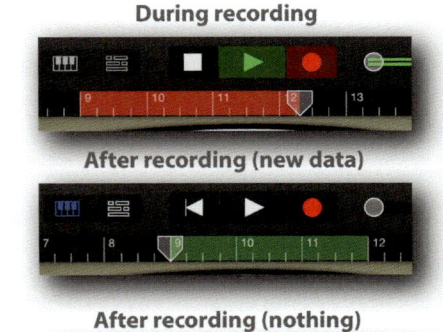

During recording

After recording (new data)

After recording (nothing)

⦿ Punch In-Out

Punch-in and Punch-out is a standard recording technique. While the song is playing, you **tap** the Record Button at a specific position to start the recording right there and **tap** the Record Button again at a specific position where you want to disable recording while the song still continues to play. This is also referred to as *drop-in* and *drop-out*.

➡ *Track Settings*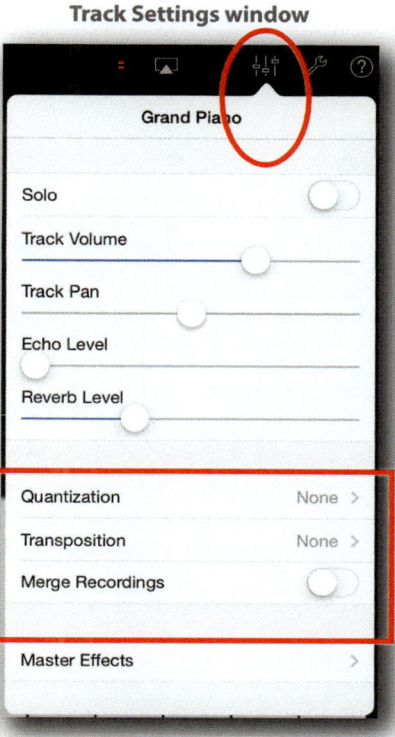

You have to be aware that there are settings in the Track Settings window, which will affect the recorded data.

⦿ Quantization

Although this is a playback parameter, make sure it is set to the value you want; otherwise, your recording might sound quite different regarding the timing. I cover the details in the Editing chapter.

⦿ Transposition

This is also just a playback parameter. However, if you have set a value while recording, then the existing Regions keep that Transposition value while the newly recorded Region will have no Transposition value. The newly displayed value will be "Multiple" without any indication of what the previous value was.

⦿ Merge Recordings

Per default, recording over an existing Region will overwrite (delete) the existing MIDI data. Enabling *Merge Recordings* will keep any existing MIDI notes and just add the new MIDI Notes to it, therefore merging both data. This is especially useful in Cycle Recording when creating drum tracks or any layered recordings.

A Drums Instrument has *Merge Recordings* enabled by default.

➡ *Cycle Recording*

GarageBand doesn't have a separate Cycle Mode where you can mark two locator positions A and B, and let GarageBand play that section repeatedly. Instead, GarageBand is always in Cycle Mode.

The locations A and B are the beginning and end of the currently selected Song Section, either a single one or all the Song Sections.

Source

The Instrument Browser contains two Instrument Types that create an Audio Track,
Audio Recorder and **_Guitar Amp_**.

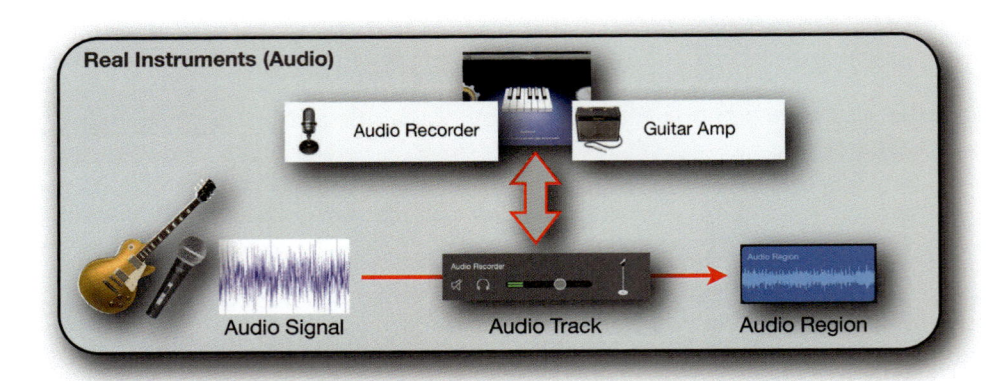

These two "Instruments" are not really instruments. You cannot "play" them on your iPad like the other Touch Instruments. The sound is also not created by a Sound Module that is part of GarageBand (Software Instruments). Instead, these two selections let you connect "Real (electric) Instruments" to your iPad or let you use a microphone that records "Real (acoustic) Instruments". Therefore, the Instrument is played "outside" of GarageBand and the Track that is assigned to these two instruments is just a standard Audio Track that you feed the Audio Signal to. The recorded Audio Signal is then placed as a blue Audio Region on the Track's Track Lane. Although Audio Recorder and Guitar Amp are both Audio Tracks, there is one little difference.

As I just mentioned, there is no Instrument (Sound Generator) "inside" the signal flow like we saw with the MIDI Track. The signal comes from "outside" as an Audio Signal. This Input signal can come from four different sources:

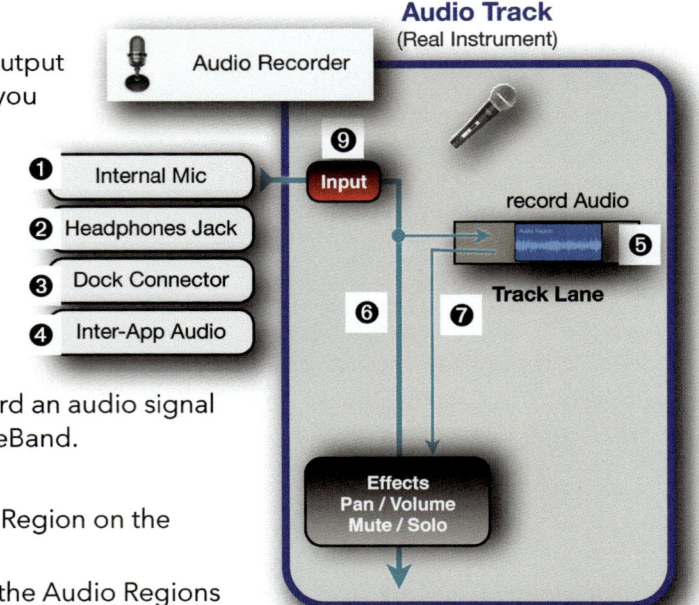

- ❶ The built-in microphone on the iPad (or iPhone).
- ❷ The Headphones Jack. Please note that this is an output +input connection. When you plug in your earbuds, you hear the output signal, but you can also use the mic on the earbuds as a microphone, sending an audio signal to the iPad through the Headphones Jack.
- ❸ The third option to send an audio signal to the iPad is via the Dock connector. These are the external devices that let you connect either a microphone or an electric instrument to send its audio signal to the Audio Track.
- ❹ Inter-App Audio is a new feature that lets you record an audio signal from a different app on your iPad directly into GarageBand.

❺ The input signal will be recorded as a blue Audio Region on the Track's Track Lane.

❻ The input signal and the signal played back from the Audio Regions

❼ goes through the usual signal processing components.

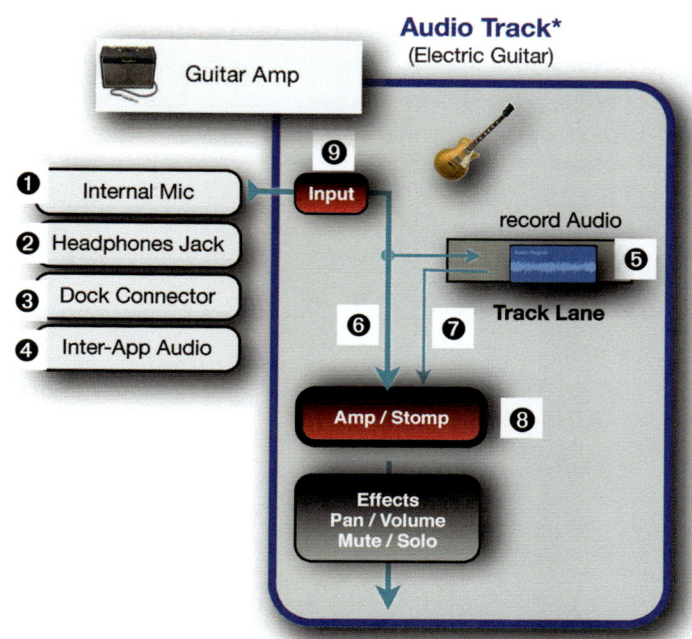

Audio Track*
(Electric Guitar)

Guitar Amp

❶ Internal Mic
❷ Headphones Jack
❸ Dock Connector
❹ Inter-App Audio

❾ Input

record Audio

❺ Track Lane

❻ ❼

Amp / Stomp ❽

Effects
Pan / Volume
Mute / Solo

❽ This is the additional component that is different in the Audio Track that is assigned to the Guitar Amp Instrument, the Amp Simulator with the Stompboxes. Technically, this is just an additional signal processor added to the Audio Track's signal flow. Although suitable for electric guitars, you can feed any audio signal to that Track if you want to experiment.

The most important fact is that the signal is recorded "dry" before the guitar amp effect. That lets you change the sound (choose different amps or stompboxes) anytime after you've recorded the guitar.

➡️ *Input Setting*

Both Audio Tracks provide an Input Settings Window that you open by *tapping* on the Input Settings Button ✐ ❾. The controls vary, depending on the connected input t device.

- **Automatic**: When enabled, GarageBand sets the audio input level automatically (the Input Slider disappears).
- **Input Slider**: *Drag* the slider to adjust the input level. An LED meter lets you view the strength of the incoming audio signal so you can avoid hitting the red "clipping" LED.
- **Inter-App Audio**: Select an audio app on your iPad as the source.
- **Monitor**: When disabled, you can't hear the input signal ❻, only the already recorded signal coming from the Regions ❼.
- **Noise Gate**: You can enable a Noise Gate, that lets you cut out noise in the background. When activated, a slider lets you adjust the threshold at what level the gate gets activated. Whatever the Noise Gate "lets through", that is what you record on that Track (*Wiki-Moment: Noise Gate*).

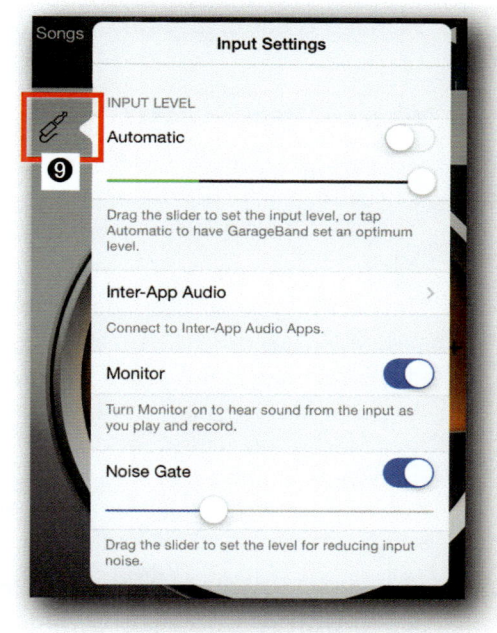

Recording Procedure

The procedure for recording on an Audio Track is almost the same as with MIDI Tracks. I will go through the steps and point out the differences. Make sure to switch to Airplane mode on your iDevice and turn off any alarms.

🔘 Select Instrument View

Recording is done in the Instrument View. If initiated in the Tracks View, then GarageBand automatically switches to the Instrument View when pressing the Record Button. It plays a one bar Count-In while it switches the view.

🔘 Select the Track/Instrument

Tap-hold the View Button, which displays all the available Tracks in your current Song. *Tap* on an Audio Track to select the one you want to record on.

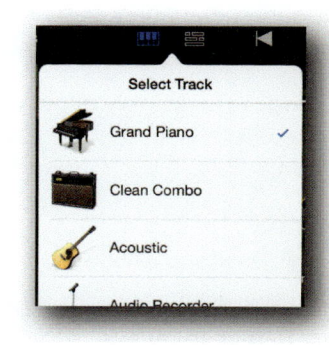

 **Input Settings:** This is the extra step when recording an Audio Track, which doesn't exist on a MIDI Track. While a MIDI Track just records a data signal that doesn't need level adjustments (either it is there or not), an Audio Signal that you record on an Audio Track requires proper level setting. For example, if the audio signal is too strong, it results in audible distortion and if the signal is too low (although not as bad) you lose valuable dynamic range. **Tap** on the Input Settings Button to open the Input Settings Window (disabled in Airplay Mode).

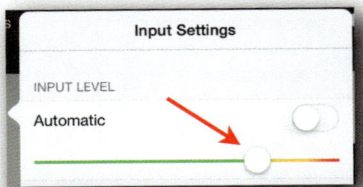

I mentioned already that the available controls vary depending on the current input device. Some of them have an Input Level slider that adjusts the level of the audio signal, which you are about to record in GarageBand. If you have no slider available (i.e. with the built-in mic) make sure you adjust the source itself (i.e. distance from the microphone, output level control on the source device).

Select the Recording Position

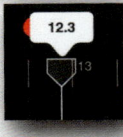

Drag the Playhead along the Time Ruler to the position where you want to start the new recording (bar).

Set Metronome and Count-In (optional)

Available in the Song Settings Window .

Start Recording

Tap the Record Button to start the recording.

What will happen next?

▶ The recording starts at the Playhead Position (after the one bar Count-In).

▶ The moving Playhead creates a red Region while it is in recording mode.

▶ The input signal will now be recorded.

▶ When you **tap** the Stop or Play Button, GarageBand stops, sets the Playhead back at the position where it started, and a new blue Audio Region appears containing the audio signal that you just recorded. Here is another difference compared to the MIDI recording. When recording an audio signal, the new Region will not be rounded to full bars at the end. The Region ends exactly where you stopped the recording.

During recording

After recording (new audio)

▶ You can tap the Undo Button to delete the Region you just recorded.

▶ If you didn't play anything while recording, the Region will still be created. You just recorded "silence".

Punch In only

Audio Tracks only allow you to punch in (start record by tapping the Record Button while in Play Mode). However, punch out doesn't work. When you tap the Record Button while in Record Mode, GarageBand stops (on a MIDI Track, GarageBand continues in Play Mode).

Replace Mode

Audio Tracks always record in Replace Mode. There is no Merge Recording with Audio Signals. However, even if you record over an existing Audio Region and "replace" the existing Audio Region, it might not be deleted. I will explain this very important behavior of Audio Regions in the next chapter about Editing.

In the last two sections I explained how to record new material in your Song, MIDI or Audio. The "problem" with that is that you have to know how to play an instrument or know how to sing. The new Smart Instruments in GarageBand make it easy to "play" an instrument even if you don't "play" an instrument by using a new intuitive user interface.

Another option is to use existing, pre-recorded Audio Files. That's what I cover in this section.

Audio Files

An Audio File is a recording of an audio signal, stored as digital audio. The content of an audio file can be for example:

- **Music**: A recording of someone humming a song or the mix of a fully produced pop song.
- **Sound Effects**: Explosions, thunder, applause, etc.
- **Dialog**: Any spoken words.

In the context of creating a song, we are focusing on the first example, music.

Phrases and Patterns

Importing an audio file of an existing song into our Song doesn't make much sense. Instead, we are looking for audio files of short musical phrases and patterns, most likely of single instruments that we can use as building blocks for our own song. This could be anything from drums or percussion grooves, strumming guitar patterns, horn riffs, or even small solo licks of a guitar or saxophone.

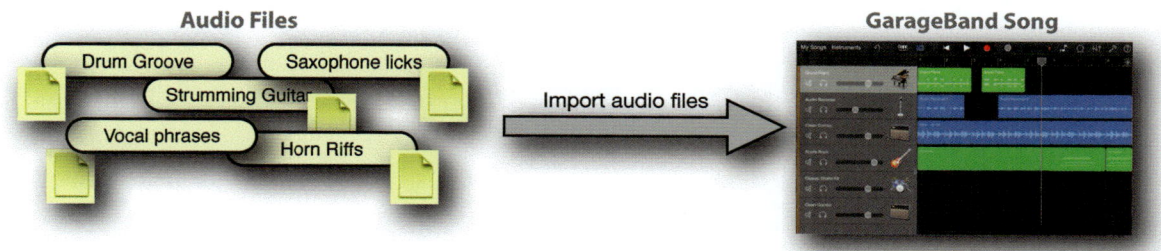

Match

There is one major obstacle when importing existing audio files into a Song. They have to match the Song Parameters!

We came across those three parameters in the Song Settings Window 🔧.
This is where we set what **Tempo** our song has, what **Key** it is in, and its **Time Signature**. The audio files we want to import have to match those parameters.

- If a saxophone phrase is recorded in C but our Song is in Eb - no match
- If a strumming pattern plays in 120bpm but our Song's Tempo is set to 130bpm - no match
- If a drum grove plays a waltz (3/4) but our Song is in 4/4 - no match

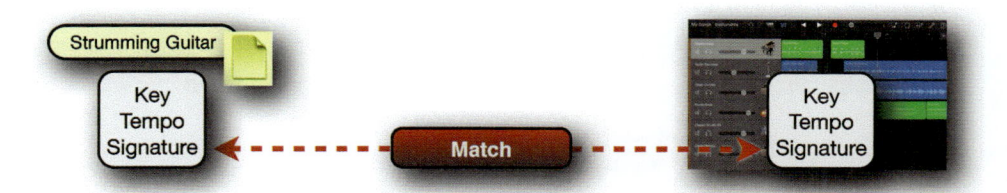

However, there is a remedy for this major restriction and it's called **Apple Loops**.

Apple Loops

Apple Loops are audio files with "special powers". On the outside, they look like regular audio files and come in standard audio formats (aiff, wav, etc.). However, besides the actual audio data, they include additional data that equip them with these two features:

☑ Keywords

This is nothing special because mp3 files also include Keywords or Metadata ("data about data") like Artist, Album, etc. that can be displayed in iTunes. Apple Loops, however, include additional information beyond that which makes them useful to search for in the context of a music production (see below).

☑ Match Tempo and Key

This is the amazing part. An Apple Loop audio file can adapt (automatically match) to the Tempo and Key of the Song it is imported into.

I'll get into much more detail in my GarageBand X manual "GarageBand X - How it Works" if you want to learn more about Apple Loops. Here is how to use them in GarageBand on the iPad:

➡ *Loop Browser*

❶ *Tap* on the Loop Browser Button 🔍 to open the Loop Browser Window. This is a highly dynamic window that lets you search and select all those Apple Loops that come installed with your GarageBand app.

The window has three sections:

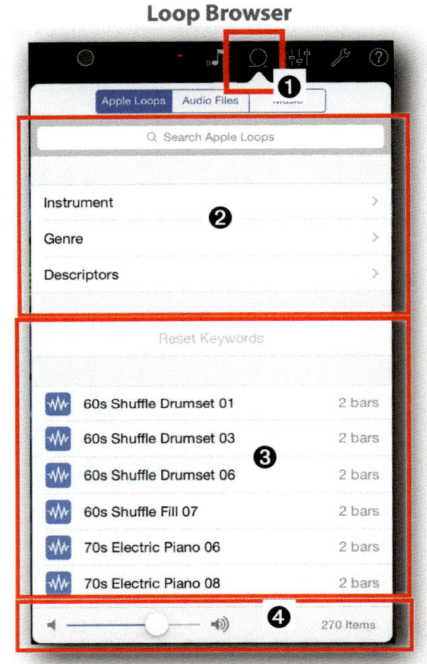

Loop Browser

🌑 Search Area ❷

In this section, you enter search criteria to find a proper Loop. Whatever selection you make here affects the Results Area ❸ below immediately. You have four categories: Name (type in the search field), Instrument, Genre, and Descriptors to add keywords for narrowing down the search. The *Reset Keywords* button removes the selection to display all Apple Loops again.

🌑 Results Area ❸

All the Apple Loops in GarageBand that match the Keywords of the selection above will be displayed in this area. On the right side, it displays how long each Loop is (in bars).

- **Browse**: *Swipe* up and down to scroll through the list.
- **Play**: *Tap* on a Loop to play it. It will repeat in Cycle Mode until you *tap* again to stop it. The Loop Icon changes to a Meters Icon ❺ while playing.
- **Match** Please note that the Loop is playing in the Tempo and Key of your Song.
- **Import**: *Tap-hold* on a Loop you want to import. The blue Apple Loop icon will separate while you are holding that Loop and will move with the movement of your finger while you are *dragging* it to the Tracks View. You can drag the Loop to the Track Lane of any Audio Track (not MIDI Track) or drag it onto an empty Track Lane (below the last Track), which will automatically create a new Audio Track for it.
  The imported Loop aligns to the bar Grid and extends to the end of the Song or the next Region. Set the Song Sections to *Automatic* to guarantee the full-length placement of the audio file. *Dragging* over an existing Region will overwrite that Region.

🌑 Control Area ❹

The Control Area at the bottom indicates how many Loops are found with the current Keywords selection. The Volume Slider lets you set the volume of the played Loop.

Search Engine

The search engine is actually a filter system. If nothing is selected, then all the available Apple Loops are displayed. With any keyword you add, you filter out the Loops that don't have that keyword embedded in their file. You can add, remove. or change the keywords selection in the Loop Browser to narrow down the displayed (found) Apple Loops.

Each of the three buttons switches to a new window to make the selection. Making a selection will switch the window back to the Browser. To deselect a Keyword, you have to go to that window again and *tap* the selection again.

- **Instruments**: This window lets you select a specific type of Instrument (i.e. only Drum Loops or only Guitar Loops
- **Genre**: This window lets you search for a specific music style. (i.e. Country, Urban, etc.).
- **Descriptors**: This window lets you set mutually exclusive pairs of buttons. Here you can make multiple selections (i.e. Single-Ensemble, Melodic-Dissonant, etc.).

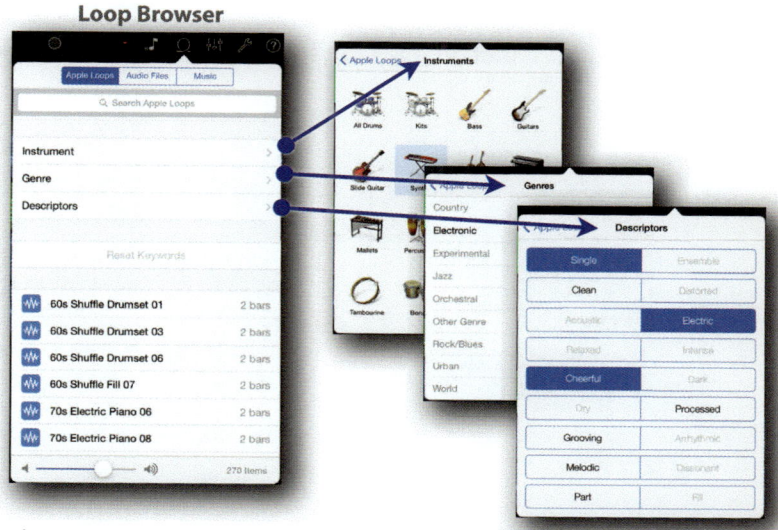

➡ *Loop Browser (Media Browser)*

The Loop Browser window functions more as a Media Browser that can display more than just Apple Loops. You can import standard audio files too. GarageBand converts audio files to 44.1kHz/16bit during the import if they are in a different format. The header of the window can display up to three tabs that lets you switch to a different view.

🔘 **Apple Loops**

The Apple Loops Tab displays the standard Loop Browser Window we just discussed.

🔘 **Audio Files**

If you have any audio files synced via iTunes File Sharing, then that tab will be visible, displaying all the Audio Files that are available via iTunes File Sharing.

🔘 **Music**

If you synced your iTunes Library to your iPad, then all those music files will be available under this tab.

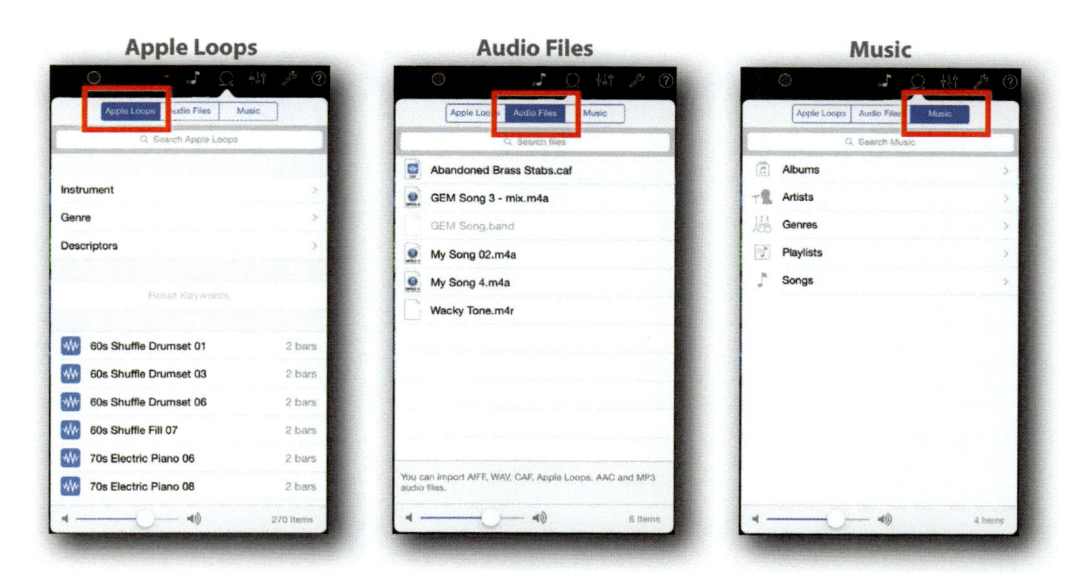

If neither the Audio Files nor the Music tab is visible because there are no files synced in that category, then the Loop Browser defaults to its original view without the tabs and displays only the Apple Loops window.

▶ Audio Files

Here is a screenshot that shows what is displayed in the Audio Files tab:

On the left is the File Sharing section in iTunes ❶ as we've seen in the chapter about File Management. All the files that are placed in the GarageBand Documents list ❷ will be displayed in the Loop Browser under the Audio Files tab ❸. This is the procedure to import more Loops from your computer into GarageBand. If you look closely, then you see that an Apple Loop has that special Loop file icon 🎵 ❹ so you can identify a file as an Apple Loop.

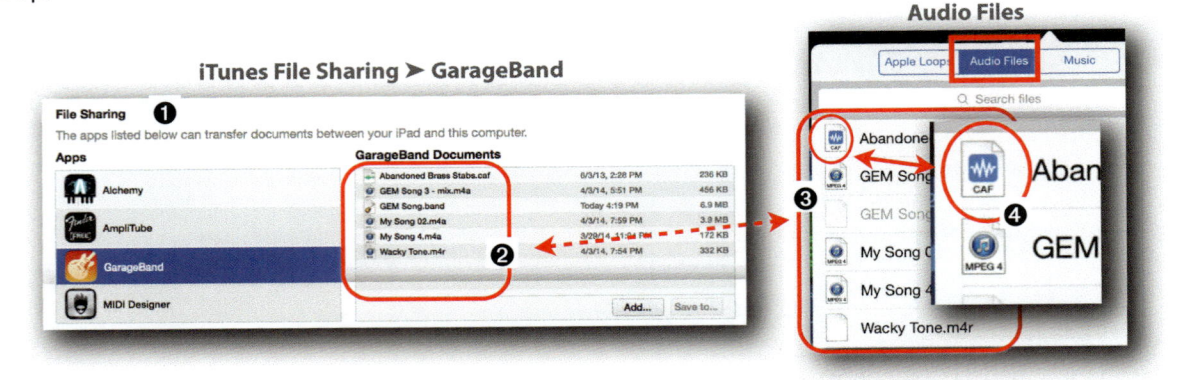

▶ Music

Whenever you select "Sync Music" ❺ in the iTunes Music tab when syncing your iDevice, the Music tab ❻ in GarageBand's Loop Browser will also be displayed. With that window you can browse your whole synced iTunes Library inside GarageBand ❼ by Albums, Artist, etc. and *drag* any audio file directly onto the Tracks View of your Song.

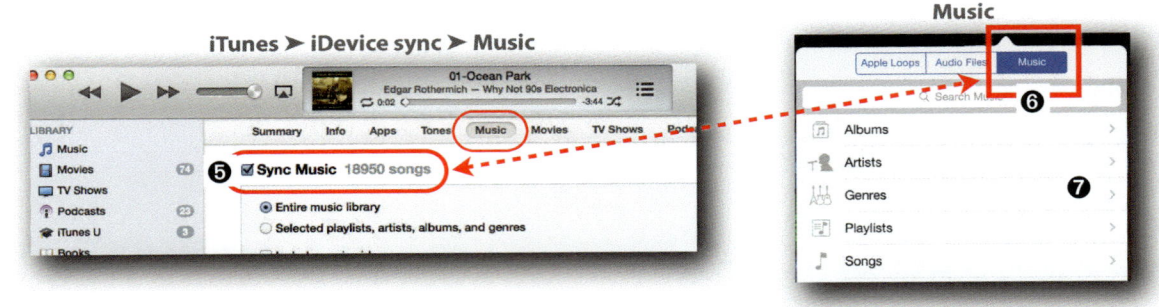

➡ New Audio Files Badge

The Loop Icon in the Control Bar can display a blue notification badge. Anytime a new audio file is placed in the iTunes File Sharing section, a badge with the number (how many files) will appear. The badge disappears automatically once you tapped on the icon to open the Loop Browser.

Please remember that there are two scenarios in which a file ends up in the iTunes File Sharing section:

New Audio Files Badge

- You add a file in the iTunes GarageBand Documents list ❷ on your desktop computer.
- You share (export, mix) a Song from the My Songs Browser in GarageBand to iTunes. This will also place it on the iTunes File Sharing list and, therefore, gets a notification batch.

After recording our material, we move now to the next step, the Editing or Arranging before we finally mix our Song.

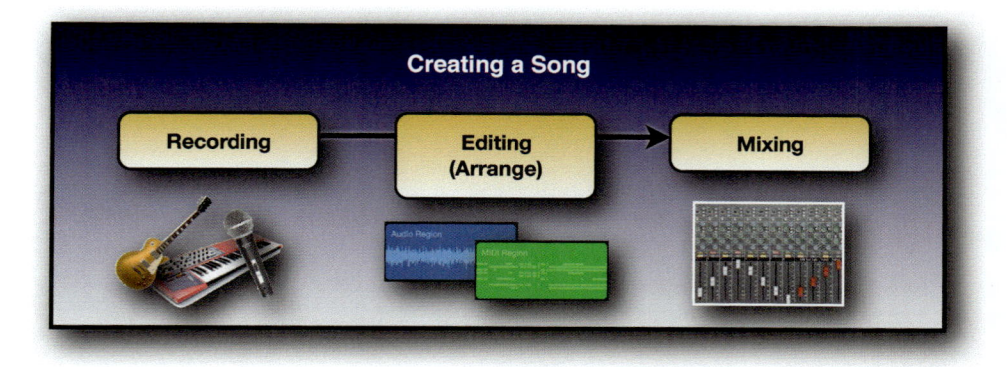

During the recording process, we produced new material or imported existing material. That material is represented as the Regions in our Song, the building blocks. In a traditional recording setup where the material was recorded onto tape, there was not much editing possible once the recording process was done. Now with DAWs, editing became the most important step in the creation process next to the actual recording.

As I mentioned before, the borders between those three steps are fluid and often you can go back and forth any time if necessary, i.e. recording some last minute changes while mixing.

Audio vs. MIDI

I've already spent quite some time creating an awareness of the difference between Audio and MIDI.

Starting with the Source, be aware of the Type of Signal it produces (Audio Signal vs. Data Signal), be aware of on what Type of Track you are recording that signal on (Audio Track vs. MIDI Track), and what Type of Region is created on that Track (Audio Region vs. MIDI Region).

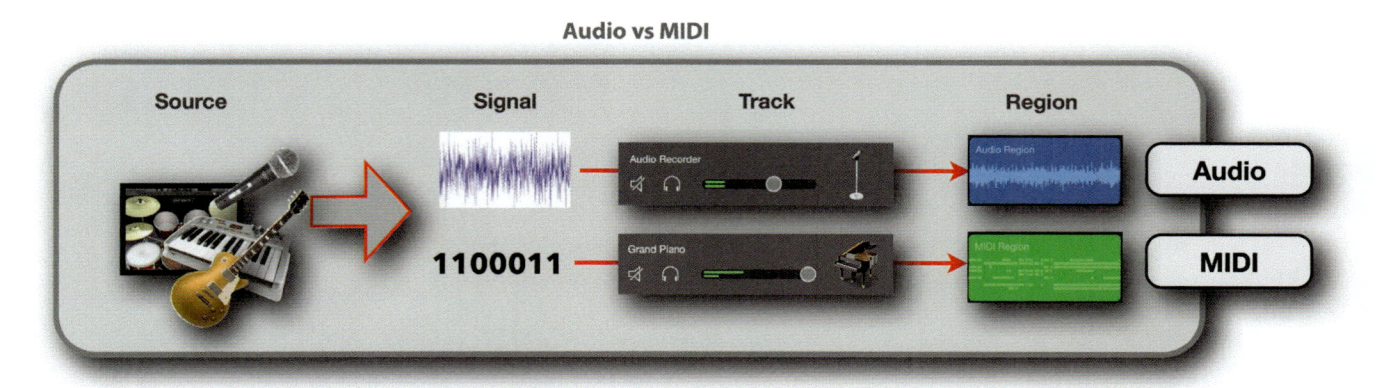

Now when we enter the editing process to work on the Regions themselves, we still have to be aware of what Region we are editing, an Audio Region or a MIDI Region. Although many tasks are the same, there are some differences you have to understand.

For that reason, I will cover the editing commands in two sections. One section with all the commands that work the same for all Regions, Audio Region and MIDI Region, and in the second section I will discuss the commands that work differently or are only available for Audio or MIDI Regions.

Here are all the commands that work the same for MIDI and Audio Regions with just a few specialties here and there:

Select

As with most computer applications, before you use any editing command, you have to tell the app what object is "receiving" the command. The object here is a Region or multiple Regions and you tell GarageBand which one to edit by selecting the Region(s). Here is how to make the selection:

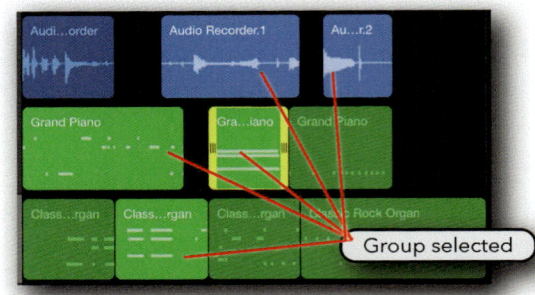

🔘 **Select a single Region**

Tap on a Region. The Region is now selected, indicated by a brighter blue or green color, plus a frame with two Trim Handles.

🔘 **Select multiple Regions**

- *Tap-hold* on a Region and while holding one finger on that Region, *tap* on one or more other Regions (either with the other fingers from the same hand or fingers from the second hand). The last tapped Region gets the frame.

- To de-select any Region from that group, *tap-hold* one of the selected Regions and *tap* on the Region you want to de-select from the group.

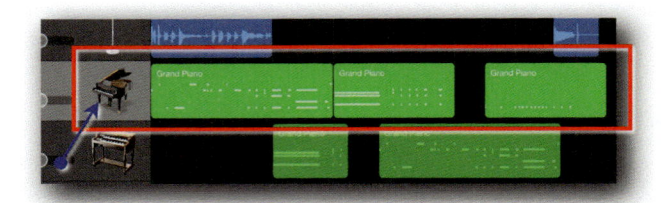

Please note that you can select Audio and MIDI Regions together in a group. However, you can only apply editing commands to that group that are available for those types of Regions.

🔘 **Select all Regions on a Track**

- *Tap* on a Track Icon to select that Track and all Regions on that Track.

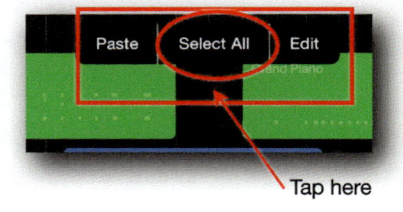

🔘 **Select all Regions**

When you *tap* on an empty Track Lane (not on a Region), a Control Strip will appear with the command "Select All". This selects all the Regions of the visible Song Section. Regions in other Song Sections that are not visible are not affected.

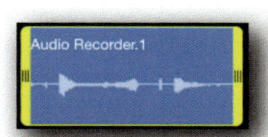

As long as you hold your finger on a single Region, its frame with the handles turn yellow in color. Now you can move it.

Move

The move command is the most intuitive on an iDevice because you *tap* directly on the Region and drag it to the place you want. Here are a few things to be aware of:

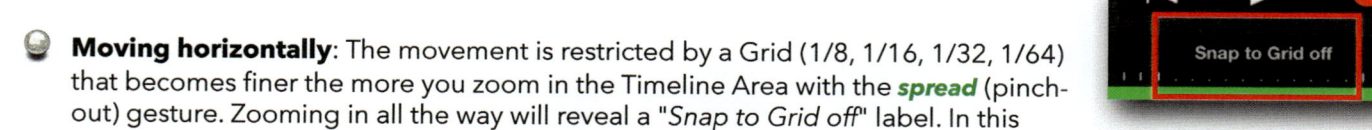

- 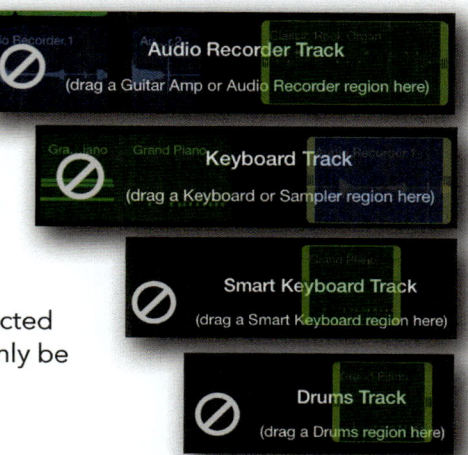 **Moving horizontally**: The movement is restricted by a Grid (1/8, 1/16, 1/32, 1/64) that becomes finer the more you zoom in the Timeline Area with the *spread* (pinch-out) gesture. Zooming in all the way will reveal a "*Snap to Grid off*" label. In this state, you can move Regions without a Grid restriction.

- **Moving vertically**: This means, moving the Region to a different Track. There are several restrictions:
  - You cannot move a MIDI Region onto an Audio Track and an Audio Region onto a MIDI Track. A white text overlay pops up with the error message when moving across "forbidden" Tracks.
  - In addition to that, there are also restrictions between specific MIDI Tracks. For example, you cannot move a MIDI Region from a Keyboard Track to a Drums Track, which expects its specific MIDI Region.

- **Moving multiple Regions horizontally**: *Dragging* one of multiple selected Regions will move all selected Regions with it. A group, however, can only be dragged horizontally to a different time position.

Cut - Copy - Paste - Delete

These four commands are the easiest to understand. They function the same way as in other applications. The commands are listed in the dynamic Control Strip. It appears when you:

  Tap on an already selected Region.

Double-tap on an unselected Region (the first tap actually selects the Region, the second tap pops up the Control Strip).

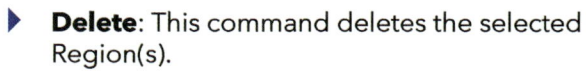

- ▶ **Delete**: This command deletes the selected Region(s).

- ▶ **Cut**: This command deletes the selected Region(s) and puts it on the clipboard (the invisible temporary storage).

- ▶ **Copy**: This command leaves the selected Region(s) and just copies it onto the clipboard.

- ▶ **Paste**: This command copies the Region(s) that is currently stored on the clipboard back to the Track Lane. Where exactly, depends on a few circumstances:
  - First of all, the command is not available if nothing has been copied to the clipboard yet.
  - A single Region will be pasted onto the Track Lane that you *tap*, at the current position of the Playhead. The same restriction as with moving Regions applies (Audio to Audio, MIDI to MIDI, etc.). If you tap on a "forbidden" Track Lane, then the Paste command will not be available.
  - If you copied a group of Regions (even a mix of Audio and MIDI Regions) to the Clipboard, then you can *tap* on any Track Lane, because the Regions are pasted onto their original Track, at the new position of the Playhead.
  - You can paste audio files from other apps that support copying audio files to the clipboard. Must be 44.1kHz/16bit.

Any action can be undone by *tapping* the Undo Icon .

Loop

The Loop function is similar to GarageBand or even Logic. For example, you have a one bar drum groove that should repeat eight times in your song. Now Instead of manually copying that Region eight times, you activate the Loop feature for that Region and just *drag* the end for how long you want to continue the repetition.

➡️ **Enable Loop**

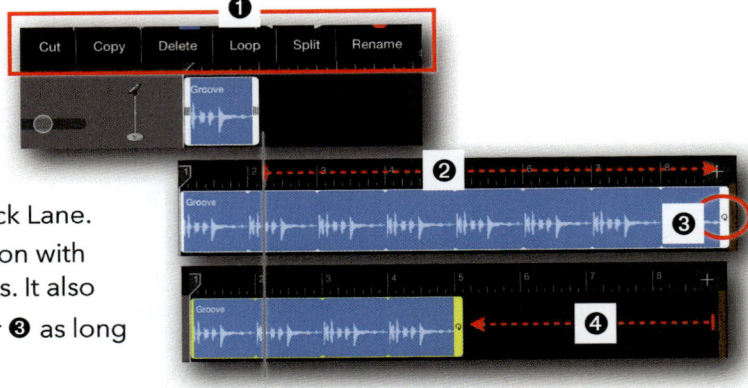

- *Double-tap* on a Region to open the Control Strip and *tap* on Loop ❶.
- The Region will loop itself ❷ all the way to the end of the current Song Section or the beginning of the next Region on the same Track Lane.
- The Region is now displayed as one long Region with notches that indicate where the Region repeats. It also displays a Loop Handle 🔁 at the right border ❸ as long as the Region is selected.
- You can resize the length of the looped Region by *dragging* that Loop Handle left or right ❹.

➡️ **Disable Loop**

There is no off or disable button to turn off the Loop feature for a Region. It requires two steps.

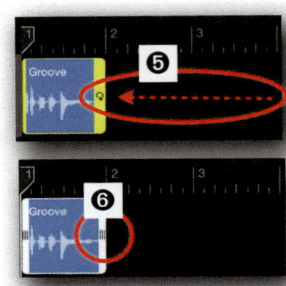

- *Drag* the Loop Handle all the way to the left so the Region once again has the same length as it did before you enabled the Loop feature ❺.
- *Tap* outside the Region to de-select it. This will turn the Loop feature off. When you *tap* on the Region now to select it again, it will display the frame with the regular Handles ❻ indicating that it is not a looped Region.

➡️ **Trim Loop**

You can trim a Region (make it shorter or longer) while Loop is enabled. Once you determine where the looped Region ends by moving the Loop Handle, it remembers that End Position. Now you can trim the actual Region, which affects only the number of repetitions, but not where the last loop ends.

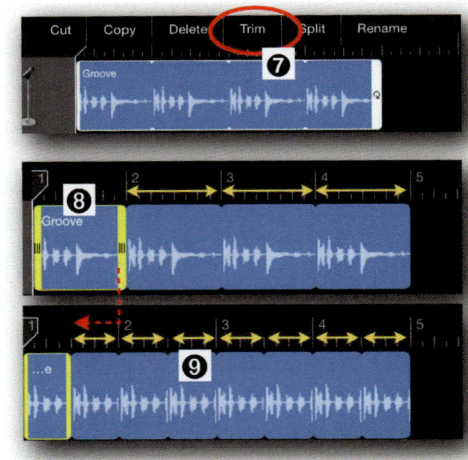

- *Double-tap* on a looped Region to bring up the Control Strip. Please note, when Loop is enabled on a Region, the Loop command changes to the Trim command ❼.
- *Tap* on the Trim command and the Region will change its appearance. The original Region is displayed with its standard Trim Handles left and right ❽. The looped segments to the right now have no borders around them.
- *Drag* the left or right Trim Handle of the Region and you will see that the looped segments adjust their length ❾ while the end position of the whole looped Region stays the same.

Please note:

- The end of a loop doesn't necessarily have to be at the end of a complete repetition of the Region.
- The Trim procedure has various restrictions, which I'll discuss in the next section.
- Don't confuse these two: *Apple Loops* are special audio files and *Loop* is a special function you can apply to any Region (not only Apple Loops).

Now let's look at the various editing commands for Regions that are different for Audio Regions and MIDI Regions.

Audio Region - MIDI Region

The reason that there are different editing rules for those two different Region Types is based on the fundamental difference between a MIDI Region and an Audio Region. Although they are both building blocks that contain recorded information and we just covered quite a few editing tools that appear identical in MIDI and Audio Regions, the "inside" of the two Region Types are totally different.

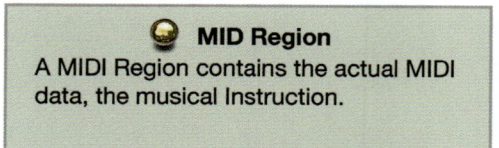
MID Region
A MIDI Region contains the actual MIDI data, the musical Instruction.

Audio Region
An Audio Region contains a link to an Audio File with the instruction on what section of that Audio File to play.

➡ *MIDI Region*

The green MIDI Region that you see in your Song is the actual container of the MIDI data, the musical information. Each individual MIDI Event inside that MIDI Region represents a note with a dedicated position, its relative time reference from the beginning of its Region. Now this reference (the beginning of the Region) is placed on the Song's Timeline and, therefore, has an absolute time reference in your Song (i.e. bar2).

Through that reference (position of the Region on the Timeline of your Song), each MIDI Event inside the MIDI Region now also has an absolute time reference in your Song (i.e. bar5, beat3, etc.). Moving the Region on the Timeline moves that whole container while keeping the relative position of all the MIDI Events (notes) inside. After you move a MIDI Region, each individual MIDI Event inside has a new absolute time reference depending upon where you place the MIDI Region on the Song's Timeline.

And in case you ever wondered, the fact that each MIDI Event is referenced to the musical time in bars and beats (and not to an absolute time in minutes and seconds), makes it possible for the MIDI Region to follow any tempo changes you make in your Song. Regardless what tempo you choose for your Song, the MIDI notes always play exactly in that tempo.

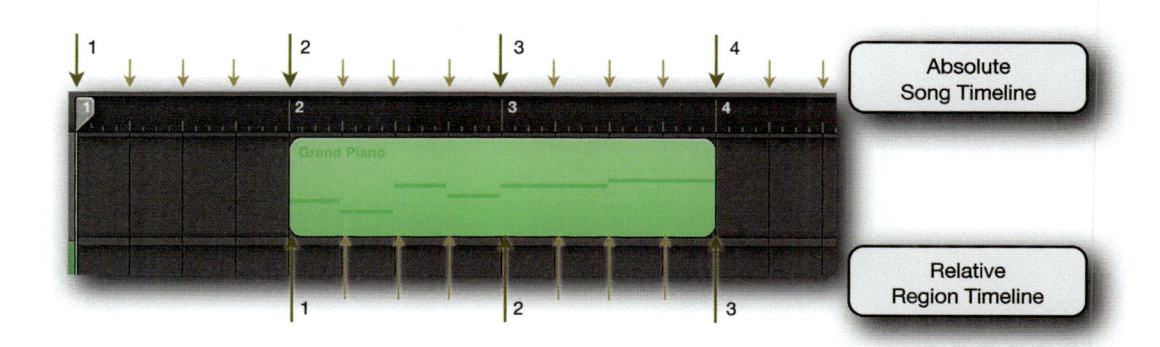

➡ *Audio Region*

The "inside" of an Audio Region is completely different from a MIDI Region. Here we have two components: The Audio File and the Audio Region:

▶ Audio File

Whenever you record an audio signal in GarageBand, it creates an Audio File (aiff). This audio file is invisible in GarageBand and you cannot access it. You could export the GarageBand Song to your computer and open the Song file; it is embedded inside
(see my manual "[GarageBand X - How it Works](#)" for details).

▶ Audio Region

Once the audio file is created (or imported), an Audio Region is created that is linked to that Audio File. That Audio Region is the only element you see in your Song. The important thing to remember is this: The Audio Region is only a **REFERENCE** to its Audio File.

Each Audio Region contains only two playback instructions for its linked Audio File:

- From what position should I actually play that linked Audio File (start from the beginning or a few seconds later)?
- How long should I continue to play that Audio File?

So the Audio Region is just a container of "Play Instructions" for the Audio File it is referenced to. Once the Playhead reaches the left border of the Audio Region, it starts to play with that instruction. The waveform you see on the Audio Region is a visual reference of that audio signal it is playing.

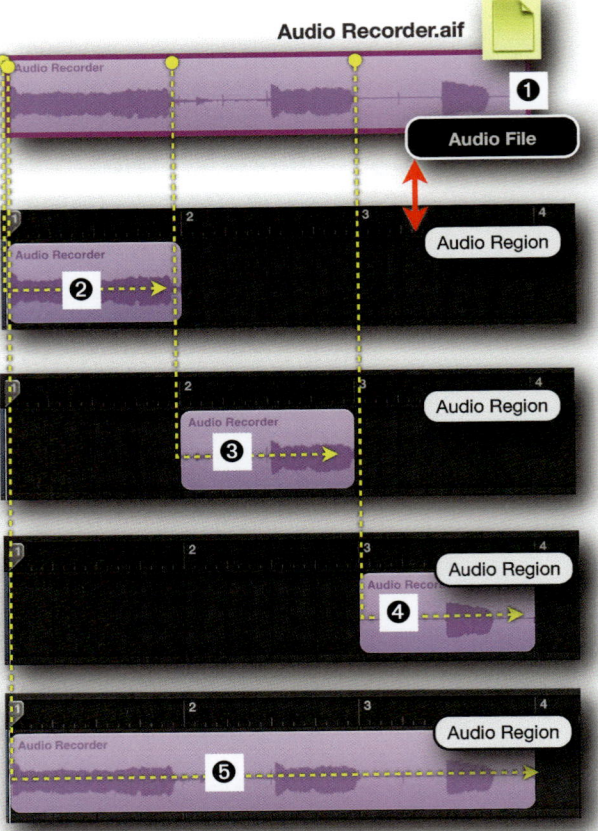

🎃 Screenshot 1

The first screenshot demonstrates the invisible Audio File ❶ and examples of four different Audio Regions. The first three examples ❷ ❸ ❹ have the instruction to play the Audio File only for one bar, each one starting at a different position from the Audio File. The last example ❺ has the instruction to play from the beginning of the Audio File all the way through.

🎃 Screenshot 2

The next example has the instruction ❻ to start the Audio File towards the end and play for one bar. The Audio Region plays that instruction at the first bar ❼ of the Song.

🎃 Screenshot 3

The next example has an Audio Region with the same play instructions ❽, but this time it is copied three times. Keep in mind that all three Audio Regions are references to the same Audio File (indicated by an incremental number in the Region's Name). The result is that the same segment of the Audio File is played back three times, at bar 1, bar 2, and bar 3 ❾.

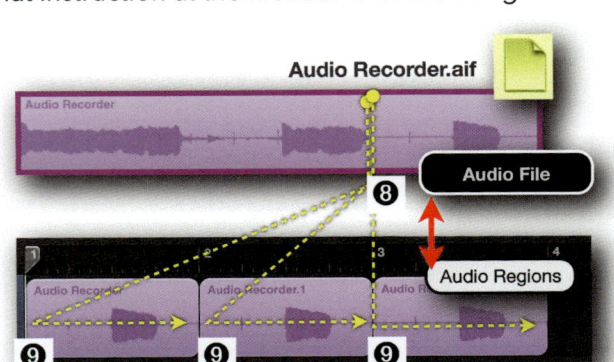

11 - Edit your Song

Audio

Now, equipped with that valuable background information, it will make sense as to why the following edit commands are different for MIDI and Audio Regions. Let's start with the Audio Regions.

➡ *Trim*

Trimming (or Resizing) a Region means changing the right border or left border of the Region. As we have already seen, selecting a Region (*tap* on it) will add a frame with the two Trim Handles on each side. This is where you drag the beginning or end of the Region left or right.

Because the Audio Region only contains the two instructions, "play the referenced Audio File from **where** and for **how long**", we now understand what actually happens when we move those Handles:

 **Drag** the left Trim Handle (beginning of the Audio Region)

This changes the first instruction "from where to play" the referenced Audio File. The more you move the Handle to the right, the later the start point will be from which the Audio Region plays back the Audio File. Moving the Handle to the left starts the Audio File earlier. Now the reason you cannot drag the Handle to the left beyond the actual start position of its referenced Audio File, and no later than the end of the file, also makes sense, there is no more signal

 **Drag** the right Trim Handle (end of the Audio Region)

This changes the duration, for how long the Audio File will be played back. Of course, you cannot move that Handle beyond the end point of the actual Audio File it is referenced to.

Tap-hold the Handle before moving and it will zoom-in the Track Lane horizontally for finer trimming resolution. Releasing your finger will zoom out to the previous zoom setting.

➡ *Split*

The Split command "cuts" a Region into two. Now with the understanding of what Audio Regions are, we understand what that actually means: We are creating two separate "Play Instructions for the same referenced Audio File".

Here is the procedure:

- **Double-tap** on the Audio Region to bring up a Control Strip and *tap* on the Split command ❶.

- A scissors arrow ❷ with an extended line through the Region (and a line on the Time Ruler) will be displayed at the center of the Region.

- **Drag** the scissors icon left-right to position where you want to make the cut (the movement is restricted to the underlying Grid). *Tap-hold* on the scissors to zoom-in to a finer resolution). **Drag** the scissors icon down ❸ to make the cut on the Audio Region.

- After the cut, the scissors icon is still visible ❹ so you can make more cuts.

- *Tap* outside the Audio Region to exit the Split Mode. The scissors icon now disappears and you will see the separate Audio Regions ❺. The new Regions have incremental numbers attached to their name to indicate that they are referring to the same Audio File.

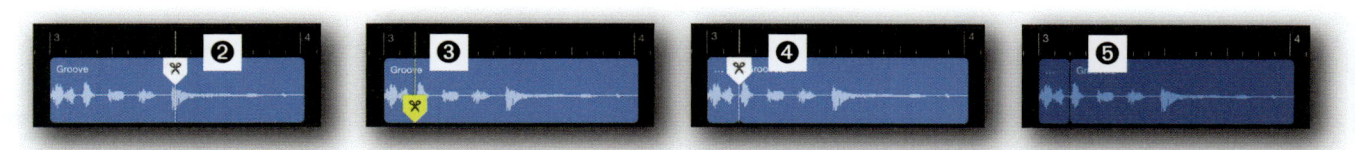

MIDI

MIDI Regions don't have a referenced relationship to a MIDI File. The MIDI Region you see on the Track Lane is the actual container that includes the MIDI Events. Therefore, the editing rules are a bit different.

➡ Trim

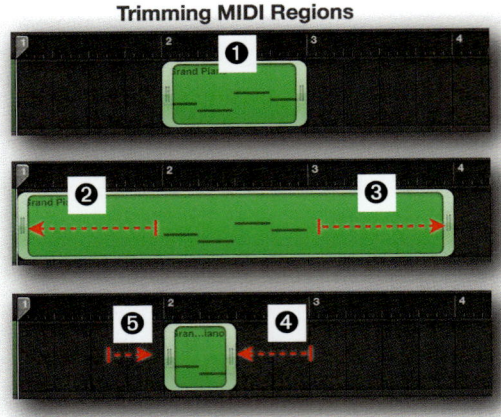

Trimming MIDI Regions

- ⚪ Here is a 1 bar MIDI Region with four MIDI Events inside ❶.
- ⚪ You can extend the Region freely on either side. *Drag* the left Handle ❷ to the left or drag the right Handle ❸ to the right. You just increase the container without changing its content. The only limitations are the boundaries of the Song Section.
- ⚪ *Dragging* the right Handle to the left can shrink the Region to as much as 1/16 in length. But here is the important part. No MIDI Events get deleted! In this example ❹, the third and fourth MIDI Event is just hidden (disabled). Once you drag the Region to the right again, all those MIDI Events will still be there.
- ⚪ *Dragging* the left Handle to the right had the restriction in previous GarageBand versions that you couldn't move the left Handle "later" than the first MIDI Event ❺. Now you can move it freely.

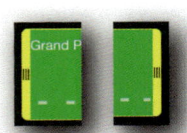 *Tap-hold* the Handle before moving and it will zoom-in the Track Lane horizontally for finer trimming resolution. Releasing your finger will zoom-out to the previous zoom setting.

➡ Split - Join

The procedure for the Split mode works the same as with Audio Regions. However, the result is different. Instead of ending up with two Regions referencing to the same file, here you create two independent MIDI Regions. Any MIDI Event that extends beyond the cut (a long Note) will be shortened to end exactly at the cut. Please note that all the MIDI Regions on a Track are named after the Track Name where they were recorded.

⚪ Join

The opposite procedure for splitting is joining. This command is not available for Audio Regions because they represent Play instructions and a join procedure would be like a bounce instruction to create a new Audio File from both instructions. A MIDI Regions on the other hand, represents just a container with MIDI Events on a Timeline. The Join command creates one big MIDI Region that includes all MIDI Events leaving their relative position untouched.

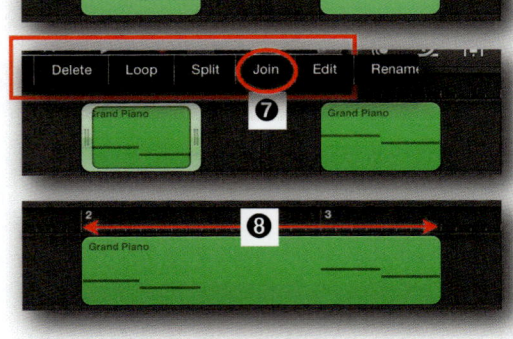

Join MIDI Regions

- ☑ Select two or more MIDI Regions on a single Track. In this example, I have a Region on the left ❺ (with two MIDI Events visible) and a second Region on the right ❻.
- ☑ *Tap* on one of the selected Regions to open the Control Strip and *tap* on Join ❼.
- ☑ This creates one single Region ❽ and you can see that the two MIDI Events from the original Regions are now included in that new joint Region.

Please note: Any "hidden" MIDI Event (due to trimmed Regions) will be deleted.

➡ Edit

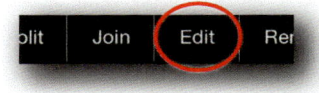

The Control Strip for MIDI Regions has one command that is not available for Audio Regions. This is the Edit command, which opens the MIDI Event Editor.

Possible Editing Dangers

There is one "side effect" you have to be aware of when editing Regions:

There are three scenarios:
- ☑ You **Move** a Region over an existing Region.
- ☑ You **Trim** the border of a Region, extending it into an existing Region.
- ☑ You **Record** a new Region over an existing Region (this is not an editing process, but has similar effects).

The effect is different for Audio and MIDI Regions based on the same principles we've just discussed:

🔘 Partial Overlay

In this case, the effect is that the existing Region will be shortened ❶ on either side or split into two Regions ❷ when the new Region is placed in the middle.

- ▶ **Audio Region**: The Audio Region will be updated with the new "play instructions", i.e. start playing the Audio File from a different starting point and/or end the playback at a different time.
- ▶ **MIDI Region**: MIDI Events that are "cut off" on the right border are just disabled (see trimming section). MIDI Events that are cut off on the left border will be deleted.

🔘 Complete Overlay

In this case, the existing Region will be completely covered by the Region you are moving or extending.

- ▶ **Audio Region**: The Audio Region will be deleted. The Audio File it is linked to will also be deleted unless there is at least one other Audio Region in your Song that is linked to the same Audio File.
- ▶ **MIDI Region**: The existing Region will be deleted.

As long as you drag the Region or its borders, nothing happens. The action is executed once you release your finger. But there is always the Undo 🔄 command.

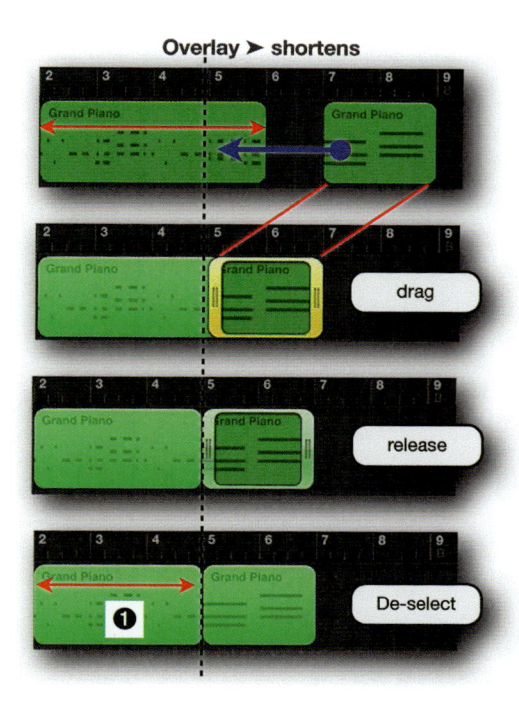

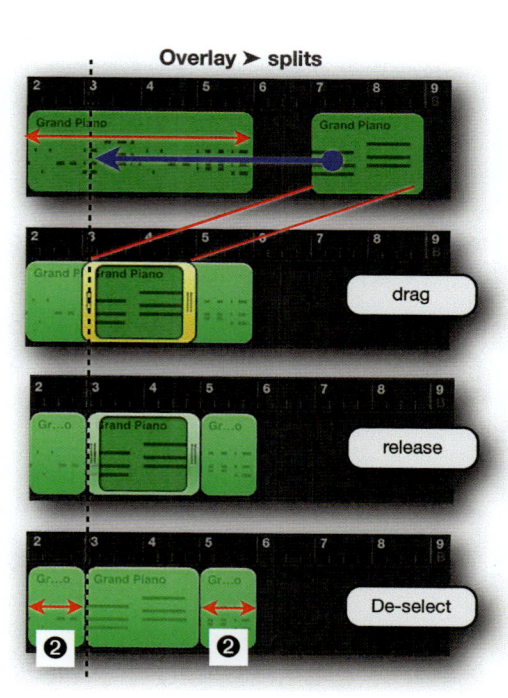

MIDI Editor Window

The MIDI Editor is the fifth full screen window in GarageBand. It is a limited version of a Piano Roll Editor, a common Editor window for editing the content of MIDI Regions. As I mentioned already in the Interface chapter, there is no main button on the Control Bar to open the Editor Window. The window can only be accessed with a **two-finger slide up** (or down) on the MIDI Region or with the *Edit* command from these two locations:

- **Tracks View**: *Double-tap* on a MIDI Region or just **tap** on the Track Lane of a MIDI Track.
- **Instrument View**: *Double-tap* on a MIDI Region or just **tap** on the Track Lane in Single Track Lane view. It becomes visible when **sliding down** the mini Track Lane. Please note: The MIDI Editor has a little section at the bottom of its window when accessed from the Instrument View. You can **slide up** from this section to return to the Instrument View.

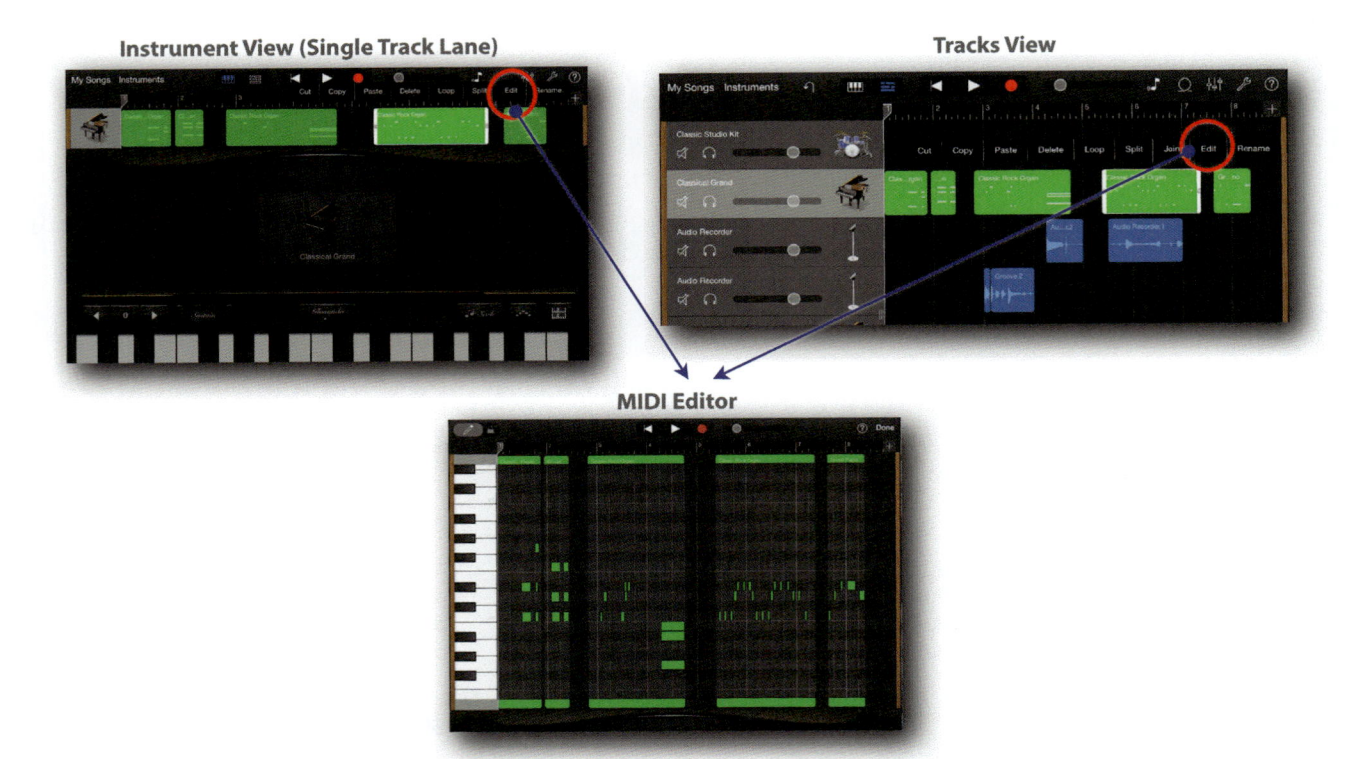

The MIDI Editor is similar to the *Piano Roll Editor* in GarageBand X.

- The window displays all the MIDI Regions that are present on that Track, not just the one from where you select the Edit command.
- *Tap* on *Done* in the upper right corner to go back to the previous window.
- The Song Section is also active so you can switch to different Sections with the Plus button or by **swiping** to the next or previous Section.
- You can use the **Pinch** and **Spread** gesture to zoom in-out both vertically and horizontally.
- All the transport controls are available (except record). The "Back To Beginning" Button ◄ functions as a "GoTo the beginning of the Previous Region".
- The window has two editing modes:
  Slide the Write Switch right or left to switch between: Write Disabled - Write Enabled

➡ **Write Disabled**

This is the default mode. You cannot write new notes (except paste). You can only edit existing ones.

▶ **Display**

- Each MIDI Region on the current Track is displayed as a shaded Range ❶ with the MIDI Events displayed inside.
- Each MIDI Event (notes) is displayed as a horizontal bar marking their start and end position.
- The horizontal position of the notes are referenced to the Time Ruler at the top.
- The vertical position of the notes are referenced against a musical keyboard on the left (or other references).
- The only displayed MIDI Event type that is not a Note is the Sustain control ❷ at the bottom.

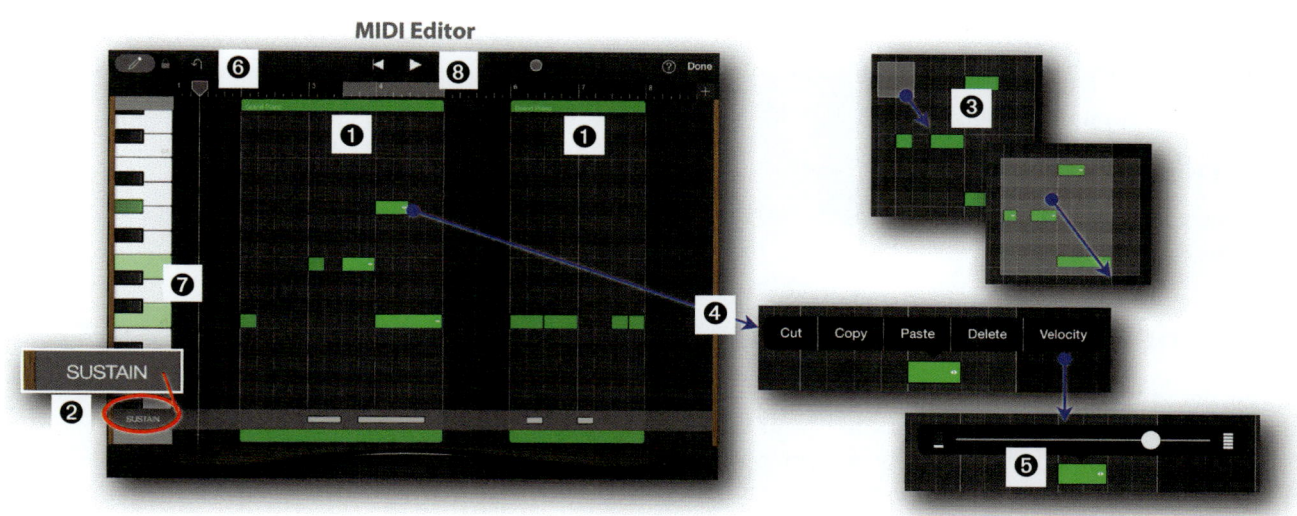

MIDI Editor

▶ **Select**

- **Single Notes**: *Tap* on a note so it turns lighter green. The corresponding key on the keyboard to the left will turn green ❼. The Ruler displays a shaded area for the length of the selected note ❽.
- **Multiple Notes**: *Tap-hold* on a note and *tap* other notes to add them to the selected group. The MIDI Editor provides an additional technique: *Tap-hold* outside a note. This will start a pulsating square underneath that point. Now *drag* your finger across to select any note inside the selected area that you create ❸.
- **Key selection**: *Tap-hold* (for a second) on a key of the musical keyboard to select all those Notes in all the MIDI Regions (if there are any).

▶ **Edit**

- **Move**: *Drag* the selected Region(s) up-down (different key) or left-right (different timing position). *Tap-hold* before dragging will automatically zoom-in for better adjustment.
- **Trim**: *Drag* the right edge of the selected Region(s) to change the duration of the Note(s). Same *tap-hold* function.
- **Cut - Copy - Paste - Delete**: *Tap* on a selected Region to popup the Control Strip with the edit commands ❹. They behave the same as editing Regions.
- **Velocity**: *Tap* on this command on the Control Strip to switch to a horizontal popup slider ❺ that lets you change the velocity of the selected Note(s). While this popup slider is open, you can *tap* on a different Note and the slider moves to that Note to quickly edit the velocity of a series of Notes.
- *Tap* the Undo Icon ❻ in the Control Bar to undo the last action or *tap-hold* the button to select the Redo command.

➡ **Write Enabled**

Slide the Write Switch to the right to switch to Write Mode. You can also **tap-hold** the button with a finger of the left hand to temporarily switch to Write mode while entering the notes with a finger of the right hand.

The Write Mode is very simple and easy to use because it provides only two actions, add or delete MIDI Events.

🌑 Add a Note

Tap on the screen inside a Region to create a single 1/4 note at the exact horizontal (start time) and vertical (key) position where you touched the screen.

Tap-hold on the screen inside a Region also creates a new 1/4 note, but this time you can **drag** your finger to move the position of the note you just created. The Playhead moves along and the Keyboard on the left displays the note as a guide while you are dragging the note around. You can't move the note outside the current Region boundary. Once you release the finger, the note is created at that position.

🌑 Delete a Note

Tap on any existing note to delete it.

🌑 Edit a Note

You can also perform a few editing procedures. **Tap-hold** to select a note. **Drag** a note to a new position or **drag** the ending to trim its length.

Smart Strings

When opening the MIDI Editor from a Region of a Smart Strings Instrument, you will see an extra edit command "***More***...". This opens a Control Strip with two more options, *Instrument* and *Articulation* with one more Control Strip to select any of the five string instruments and set the articulation between Legato, Staccato, and Pizzicato.

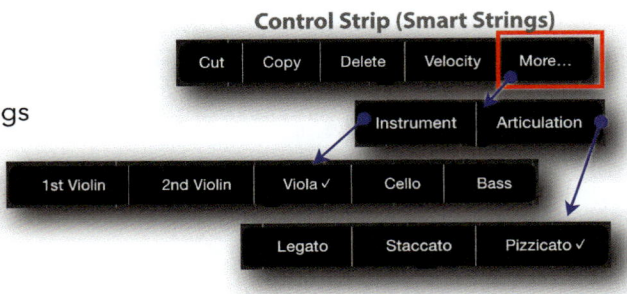

Control Strip (Smart Strings)

Note Axis

The upright Keyboard on the left (y-axis) that references the pitch of a MIDI note in the MIDI Editor is only displayed for the Keyboard Instruments. The MIDI Editor changes to different axis for different MIDI Instruments, i.e. Drums, Smart Guitars, or Smart Strings.

Smart Instruments

Please note that the Smart Drums instrument is different. Although it is a MIDI Track and the Regions are green MIDI Regions, you cannot access the MIDI Editor to edit those MIDI Events because they are based on patterns, not individual MIDI notes.

Y-axis for various Instruments

These two parameters are playback parameters, because they don't permanently change the MIDI Notes in a Region. They are applied during the playback as an offset to the actual MIDI Notes. Those Track Settings affect ALL the Regions of the selected Track, <u>but only for the current Song Section</u>! If you have set different values in different Song Sections and display All Song Sections, then the parameter will display the value "*Multiple*".

You access those parameters by selecting the Track and then opening the Track Settings Window by *tapping* the Track Settings Button (mixer icon) ❶.

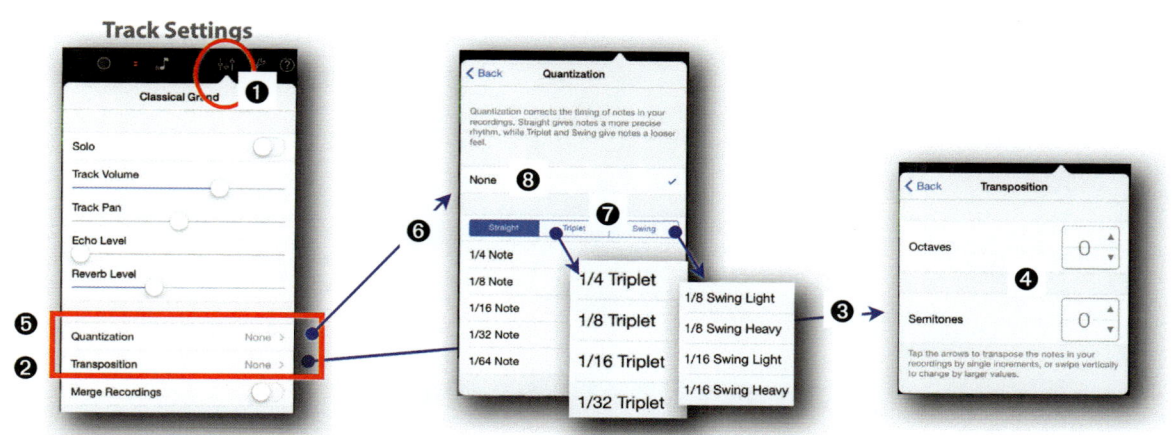

Transpose

Tap the Transposition Button ❷ to switch to the Transposition Window where you can set the transposition value ❹ in Semitones and Octaves (1 octave = 12 semitones). Maximum value is plus or minus 3 octaves.

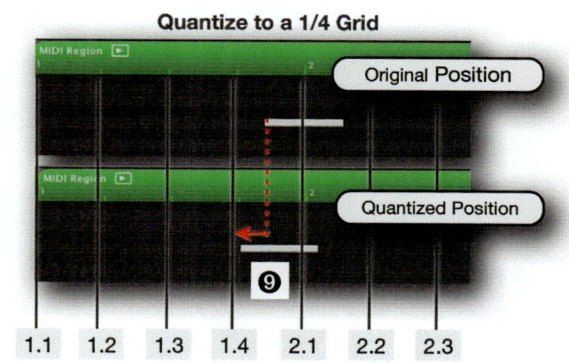

Be careful when you have set a Transposition value for existing Regions on a Track and record a new Region because the new Region will stay in its original pitch. If you look at the Track Settings Window, you will see the value "Multiple" indicating that some Regions are transposed (the existing ones) and some are not (the ones recorded after you set the transposition value).

Quantize

To "apply quantization" means to let GarageBand move all the MIDI notes on that Track to a specific timing Grid. The Quantization window lets you choose the Grid (quantization value). For example, selecting "1/4 Notes" for a drum track will move every note to the closest 1/4 note value of your Song. For a MIDI drum groove, this ensures that all the notes have a perfect timing.

Quantization helps to correct the timing of a sloppy performance on a Track. However, if the notes are too far off, then you have to manually correct them. You see the quantization effect in the MIDI Editor ❾.

Tap the Quantization Button ❺ in the Track Settings Window to switch to the Quantization Window ❻. Select a value from three types of Grids, *Straight*, *Triplet*, and *Swing* ❼. Selecting "*None*" ❽ will move all the notes back to their original position the way you recorded them, or manual positioned them.

The Quantization setting on a Track will automatically be applied to every newly recorded Region.

I discuss the concept of Quantization in much more detail in my manual "GarageBand X - How it Works".

Now we are at the last step before we can send our Song off to the iTunes charts - the Mixing.

This is the process where we get the balance right between the different Tracks/Instruments and add some effects to individual Tracks to make the Song sound interesting.

Mixing - the traditional way

In a big recording studio and even with a regular DAW on a computer, you have a mixing console (real or virtual). That is the tool you use for mixing.

Mixing - the GarageBand way

In GarageBand, there is no mixer. The mixing is done "computer style" with windows, popup menus, and lists. However, all those controls, scattered over various places, still replicate the controls of a real mixer. The funny thing is that this type of "computer style" mixing is supposed to be easier and more intuitive for the casual user. Look at the diagram - you'll be the judge:

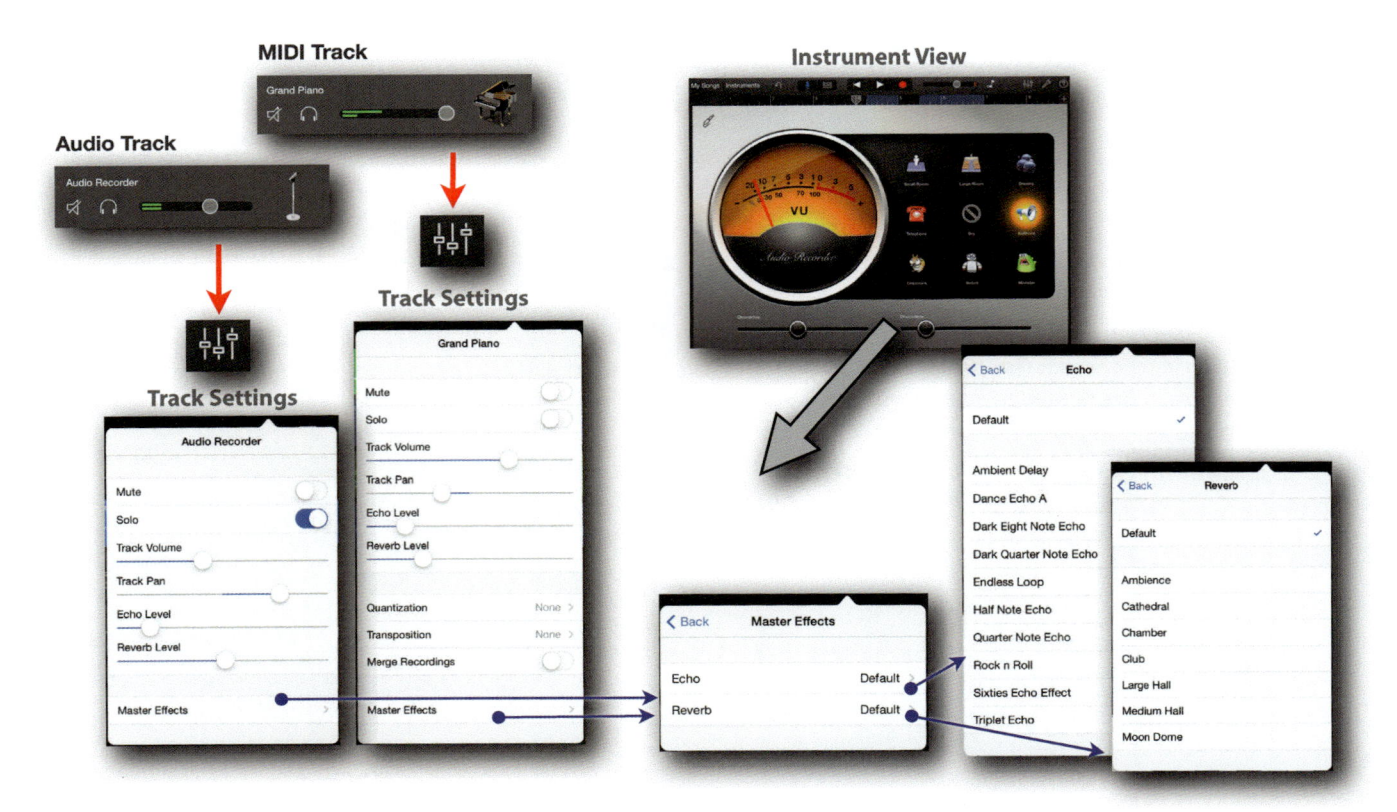

All those various controls that are available to mix your Song are located in three main locations:

Instrument View

GarageBand doesn't provide any effect rack or plugins for signal processing. Instead, you have to do the signal processing at the source, the Instrument, in the Instrument View window.

Each Instrument has a unique interface with a set of individual signal processing controls common for that type of Instrument/Track. This is the first place where you make the most drastic sound changes:

Instrument View - sound controls

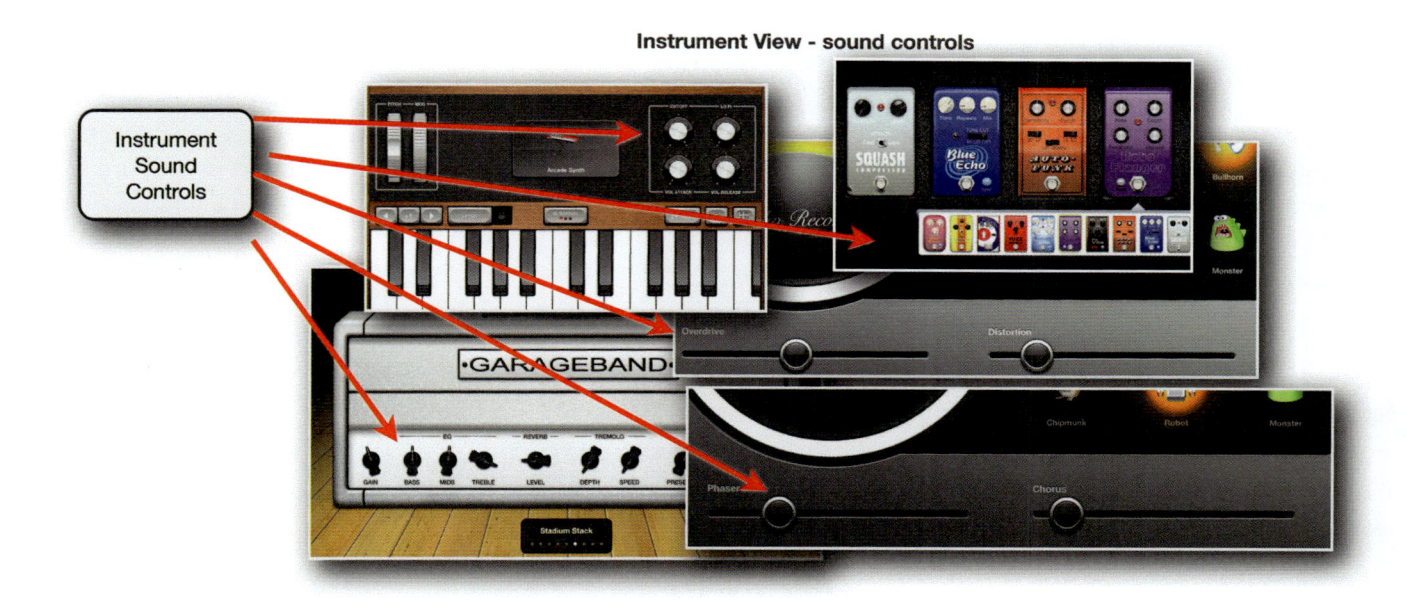

Track Header

The Track Header is the only place where you can view and access mixing controls for at least eight Tracks at the same time. This is like the mini-Mixer in GarageBand in the traditional way.

Audio and MIDI Tracks behave the same because at this point, a MIDI Track is controlling the audio signal, the audio output of the MIDI Sound Module.

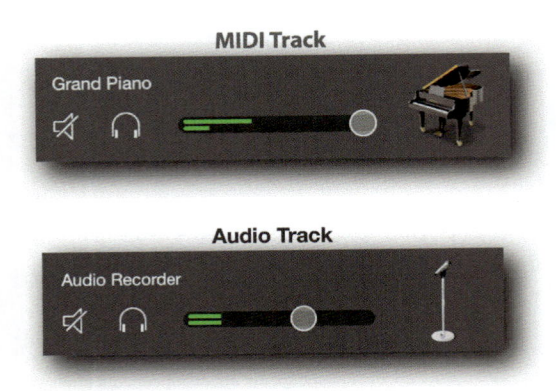

There are four controls available on the Track Header that I already covered in the Interface chapter:

 **Mute**

Tap the Mute Button to disable (silence) this Track. The button will turn blue when enabled (muted). This button lets you quickly turn off the signal on a specific Track. To mute a few Tracks at once, **tap-hold** on a Mute Button and **slide** up or down across the other Track's Mute Button. You can do the same procedure to deselect multiple Mute Buttons in one "swoop".

 **Solo**

Tap the Solo Button to mute all other Tracks. You can enable Solo Mode on more than one Track. **Tap** again to disable Solo Mode. This lets you quickly listen to a single Track in isolation. To solo a few Tracks at once, **tap-hold** on a Solo Button and **slide** up or down across the other Track's Solo Button. You can do the same procedure to deselect multiple Solo Buttons in one "swoop".

 **Meter**

The Meter displays the signal level of that Track with colored LEDs from green to red (low level to high level).

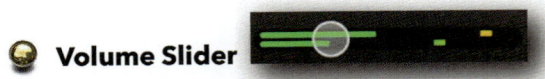 **Volume Slider**

The Volume Slider represents the Fader on a Channel Strip. Here it is a transparent circle (on top of the Meter) that you can **swipe** left and right on the Meter to raise or lower the volume of that Track. **Double-tap** to reset the level to 0dB (WIKI-Moment: dB, Decibel). Please note that the Meter displays the signal after the Volume Slider, which means the lower the volume control, the lower the resulting level.

Track Settings

The Track Settings Window functions like an Inspector window. You select an object (a Track) and open the Track Settings Window. This window displays the Track's parameter that you can edit with the available controls. Now you can leave that window open and select a different Track, which switches the content of the window to display the new Track's parameters so you can edit them.

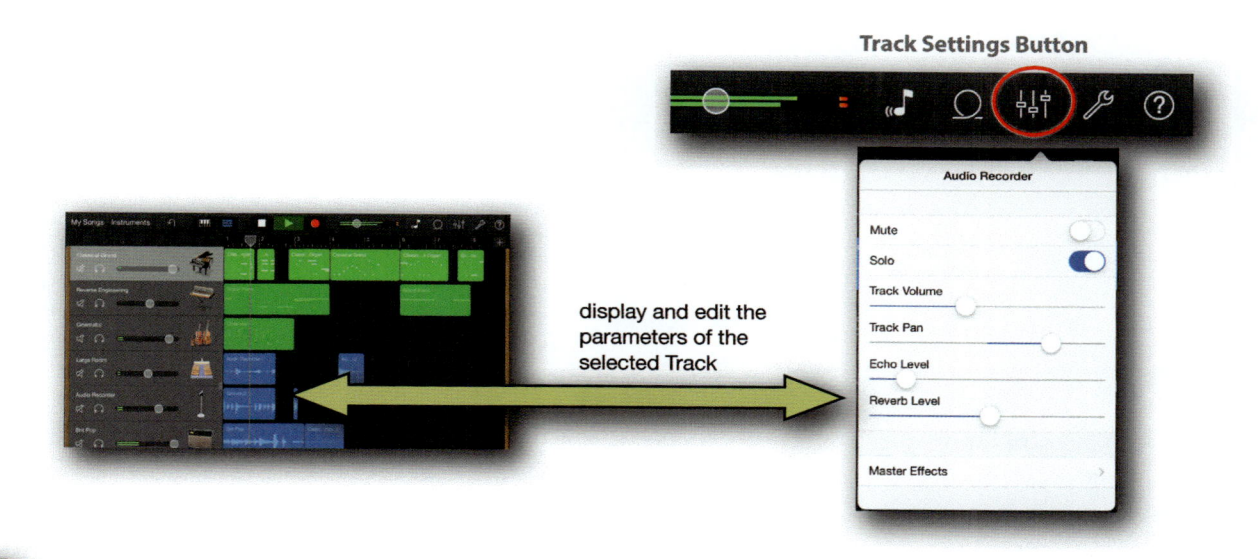

Track Settings Button

display and edit the parameters of the selected Track

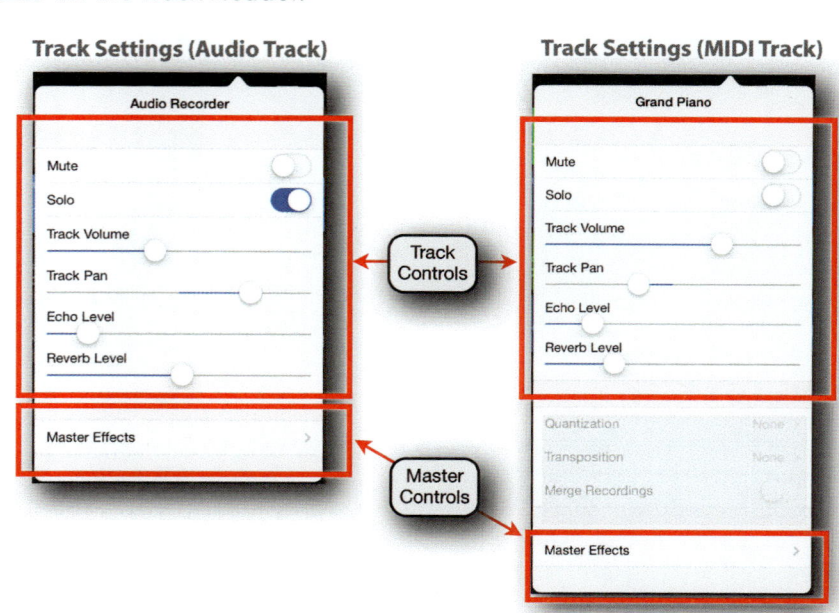

Tab on the Track Settings Button (mixer icon) in the Control Bar to open the Track Settings Window.

There are six Parameters available, plus one Master Effects Button that affects all Tracks, not just the currently selected one. The window for a MIDI Track displays a few more parameters that are related to MIDI editing, which I covered in the Editing chapter.

Mute

This switch is the same as the Mute Button on the Track Header.

Solo

This switch is the same as the Solo Button on the Track Header.

Track Volume

This is the same slider as the Volume Slider on the Track Header.

Track Pan

This slider positions the signal between the left and right channel of the stereo panorama.

Track Settings (Audio Track)

Track Settings (MIDI Track)

Track Controls

Master Controls

➡ Master Effects

The next three parameters need an understanding of the concept of Master Effects or "Aux Sends" as they are referred to on a standard mixing console.

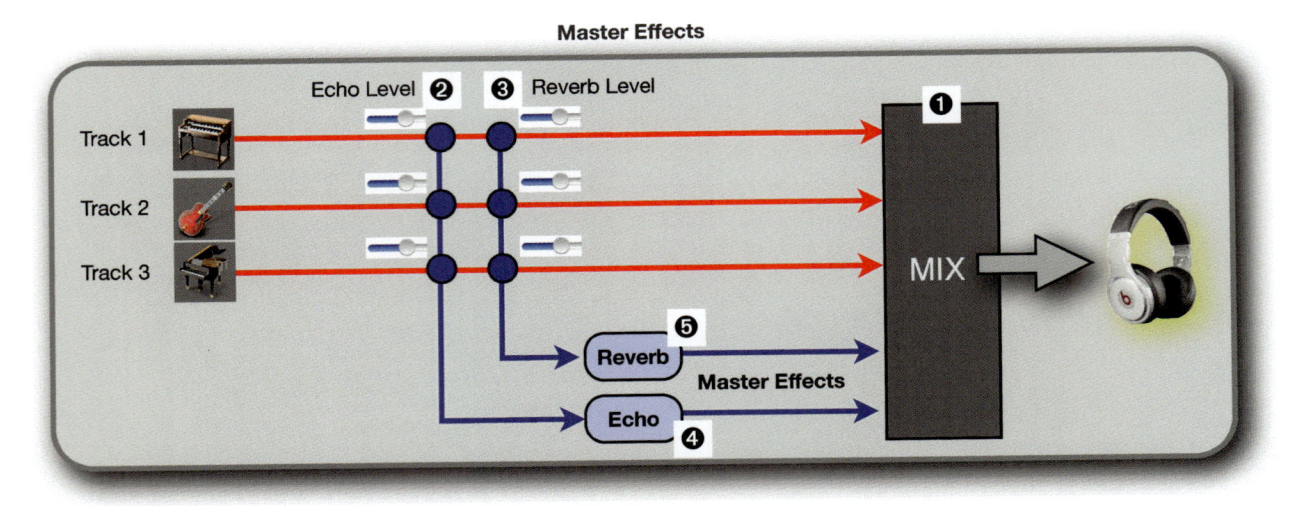

The signal of each Instrument on a Track gets sent to its final destination ❶ where they are mixed together and that's what you hear.

However, each signal can also go to two other destinations. The important part is "*also,*" which means sending the signal to that route won't affect its main route. A slider lets you control the signal level or the amount (how much of the signal you want to send to that route). Each Track has two sliders, the Echo Level ❷ and the Reverb Level ❸, that controls how much that Track sends to those two individual routes.

Those two side signals (blue) also end up at the final destination ❶ where they are mixed together with the signal of each Track.

And here comes the important part: Each of these two signal routes (blue) pass through an effects module (Master Effects) before reaching the final destination. One is processed with an Echo Effect ❹ and the other one with a Reverb Effect ❺.

⦿ Echo Level

This slider ❷ determines how much (the level) of the Track's signal is sent to the Master Echo Effect ❹.

⦿ Reverb Level

This slider ❸ determines how much (the level) of the Track's signal is sent to the Master Reverb Effect ❺.

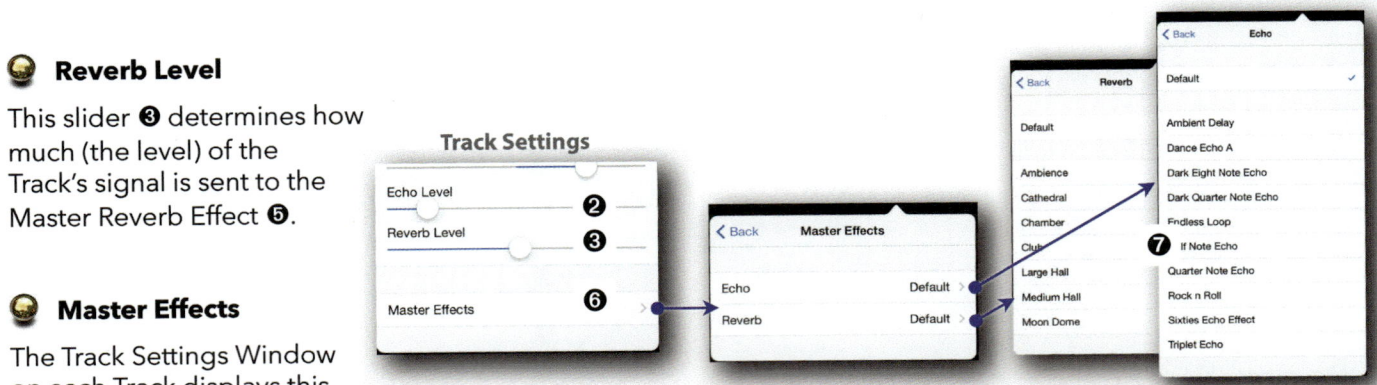

⦿ Master Effects

The Track Settings Window on each Track displays this Master Effects Button ❻. However, this is a global setting. It controls the same two modules, the Echo Effect module ❹ and the Reverb Effect module ❺. Switching to the next window lets you select different effects presets from a list ❼.

I touched on the various Instrument Types in the Instrument Browser chapter already, so you know by now that not only are there 10 different Instrument Types, but that they belong to different groups with fundamentally different behaviors. You also might understand my reluctance to even call some of them "Instruments".

In this chapter, I will go through the various Instruments in more detail.

Each Instrument has its own interface with its own sets of controls. This can be a bit overwhelming. So to make this learning process easier, I introduce the Instruments in a special order so you can recognize similar controls and playing techniques.

➡ *Audio "Instruments"*

➡ *Standard MIDI Instruments*

➡ *Sampler MIDI Instrument*

➡ *Smart MIDI Instruments*

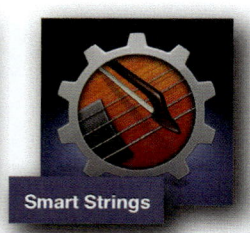

Here are some points you have to be aware of when comparing what the Instruments have in common and how they are different:

- **Patches**: All Instruments provide Patches (similar to the Patches in the Library of GarageBand X) and with the exception of the Smart Instruments, you can even save your own Patches.
- **Sound Controls**: Look out for the controls that let you change the sound of the Instruments.
- **Play Controls**: Look out for the controls that let you change the way you can play the instrument.
- **Track Settings**: Keep an eye on the Track Settings Window because different Instruments may have specific settings available.
- **MIDI Regions**: Eight of the ten Instruments create MIDI Regions. Keep in mind that some Regions cannot be edited in the MIDI Editor and not all MIDI Regions can be moved between Tracks (i.e. move a MIDI Region from a Smart Keyboard to a Standard Keyboard Track).

Audio "Instruments"

 Audio Recorder

This is the Instrument/Track for recording any audio signal. That can be an acoustic signal recorded with a microphone or an electric signal recorded from an electric guitar or a keyboard connected to your iPad.

The Audio Recorder window has two different views:

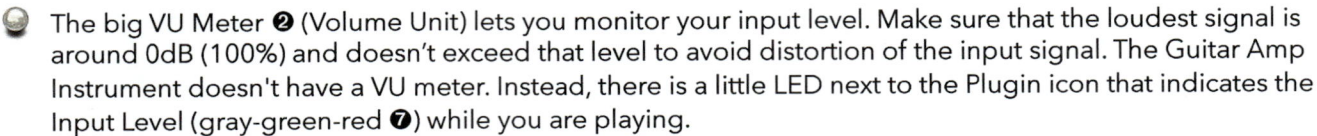

➡ Before the first Recording

This is the view when you first select that "Instrument" and haven't recorded anything yet.

- The Plug ✎ Icon ❶ opens the Input Settings Window for adjusting the Input Level and Noise Gate for reducing any background noise. The Monitor Switch lets you listen ("monitor") to the input signal. Which controls are available depends on the input device. GarageBand detects your input device automatically.

- The big VU Meter ❷ (Volume Unit) lets you monitor your input level. Make sure that the loudest signal is around 0dB (100%) and doesn't exceed that level to avoid distortion of the input signal. The Guitar Amp Instrument doesn't have a VU meter. Instead, there is a little LED next to the Plugin icon that indicates the Input Level (gray-green-red ❼) while you are playing.

- The text with instructions on the right ❸ changes depending on what input device you use. If nothing is connected, then GarageBand uses the built-in iPad Microphone.

➡ After the first Recording

After you recorded your first signal on that Track, the window view switches to display the following:

- The right side of the window now displays nine icons ❹ that represent nine Effect Presets.

- *Tap* on an icon to select that Preset. The name and the icon will be displayed on the Track Header in the Tracks View.

- Each Preset has two sliders ❺ that lets you adjust its two Effects. "Dry" ❻ is the only Preset with no Effects. It is the default Preset after you record your first take. Different Presets provide different Effects (Compressor, Distortion, Chorus, etc.). This is the only place where you can manipulate the recorded sound of the Audio Recorder Track (besides the two Master Effects).

Input Settings

Here is a closer look at the Input Settings Window. It is highly dynamic, meaning that it displays different controls, depending on various conditions.

At the beginning of the book I discussed external hardware devices that you can connect to your iPad. GarageBand automatically detects what is connected and provides the necessary controls. The text ❶ on the Audio Recorder Instrument also changes accordingly when you first record on a new Track.

The Input Settings Window will also display the "Inter-App Audio" ❷ Button if you have at least one Inter-App Audio app installed on your iPad. I will discuss this new feature in the last chapter.

➡ Nothing connected (built-in Mic only)

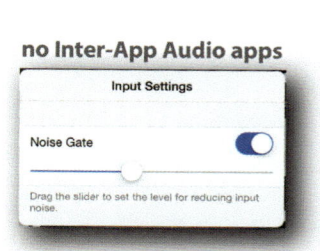
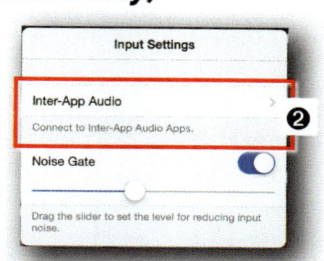

Point your iPad towards the sound you want to record then tap the Record button above to begin. ❶

➡ Cable/Device connected to the Headphones Jack

The window provides an optional Input Level ❸ control and the Monitor Switch ❹.

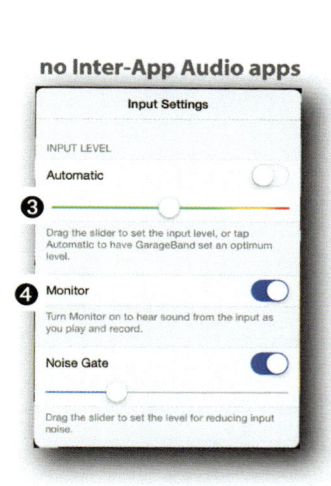
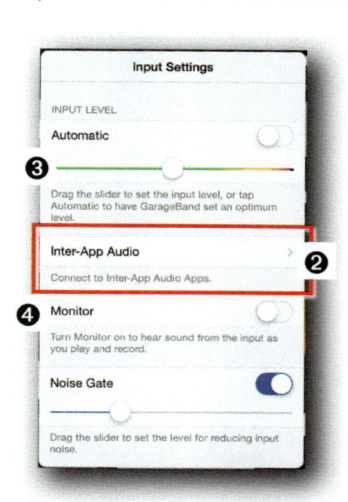

Tap the Record button above to start recording using the device connected to the headphones jack. ❶

➡ Device connected to the Dock Connector

If the external Audio Device has multiple Input Channels, then the Input Settings Window will have an additional Channel Button ❺ to select a specific input channel ❻ that you want to record on that Track.

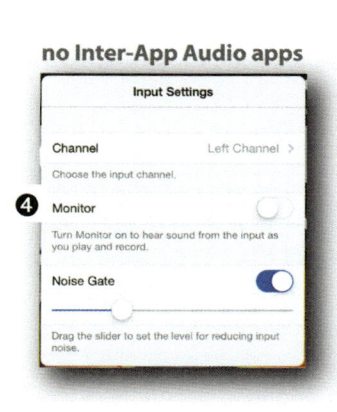
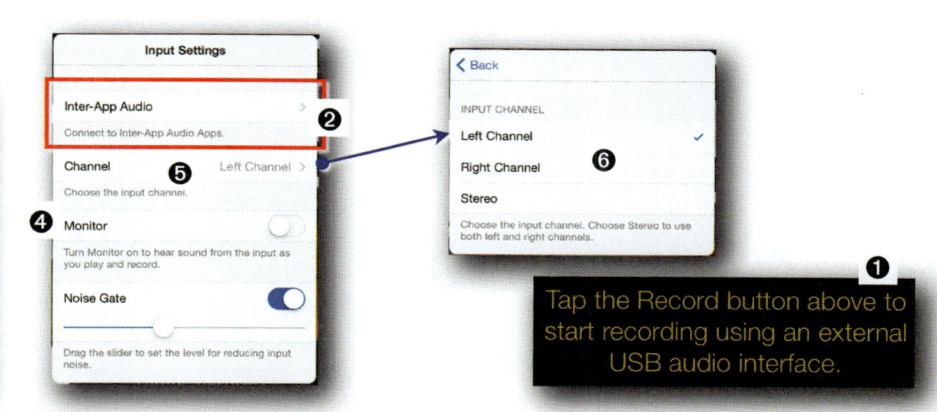

Tap the Record button above to start recording using an external USB audio interface. ❶

 Guitar Amp

The Guitar Amp is the second Instrument Type that creates an Audio Track. Please note that the actual *instrument* is "outside" the GarageBand app. It is your electric guitar that you connect to your iPad. The Guitar Amp "Instrument" just provides the signal processing components that make your guitar signal sound like it was played through some real amplifier, speaker cabinets, and stompboxes.

Also keep in mind that you can feed any audio signal to a Guitar Amp Instrument (even a microphone) if you want to experiment with it.

Overview

This Instrument has two different views that can be switched with the button in the upper right corner.

- **Amp** button : ***Tap*** on the Amp Button ❶ to switch to the Amp View.
- **Stompbox** button : ***Tap*** on the Stompbox Button ❷ to switch to the Stompbox View.

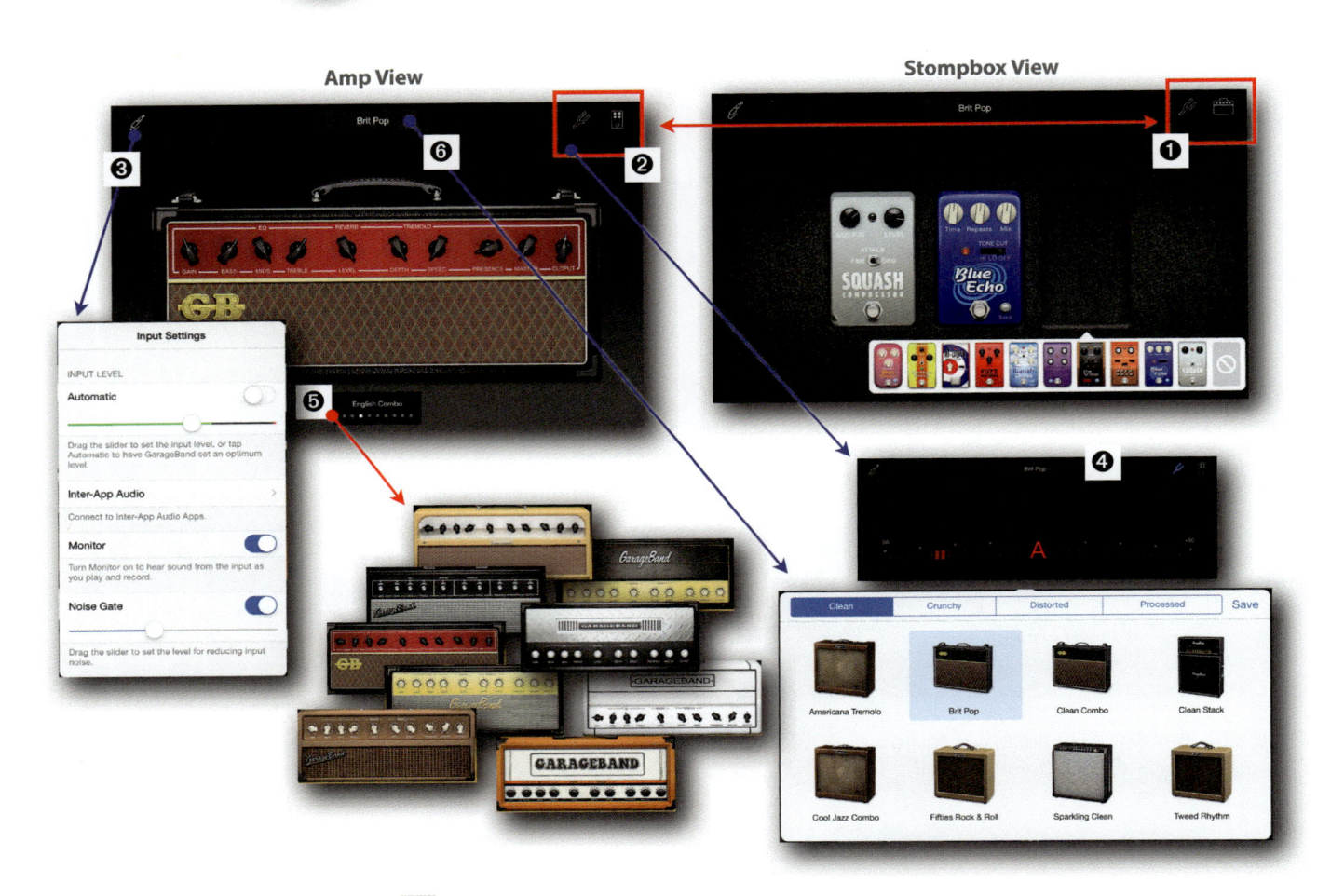

Tap on the Input Settings Button ❸ to open the Input Settings Window.

Tap on the Tuning Fork Button ❹, which overlays a large Tuner display so you can tune your guitar.

Swipe the window left or right to change to a different Amp. A little popup display ❺ temporarily shows the name of the current amp and the nine dots which represent the nine available amps. ***Tap*** on the main window to show that popup display again to see what the name of the amp is. This is the name of the Amp, but don't get confused with the name of the Patch from the Library Window that uses one of those nine Amps.

Tap the Patch Button ❻ at the top to open the Library Window to select and manage the Patches.

Amp Models

The Guitar Amp Instrument provides nine different amp models. Each one simulates the sonic characteristics of a famous guitar amp. Each amp picture is a clue as to what real guitar amp it is copying.

How it works

Amp Controls

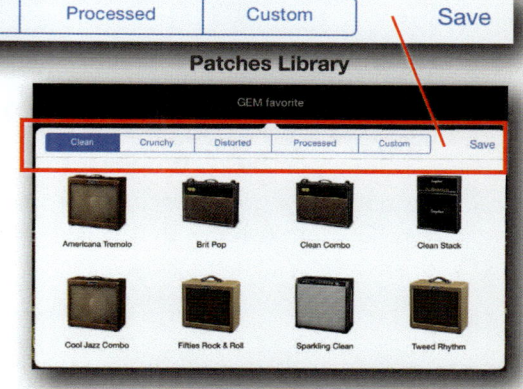

- Each amp has ten controls, the knobs on the front (Gain, Bass, Mids, etc.). You can set those controls with your finger using the *swiping* gesture. The exact type of movement can be set in the iPad Settings app for GarageBand.

- When you change to a different amp model, the settings of those 10 controls stay the same. This would be the same as when you have two different amps next to each other and set their controls to the same position. Even with those same settings, they would sound differently because each amp has its own sonic characteristics.

Stompboxes

Stompbox View

The Stompbox View lets you add little pedal effects, called Stompboxes to your sound.

- *Tap* on a Stompbox Icon to change the window to select from 10 popular Stompboxes.
- **Add**: *Drag* a Stompbox up to an empty slot.
- **Replace**: *Drag* a Stompbox over an existing slot.
- **Swap**: *Drag* the slots left or right to swap those Stompboxes. The signal "travels" from left to right and the order of the boxes could make a big difference.
- All the knobs and buttons on the Stompboxes can be controlled with your touch gestures.

Patches

Clean	Crunchy	Distorted	Processed	Custom	Save

Patches Library

A Patch is the combination of a specific Amp Model (and its settings), plus the additional Stompboxes (and their settings). Once you select a Patch, you can change any of those components (different Amp, different Stompboxes, different settings). In addition, you can save that "new sound" you created as a new Custom Patch.

Tapping on the Patch Button (available in Amp View and Stompbox View) opens a popup window that functions like the Library Window in GarageBand X.

- The different Patches are organized in four categories (Clean, Crunchy, Distorted, and Processed). *Tap* on one of the tabs to select that group.
- Each Category contains eight Patches. *Tab* on one to select that Patch.

Custom Patches:

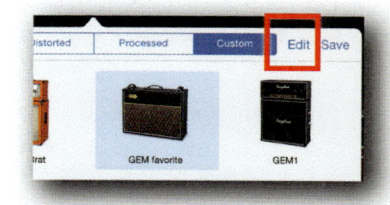

- *Tap* the Save Button to save the current settings as your Custom Patch. All your own Patches are listed under the Customs tab.
- You can give a Custom Patch your own name, but the picture is used from the Patch where it was originated.
- If you have more than eight Custom Patches, just *swipe* to the next page.
- If you select the Customs tab, then the header will display an additional Edit Button that lets you rename or delete a Custom Patch.

The Instrument Types I include in this category are the *Keyboard Instrument* and the *Drums Instrument*. Let's start with the Drums because it has the easiest interface.

 Drums

The Drums Instrument has two different user interfaces depending on the Drums Patch you select.

➡ *Drum Set*

Drums Set

The window is a replication of a real drum set ❶ from the point of view of the drummer. This is the most intuitive graphical interface. You just *tap* on a drum or cymbal you want to hit, almost as if you played the real drums.

The sound varies depending on how hard you tap and which area of the individual drum or cymbal you tap. Activate the Smart Guides by *tapping* on the question mark ❓ in the upper right corner of the Control Bar to see all the detailed touch gestures explained.

➡ *Drum Machine*

Drums Machine

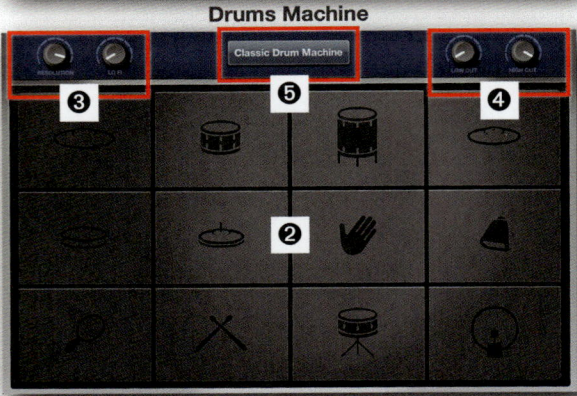

This window is a replication of the drum pads of a drum machine ❷. The sound also responds to the intensity of your tap. In addition, here you have four controls: *Resolution* and *LoFi* changes the sonic quality ❸ while *Low Cut* and *High Cut* are equalizer controls to change the frequency response ❹ of all sounds.

Both views have the Patch Button ❺ in the upper middle section to open the Library Window. It contains only three drum sets and three drum machines. You can also save your setting as a Custom Patch with the Save Button ❻. This will add the Custom tab ❼ to the Library Window.

Patches

Custom Patches

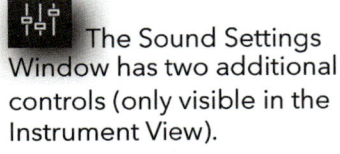 The Sound Settings Window has two additional controls (only visible in the Instrument View).

- The Velocity Sensitivity setting determines the generated velocity value based on how hard you tap on the iPad.
- Turning on "Bass drum with cymbal" will trigger the Bass Drum whenever you hit the crash cymbal.

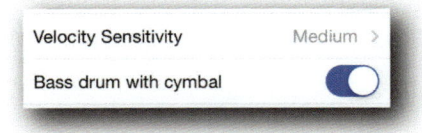

 Keyboard

The Keyboard Instrument is one of the most important Instruments in GarageBand. It offers a variety of synthesized and sampled instruments that you can play with the virtual touch keyboard or with an external MIDI keyboard connected to the iPad.

All the various keyboard sounds have the same three interface elements:
- **Touch Keyboard**: The virtual touch keyboard is the same on any Patch.
- **Play Controls**: In the center is a row of controls and switches that affect various elements of how you play the keyboard. The controls are almost the same for all Patches.
- **Sound Controls**: The upper portion of the window contains the big Patch button to open the Library Window. The rest of that section holds the various controls specific for the selected type of keyboard.

Type of Keyboard

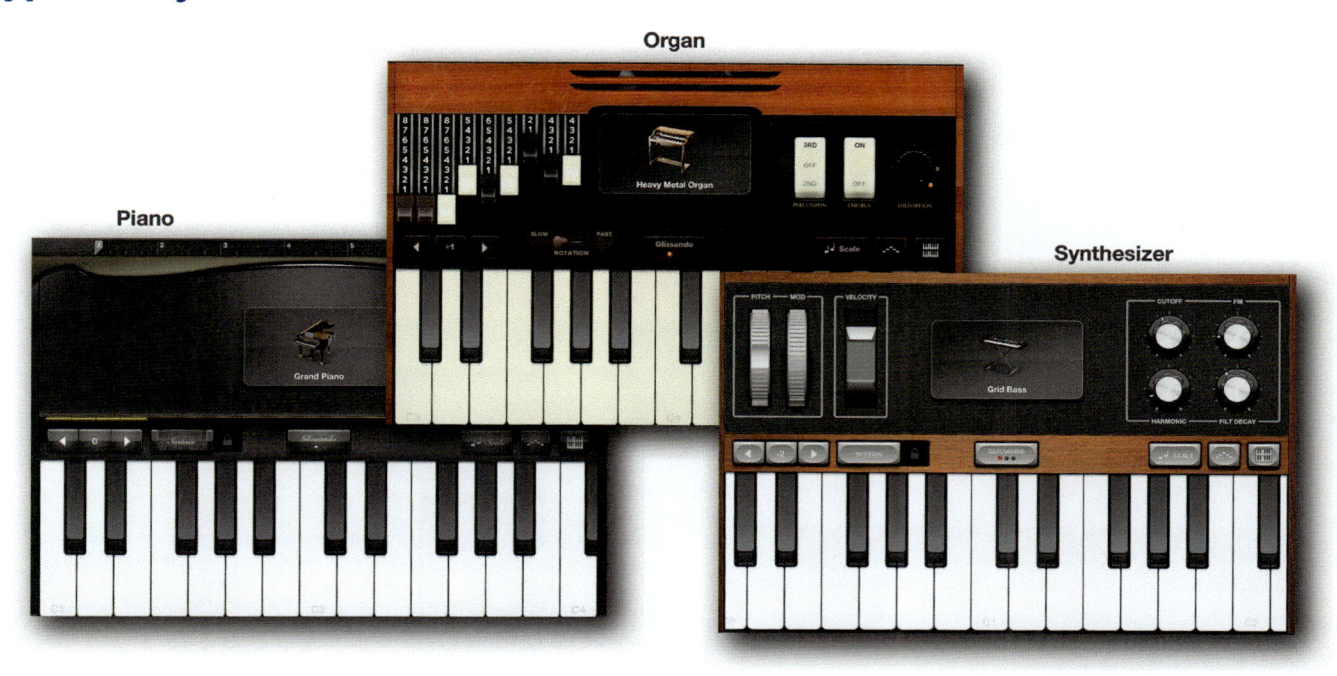

Although the interface is similar for the various Keyboard Patches, there are three types of Keyboards and they differ mainly in the upper part of the window, the Sound Controls.

Piano

Most of the Piano Patches have no additional controls to alter the sound, only the Electric Pianos.

Organ

The Organ Patches provide most of the controls of a real Hammond Organ: Drawbars, controls for a Leslie cabinet, etc.

Synthesizer

The various Synth Patches provide the pitch bend and modulation wheel on the left and sound control knobs on the right (Cutoff, Resonance, Attack, Release).

Library Window

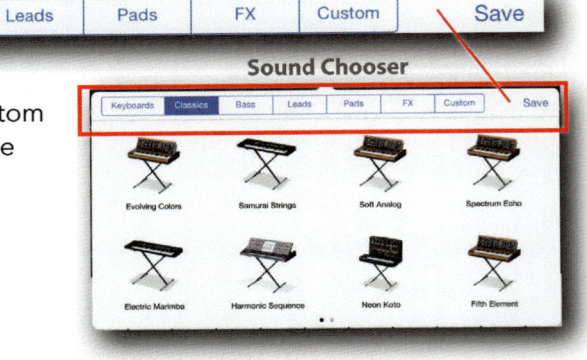

Sound Chooser

The Library Window provides six tabs that represent the various groups of keyboards, plus the Custom tab that contains your own Patches. Many tabs have more than one window of Patches. **Swipe** to the left or right to get to the next or previous window.

Keyboard Controls

 Keyboard Range

Tap the left-right button to set the playable range of the virtual Keyboard. **Tap** the middle button to reset the offset.

 Sustain Switch

Tap-hold the Sustain Switch to simulate pressing the sustain pedal. **Slide** the switch to the right to lock the "Sustain Pedal". If the Sustain switch is locked, then **tap-hold** on it to temporarily "lift" the Sustain pedal.

 Keys Control

This button determines the behavior when you **swipe** across the keys instead of tapping them. _Scroll_ lets you shift the playable keyboard range while _Glissando_ lets you play a glissando. Some Patches have a _Pitch_ mode that creates a portamento effect like the Pitch Bend wheel (Wiki-Moment: Glissando, Portamento).

 Scale

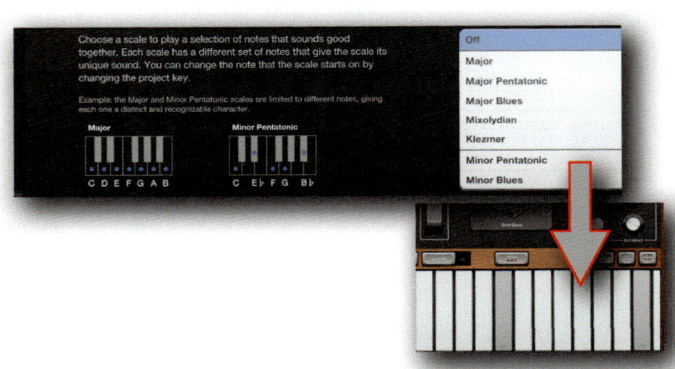

The Scale Button switches the keyboard section with a setup window to choose a specific scale. The black and white keys change to a single bar layout representing only the notes of that scale to avoid "unwanted" notes. Please note that the scale depends on the Song Settings (Key).

 **Arpeggiator**

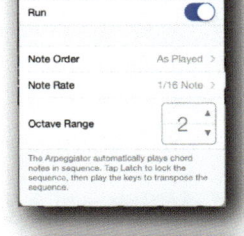

The Arpeggiator is a common module on synthesizers that lets you create electronic grooves and sequencer patterns. When you **tap** a note or a chord on the keyboard, the Arpeggiator will then play those note(s) in a sequence determined by a set of parameters:

- _Note Order_: Play in what order or direction.
- _Note Rate_: The length of the notes.
- Note Range: Spread over how many octaves. The sustain control changes to a Latch control so the note(s) repeat until you tap the next note(s).

 **Keyboard Layout and Controls**

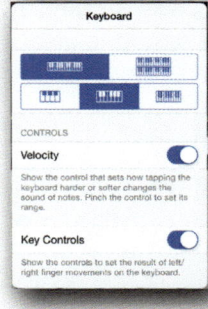

This opens a window that lets you set the layout of the keyboard, plus two display controls:

- _Velocity_: If turned on, it displays the Velocity Bar that lets you set the Velocity Range for the notes you play on the touch keyboard.
- _Key Controls_: If turned on, it displays the control for _Scroll_, _Glissando_, and _Portamento_.

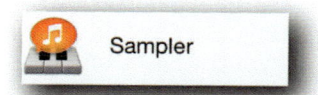 Sampler

A Sampler is a special Keyboard Instrument. Instead of playing a synthesized sound as the sound source, this instrument lets you record an audio signal, a "Sample". But unlike an Audio Recorder where you also record an audio signal, the recorded signal in a Sampler will be played back (triggered) with a musical keyboard. This way, you can "play" your recording musically, because the recorded sample follows the pitch of the key. Now you can play melodies with your sample and even chords. Please note that you can use only one sample per Sampler Instrument in GarageBand.

The Instrument has two main views:

New Sample View

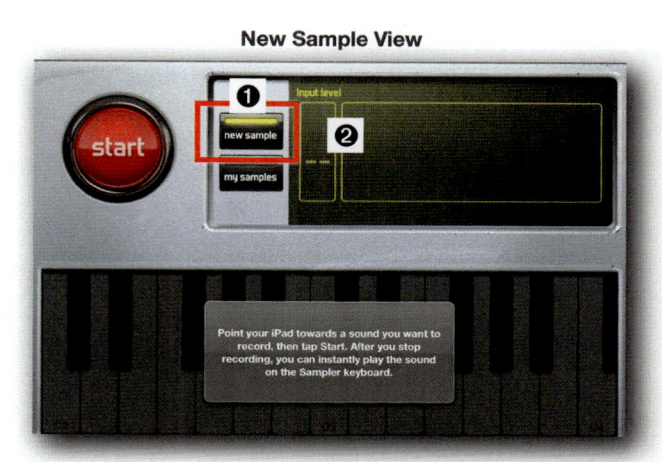

➡ *New Sample*

This is the default window. It can be switched to at any time with the *"new sample"* Button ❶. This view has one big red button to start-stop your recording. The right side ❷ shows the input level and the waveform when you are recording. The bottom displays instructions depending on the connected input device, even the Input Settings Button when applicable.

➡ *My Samples*

When you stop the recording, the Sampler changes automatically to the My Samples View indicated by the *"my samples"* Button ❸. This window can switch between two sections.

⦿ Sample Edit

The window provides various controls ❹ to treat the recorded signal: Trim it, tune it, loop it, reverse it, and even shape it (apply an ADSR envelope to it). And everything with the ease of your finger touch.

⦿ Sample Library

Each recorded Sample is stored with your Song. When you record a new Sample, it will not be overwritten, but added to the Songs list ❺. You can add another Sampler Instrument to your Song and have access to those Samples from that Song list.

But you can also add any recorded Sample to the Library list ❻. This will store the Sample with the GarageBand app so you can have access to it from other Songs in GarageBand.

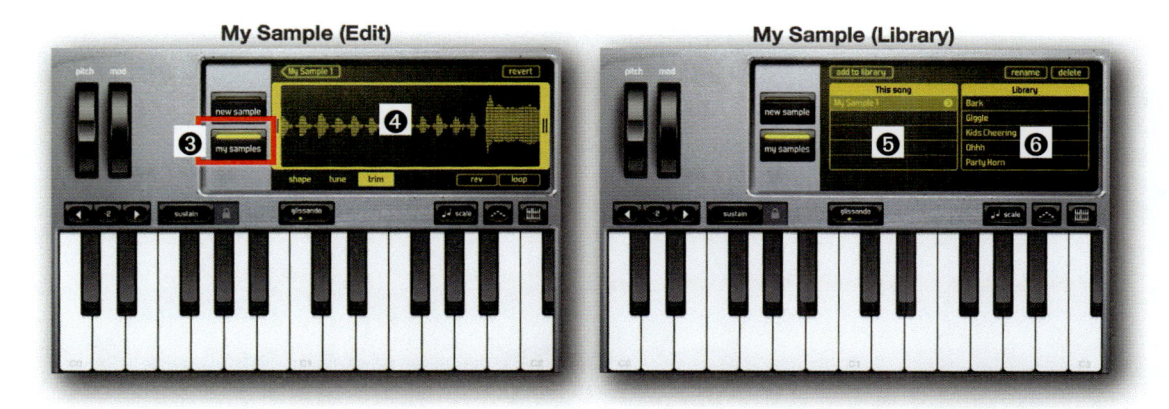

MIDI Instrument (Smart)

Standard MIDI Instruments use either a musical keyboard or pads that generate the MIDI notes when you play on that common user interface. This can be a virtual keyboard or a real MIDI keyboard connected to the iPad.

The Smart Instruments in GarageBand provide new and unique interfaces that enable the player to create much more realistic parts. And on top of that, playing those instruments doesn't require the knowledge of how to play a musical keyboard or any other instrument. The new concepts are fast, intuitive, and easy to learn.

Please note that Smart Instruments won't allow you to create your own Patches.

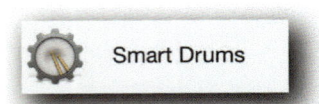 Smart Drums

This is actually a pattern based drum sequencer. To program those patterns you just define basic parameters.

➡ Create

- ⚪ On the right side, you have up to ten individual drums or percussion instruments ❶. *Tap* on them to hear how they sound.
- ⚪ *Drag* the instruments to the big center square ❷ if you want them to be played in your drum pattern. What specific pattern that instrument will play is determined by two parameters:
  - **Loud-Soft**: The higher you place that instrument on the square, the louder it will play.
  - **Simple-Complex**: Moving the instrument more to the left will let it play a simpler pattern, moving it more to the right will have it play a more complex pattern.
- ⚪ That's how simple it is to construct your pattern. You can *drag* the instruments around (or back to the right side to remove them from the pattern) to find the correct balance.
- ⚪ *Tap* the On-Off Button ❸ to listen to the pattern. You can play it by itself or together with your Song.
- ⚪ *Tap* the Dice Button ❹ to let GarageBand create a pattern for you. If you don't like it, *tap* it again for another variation. The Reset Button ❺ clears all the patterns (every instrument back to their place).

➡ Record

- ⚪ *Tap* the Record Button in GarageBand to record the pattern on that Track as a MIDI Region. You can even move the Instruments around while recording. Use the punch-in while playing to record over an existing Region to change the existing pattern at some point.
- ⚪ You can't open those MIDI Regions in the MIDI Editor!

➡ Patches

The Patch Button ❻ opens a Library Window with six types of Drums Sets and Drum Machines.

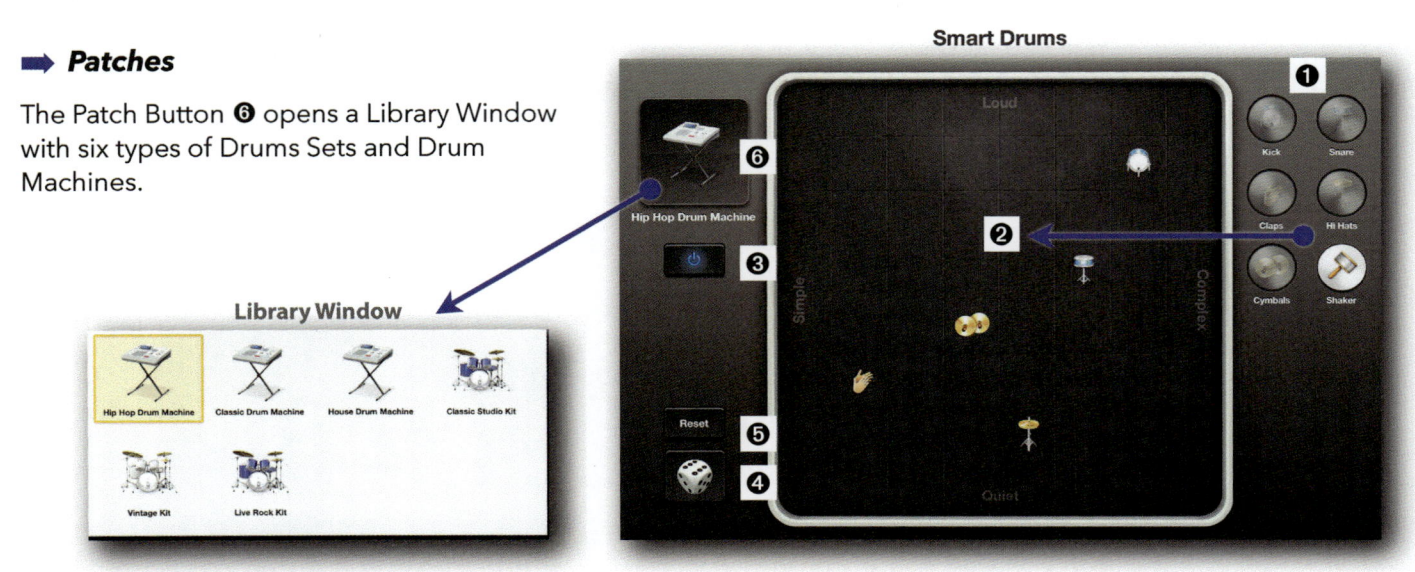

13 - Instruments

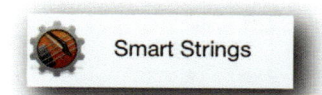 Smart Strings

Let's first have a look at the concept how Smart Strings make it possible to achieve such a high level of realism. How can you play various techniques without the knowledge of playing any strings instrument in the first place? Think of it as four levels:

❶ Patches

The Patch Button in the upper left corner lets you select from 4 different "sounds". Although the sounds are not dramatically different when you play them, they have more of an effect on the chord pattern when using the *Autoplay* mode.

❷ Instruments

The available Instruments are from a standard string section (1.Violin, 2.Violin, Viola, Cello, Bass). Even when selecting the Chord mode, which plays the String Ensemble, you still can choose which instrument is part of the Ensemble.

❸ Chord - Notes

Selecting Notes allows you to play a single Instrument with the available techniques. Selecting Chords lets you play chords also with various techniques, but you have an additional "Autoplay" option to have GarageBand play four different chord patterns. Chords also allows you to choose a single instrument or any combination of a string ensemble.

❹ Techniques

This is the actual part where you play the instrument. You have different touch gestures to simulate typical playing techniques for string instruments.

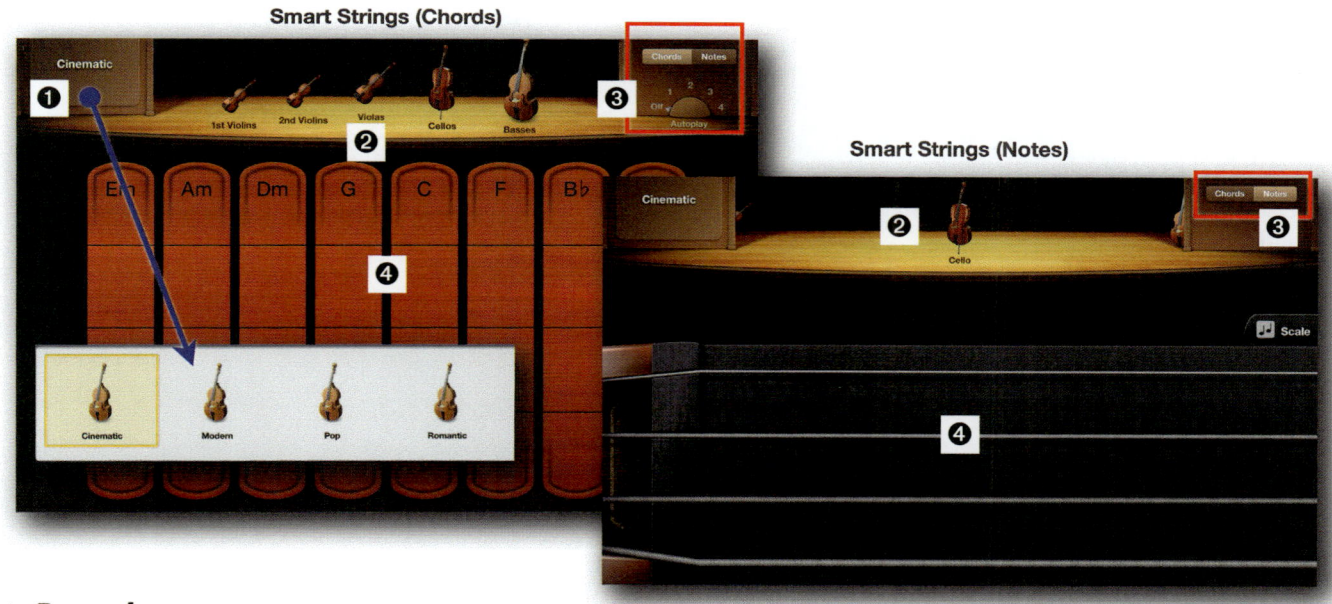

➡ Record

You can play different techniques and change instruments while you are recording. Whatever you perform with those touch gesture techniques will be recorded in a MIDI Region as real MIDI Events.

You can open those MIDI Regions in the MIDI Editor and edit each individual note. This way you can record an Autoplay pattern, but further edit it to create your own variation.

Techniques: Chords

- **Chords**: The eight vertical strips represent the available chords for the current key of your Song (selected in the Song Settings). You can change the default Chords by choosing "Edit Chords" in the Song Settings .
- **Chord variations**: Each strip is divided into four sections ❶. Each one represents a variation of that specific chord.
- **Pizzicato**: *Tap* on a chord strip to play that chord in pizzicato. They have only one level of dynamics.
- **Staccato**: *Swipe quickly* on a section to play a staccato (*arco*) chord.
- **Legato**: *Tap-hold* on a specific chord section and keep *sliding* up and down. The section where you *tap* is important for the type of chord, the sliding movement then can span across the whole strip.
- **Crescendo - Decrescendo**: You can increase the dynamic of the played chord by moving your finger faster up and down. Slowing down the movement will decrease the dynamic.
- **Change Ensemble**: You can tap on an instrument on the stage to select or deselect it ❷ while you are playing a chord. This will affect the next chord you play.

➡️ *Autoplay*

You have four Autoplay variations ❸. In addition, you still can choose the Instruments on the stage to get even more variations. The Chord Strips now have no divisions ❹. You **tap** once to start the pattern and **tap** again to stop the pattern or **tap** a different Chord Strip. Of course, the pattern follows the tempo of your Song.

Techniques: Notes

- **Instrument Selection**: *Slide* left or right on the stage to select one of the four string instruments. Notes can only be played by a single instrument.
- **Scale**: *Tap* on the Scale Button ❺ to open the window for selecting a specific scale. This is the same window we saw for the Keyboard Instruments. A scale restricts the played note to its scale, avoiding any "unwanted" notes.

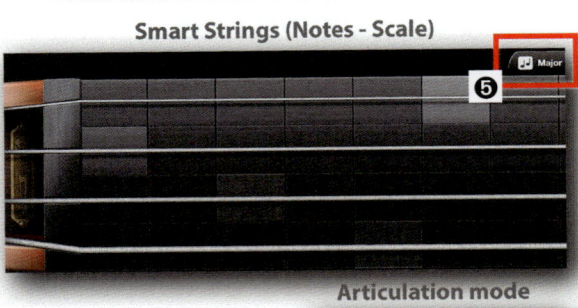

- **Standard Play**: *Tap* a string to play a short note or *tap-hold* a note to play a sustained note (until you release the note). Like on a real fretless instrument, you can *slide* your finger up and down for a portamento effect. Please note that this is not possible when a scale is selected. You can even play polyphonic (more than one note) by using more than one finger.

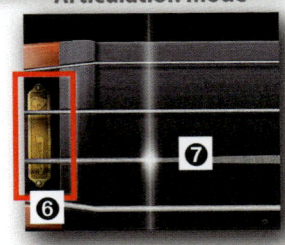

- **Articulation Play**: On the left side of the strings is an Articulation Button ❻. *Tap* it to temporarily switch the articulation or *double-tap* it to latch the Articulation Mode. *Tap* again to turn it off. When activated, you have two different styles:
  - **Pizzicato**: *Tap* a string(s) to play it pizzicato.
  - **Crescendo-Decrescendo**: *Tap-hold* with one finger on a string and slide up or down. A vertical light beam ❼ will appear and you will hear a sustain note. Now the faster you *slide up-down*, the more you increase the note's intensity (crescendo) and the slower you *slide up-down*, the more you decrease the note's intensity (decrescendo).

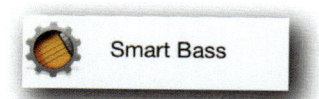 Smart Bass

The Smart Bass follows a similar concept.

The Library ❶ lets you choose from eight different bass sounds: Three electric basses, one upright bass and four synth basses.

You can switch between Notes and Chords ❷ that provide a different user interface and different playing techniques.

Techniques: Notes

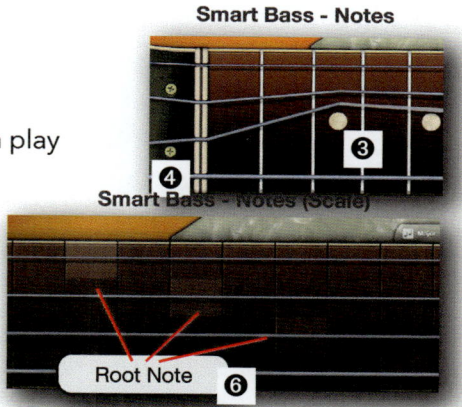

Smart Bass - Notes

Smart Bass - Notes (Scale)

Root Note ❻

- 🔘 **Tap** the strings to play the note.
- 🔘 **Tap-hold** on a string and **drag** it up or down to bend ❸ that note. You can play multiple notes, but bend only one at a time.
- 🔘 **Tap** on a string above the neck ❹ to play the empty string.
- 🔘 **Tap** the Scale Button ❺ to select a specific Scale. The root notes of the Scale are highlighted ❻ with a lighter shade on the frets.

Techniques: Chords

The Smart Bass Instrument also has a Chord Mode (even though a bass player plays single note lines most of the time).

- 🔘 The Chord strips can be used to easily play a bass line for the main chord. This comes in handy if you don't know how to play the bass guitar and don't know which note is which on the fret board. The Chord Strips ❼ indicate the root note and the four strings on a strip provide the individual notes for that chord. This way you can play simple bass lines or even **tap** two or three strings at the same time to play a chord.
- 🔘 The Autoplay Mode ❽ provides four variations of standard bass patterns. Please note that the patterns are different for the different Bass Patches. This takes into account that an electric bass plays different phrases than an upright bass or even a synth bass. In this mode, there are no strings displayed, and the Chord Strip. They just just functions as an on-off button.

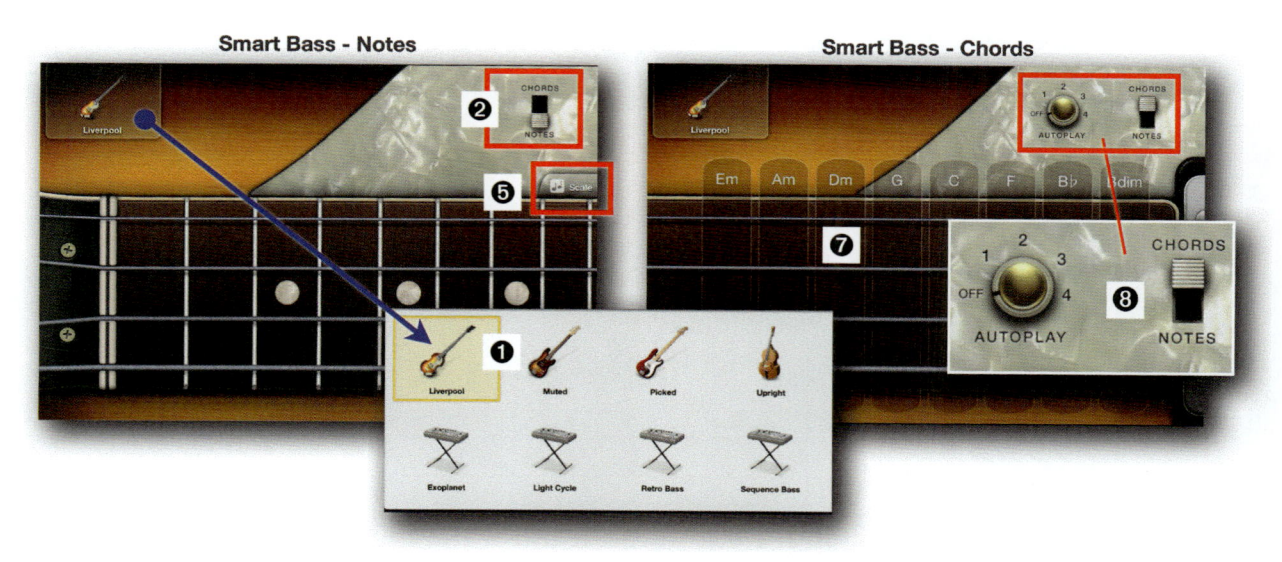

Smart Bass - Notes   Smart Bass - Chords

➡️ *Record*

Recorded MIDI Regions created by the Smart Bass can also be opened with the MIDI Editor and all the MIDI Notes can be edited.

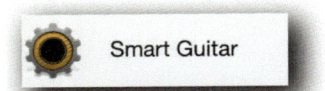 Smart Guitar

The Smart Guitar functions almost the same as the Smart Bass Instrument.

The Library ❶ lets you choose from four different guitar models, one acoustic and three electric guitars. The Electric Guitars have an additional element, two stompboxes ❷.

You switch between Notes and Chords ❸ for the different user interface and different playing techniques.

Techniques: Notes

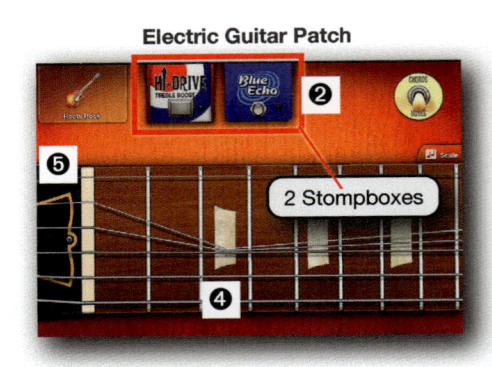

Electric Guitar Patch

2 Stompboxes

- 🔘 *Tap* the strings to play the note.
- 🔘 *Tap-hold* on a string and *drag* it up or down ❹ to bend that note. You can play multiple notes, but bend only one at a time.
- 🔘 *Tap* on a string above the neck ❺ to play the empty string.
- 🔘 *Tap* the Scale button ❻ to select a specific Scale.

Techniques: Chords

The Chord Mode provides some amazingly realistic playing techniques. The available chord symbols depend on the Key of the current Song (key and major-minor). The root chord is the fifth Chord Strip.

- 🔘 You can use different playing techniques.
  - **Single Note picking**: *Tap* individual notes inside a chord strip to create some easy chord picking.
  - **Automatic Strumming:** *Tap* on the chord symbol ❼ at the top of each Chord Strip to trigger a single strummed chord. *Tap* those areas in a rhythmical fashion to create some realistic sounding strumming patterns.
  - **Manual Strumming**: *Swipe* the strings up and down ❽ along a Chord Strip to create an arpeggiated chord. The speed of your swipe controls the arpeggio the way you would actually play the guitar.

  Everything Together: You can mix and match all three styles together to create some realistic patterns.

- 🔘 The Autoplay Mode ❾ provides four variations of standard rhythm guitar patterns. Again, the patterns are different for the different Guitar Patches. In this mode, there are no strings displayed and the chord strip just functions as an on and off button.

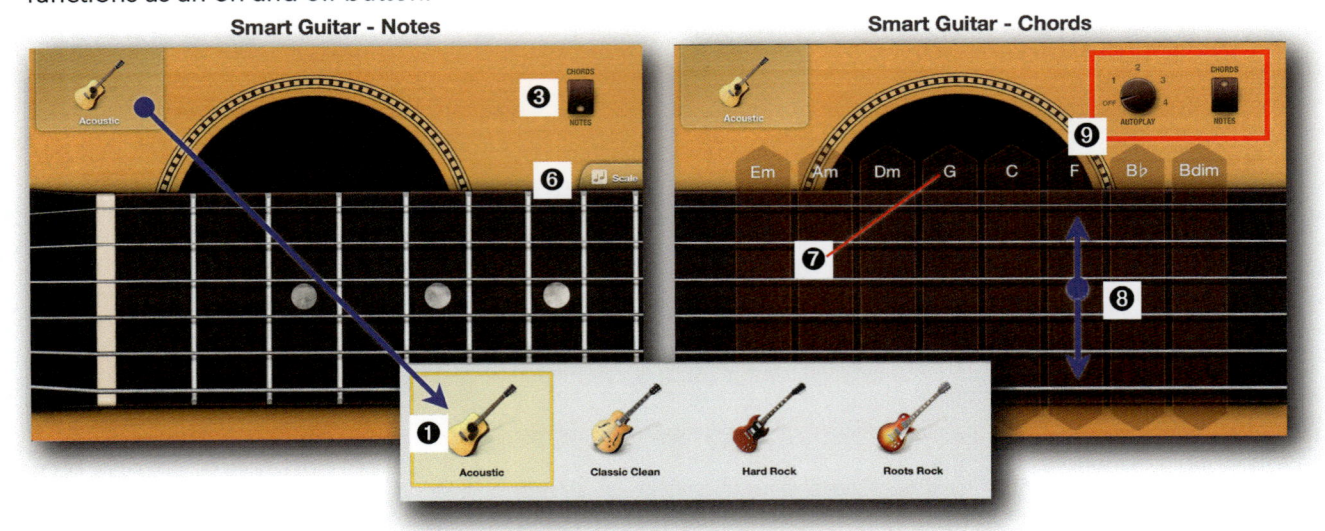

Smart Guitar - Notes   Smart Guitar - Chords

MIDI Regions created with the Smart Guitar can also be edited in the MIDI Editor to manipulate individual MIDI Notes for an even greater variety.

 **Smart Keyboard**

The Smart Keyboard has similar elements as the other Smart Instruments, but the main difference is that there is no switch between Notes and Chords. You are always in Chord mode.

The Library ❶ lets you choose from eight different keyboards. These are the same types as in the Standard Keyboard Instrument. The different types of keyboards have individual controls available to change their sound ❷ and the way you play them.

Keyboard Patches - different Controls

Manual Play

With Autoplay off, you have the standard eight chord strips that depend on the current Song's key. The strips are divided again, this time into eight sections with two different shades.

▶ **Chord**: *Tap* on any of the upper five sections ❸ to play a chord. The higher the section the higher sounding the chord is.

▶ **Bass**: *Tap* on any of the bottom three sections ❹ in gray to play a bass note for that chord.

- You simulate a typical rhythm pattern on a piano by tapping the bass notes with the left hand finger and the chords with the right hand finger. In addition, you can use the Sustain switch ❺ to simulate the sustain pedal of a piano. The sound of some keyboards depends on how hard you tap.
- *Swipe* a chord strip up or down to play that chord arpeggiated.
- Use the Arpeggiator module ❻ to quickly create some interesting sequences while swiping along the strips (with or without sustain).

Autoplay

Autoplay functions like it does with the other Smart Instruments. Select from different patterns that are specific for each Keyboard Patch. However, there is one unique thing. The Chord Strips are divided into three sections:

- **Chord and Bass**: *Tap* on the top section ❼ to play the full pattern in that key (all three segments are lit).
- **Chord only**: *Tap* on the middle section ❽ to play the Chord part of that pattern in that key.
- **Bass only**: *Tap* on the lower section ❾ to play the Bass part of that pattern in that key.

You can mix and match those sections to create a greater chord variety with your Autoplay pattern. Please note that each section functions as an on-off switch for that part of the sequence.

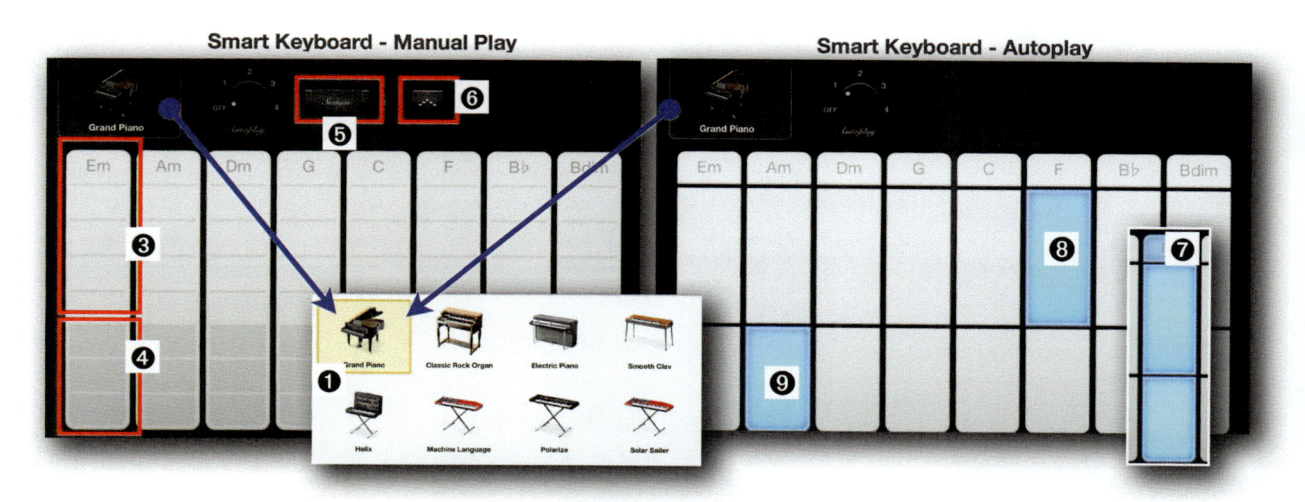

Smart Keyboard - Manual Play | Smart Keyboard - Autoplay

Jam with other Users

The Jam feature in GarageBand allows you to play and record together with up to three other users on their iDevices. Each Device is running a GarageBand Song that is synchronized over Wi-Fi or Bluetooth (minimum requirement iPhone 4, iPod 5, or any iPad).

Purpose

- Play together on multiple devices (playing through their own speaker), synchronized to their shared song.
- Create a Song on one iDevice (*Bandleader*) and have other iDevices (*Band Member*) remotely record into that Song.

Network requirement

The communication can run either over Wi-Fi if all iDevices are on the same Wi-Fi network or over Bluetooth if all iDevices have Bluetooth enabled. For best performance, use only one network and disable the other networks on the Devices. Please note that this has nothing to do with the Bluetooth playback setting in the Song Settings. That switch has to be turned off anyway in order to use the Jam Session.

Configuration

The iDevice that initiates the Session is the *Bandleader* and the iDevices that join the Session are the *Band Members*.

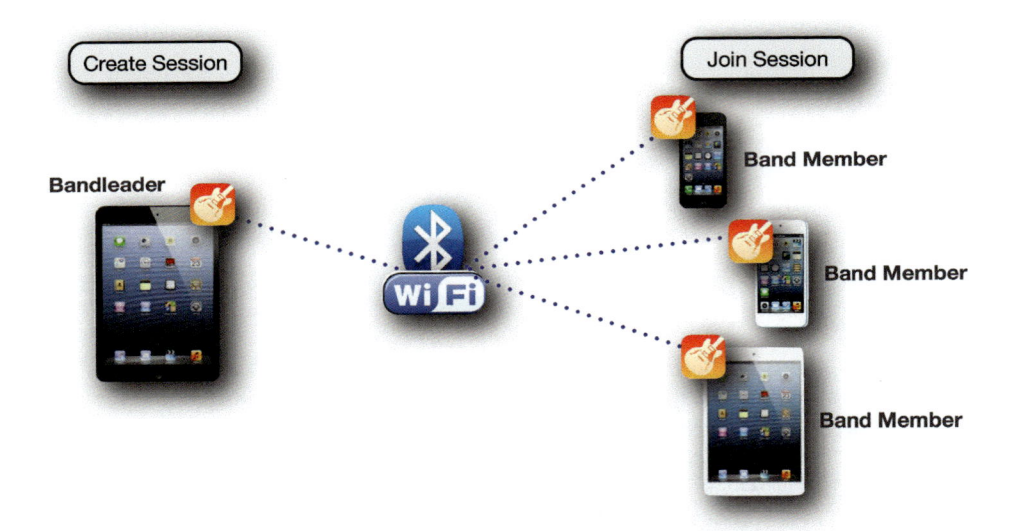

▶ If *Bandleader Control* is set to on, then only the Bandleader controls the Transport Controls and the Band Members just follow. If all participating iDevices want to control the Transport Controls, set it to off.

▶ If *Auto-Collect Recording* is on, then all recordings done on the Band Members Devices are transferred to the Song of the Bandleader.

Here is a step-by-step example for the setup of an iPad (*iPad - Ed*) and an iPhone 5 (*iPhone5 - Ed*):

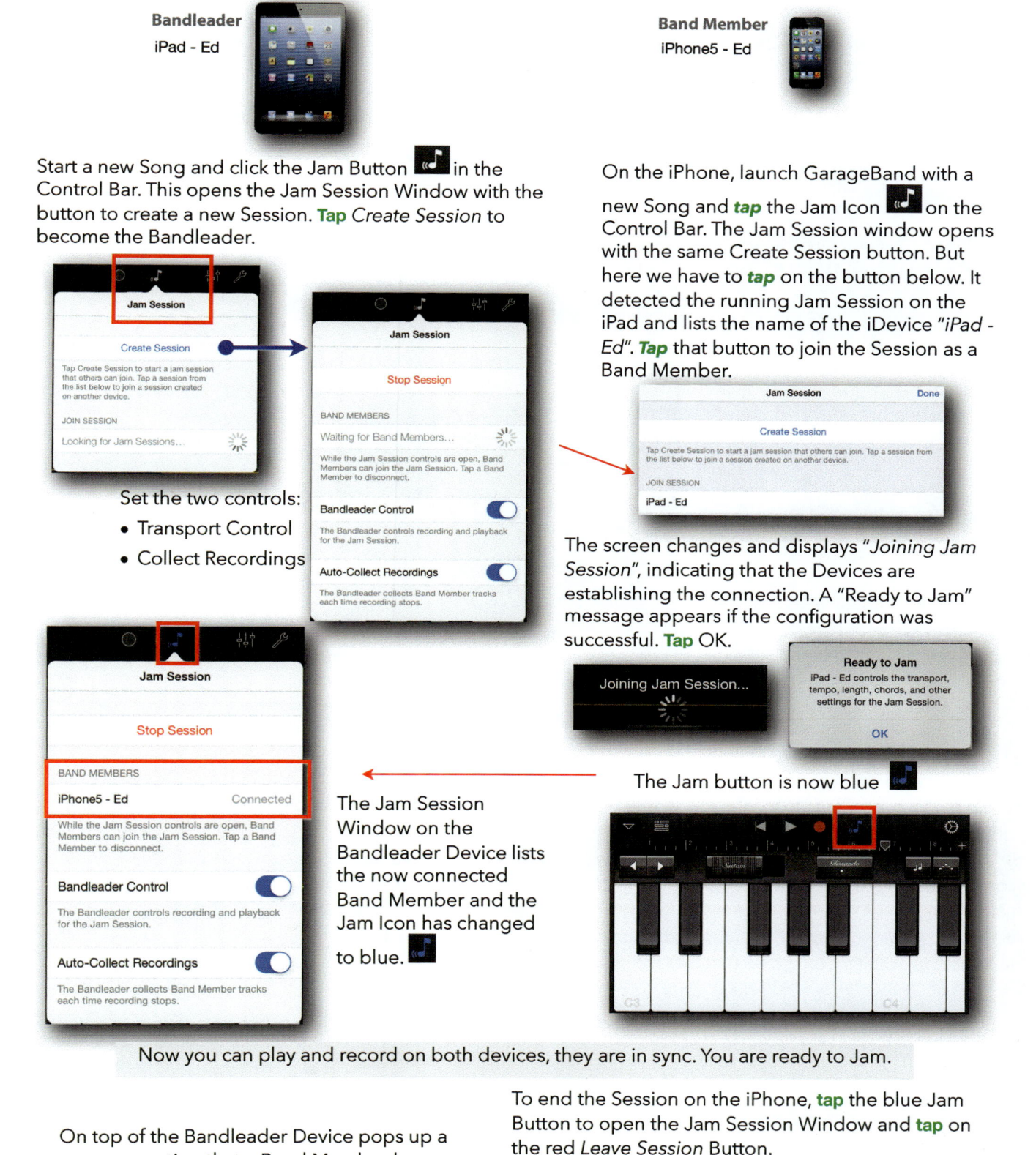

Bandleader
iPad - Ed

Band Member
iPhone5 - Ed

Start a new Song and click the Jam Button in the Control Bar. This opens the Jam Session Window with the button to create a new Session. **Tap** *Create Session* to become the Bandleader.

Set the two controls:
- Transport Control
- Collect Recordings

The Jam Session Window on the Bandleader Device lists the now connected Band Member and the Jam Icon has changed to blue.

On the iPhone, launch GarageBand with a new Song and **tap** the Jam Icon on the Control Bar. The Jam Session window opens with the same Create Session button. But here we have to **tap** on the button below. It detected the running Jam Session on the iPad and lists the name of the iDevice "*iPad - Ed*". **Tap** that button to join the Session as a Band Member.

The screen changes and displays "*Joining Jam Session*", indicating that the Devices are establishing the connection. A "Ready to Jam" message appears if the configuration was successful. **Tap** OK.

The Jam button is now blue

Now you can play and record on both devices, they are in sync. You are ready to Jam.

On top of the Bandleader Device pops up a message noting that a Band Member has left the Session.

To end the Session on the iPhone, **tap** the blue Jam Button to open the Jam Session Window and **tap** on the red *Leave Session* Button.

GarageBand is a Universal iOS app that runs on the iPad and on the smaller iPhone (4 or later) or iPod touch 5. Instead of just shrinking or blowing up the graphics, both Device types have their individual (optimized) GarageBand interface.

Throughout the manual I was referring to the iPad version of the GarageBand interface. In this section, I just want to point out a few changes of the interface when running GarageBand on those smaller iPhone and iPod devices.

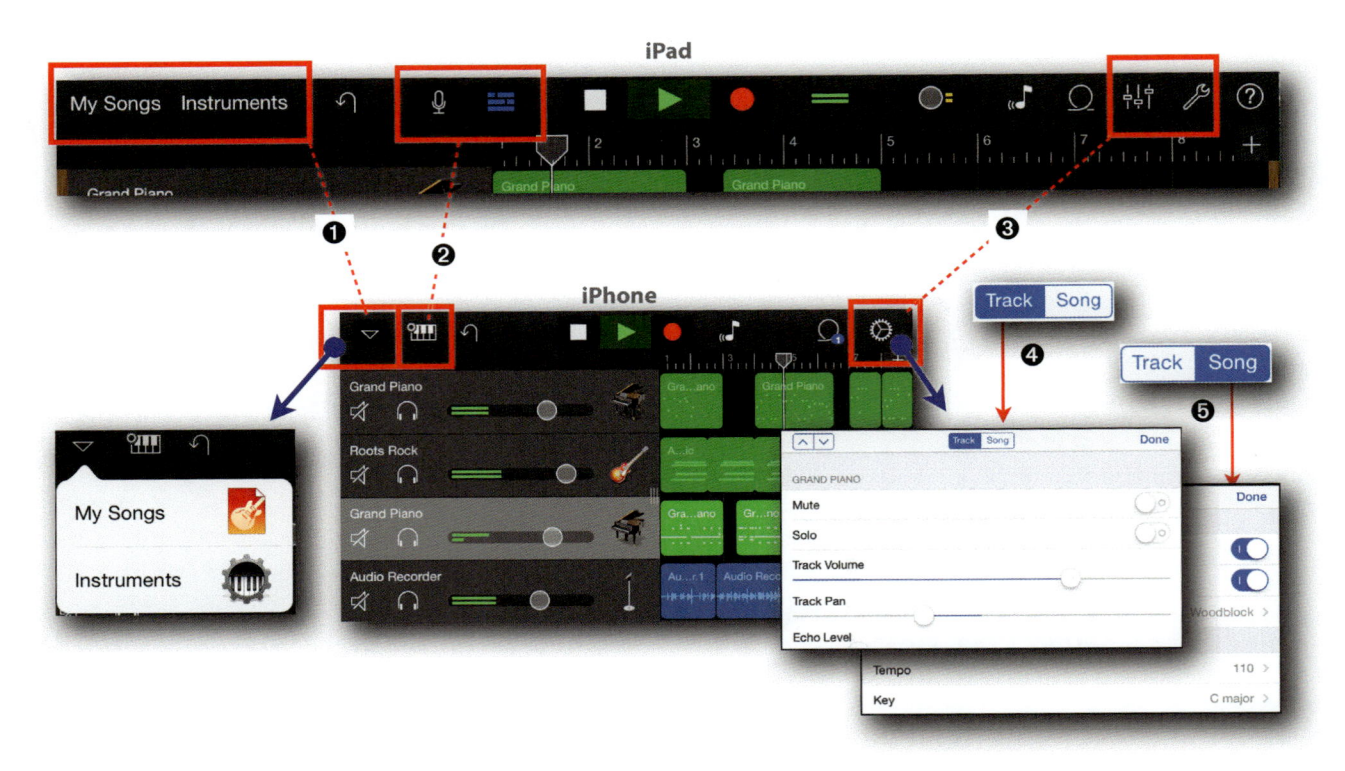

Control Bar

❶ The *My Songs* and *Instruments* Button are merged into a new DownArrow Button. This button opens a popup window containing the actual *My Songs* and *Instruments* Button.

❷ The View Button, which looks like two buttons (it functions as a single toggle button), now only has a single icon. In Tracks View, it displays the Instrument Icon of the selected Track and when *tapped* on, it switches to the Instrument View. In Instrument View, it displays the Tracks Icon to switch back to the Tracks View.

❸ The *Track Settings* and *Song Settings* buttons have also merged into a new "*Gear*" Icon. *Tap* on it to switch to a new window with two tabs, one that lists the Track Settings ❹ parameters and the other one listing the Song Settings ❺ parameters. The Track Settings window has some new extras:

Track Settings

Accessing the Track Settings Window from the Tracks View will display an up and down arrow ❻ to step through the available Tracks. The Header displays the name ❼ of the currently viewed Track.

Accessing the Track Settings Window from the Instrument View will display an extra "Listen" Button ❽ in the upper left corner. *Tap* on it to play some notes on the current Instrument to check its volume (only available for MIDI Tracks).

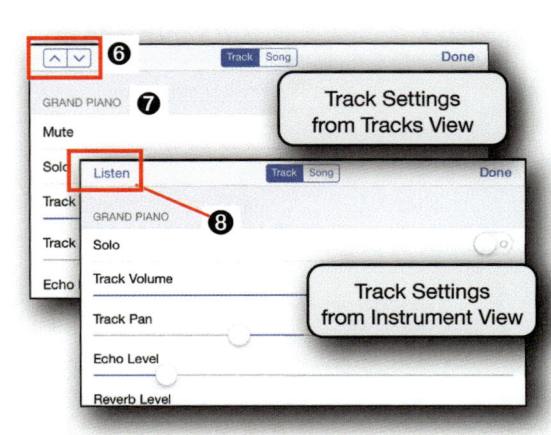

Instrument View

The Instrument View also has a few interface changes and specialties.

- You cannot access the sound controls directly in that View. For that, you have an extra button (Knob Icon) ❶ that opens a new window. It is like a zoomed in window ❷ where the knobs and switches are bigger so you can control them better with your finger. The Knob Icon on the Control Bar turns blue ❸ to indicate that you are in the Control window.
- The popup window that opens with the DownArrow ❹ Button in the upper left corner of the Control Bar gets a third button. This is the Patch Button ❺ that is part of the Instrument layout in the iPad version. This button opens the Library Window ❻ to load or save Patches.
- *Sliding* down the mini-Time Ruler in the Instrument View will also expand to display the Single Track Lane View ❼.

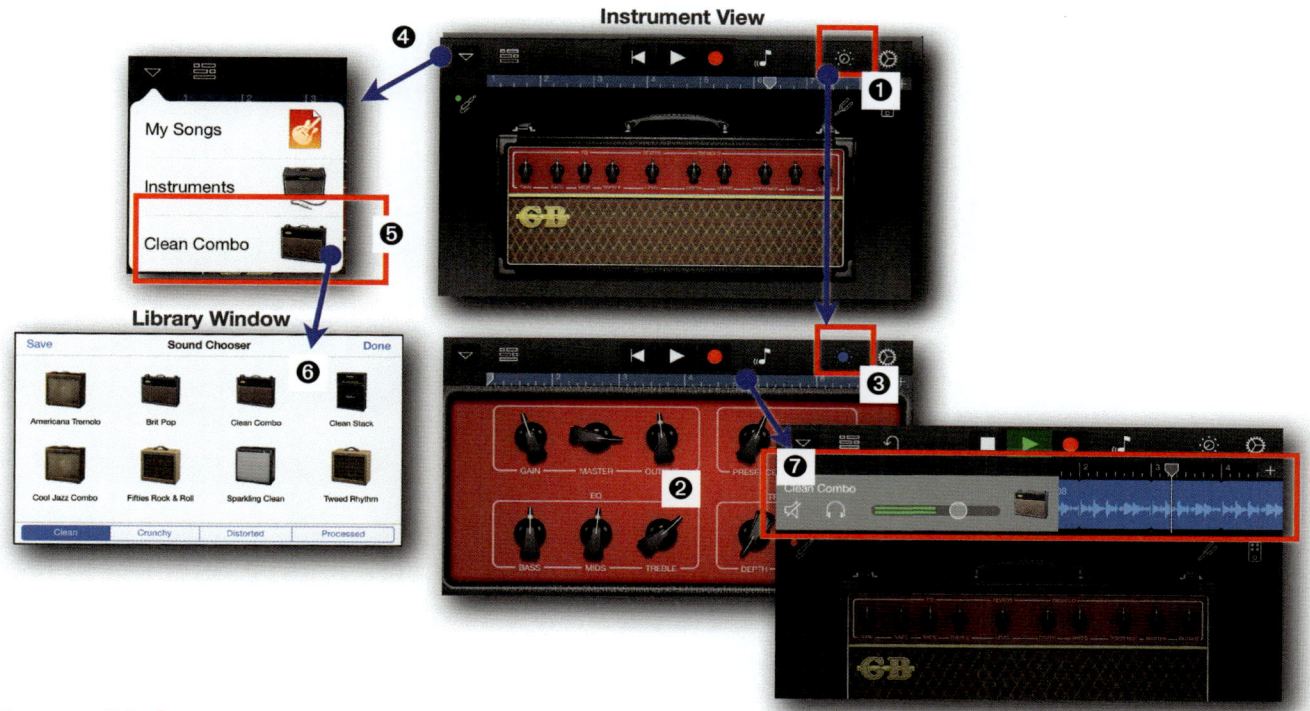

Master Volume

The Playback Volume Slider on the Control Bar is not available on the iPhone. This was just the remote control for the iPad's speaker volume (playback) anyway with no effect on the Song's actual volume.

Undo - Redo

The Undo button ⤺ is visible after you made the first change/edit/ record. *Tap-hold* to bring up the menu to redo an undo.

Loop Browser

The Loop Browser window keeps all its functionality on the iPhone version with the exception of the Playback Volume slider.

Tap-hold on a Loop or Audio File and the screen switches to the Tracks View so you can drop the file to the Track Lane position you want.

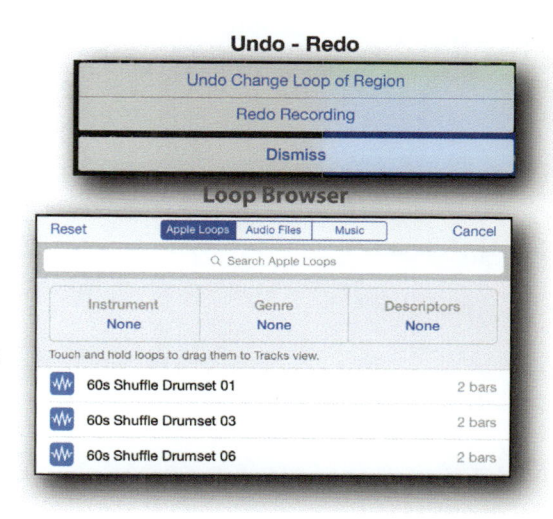

GarageBand Settings

GarageBand, like most of the iOS apps, doesn't have a specific Preferences window itself. However, GarageBand is listed in the iOS Settings App with four Global Preferences:

- **Use iCloud**: This enables the connection with your iCloud account to open and save GarageBand Songs stored on your iCloud account.
- **Knob Gestures**: Select the gesture for turning knobs: Automatic, Linear, and Circular.
- **Crosstalk Protection**: Protect against crosstalk from a guitar connected to the Headphones Jack while Monitoring is set to On in the Input Settings. Especially when using guitar settings with a high gain on the amp or stompboxes, crosstalk can cause unwanted feedback. Please note that crosstalk protection can alter the sound while Monitoring is On.
- **Reset GarageBand**: Restores to the original GarageBand settings (sounds, samples).

iPad Settings app ➤ GarageBand

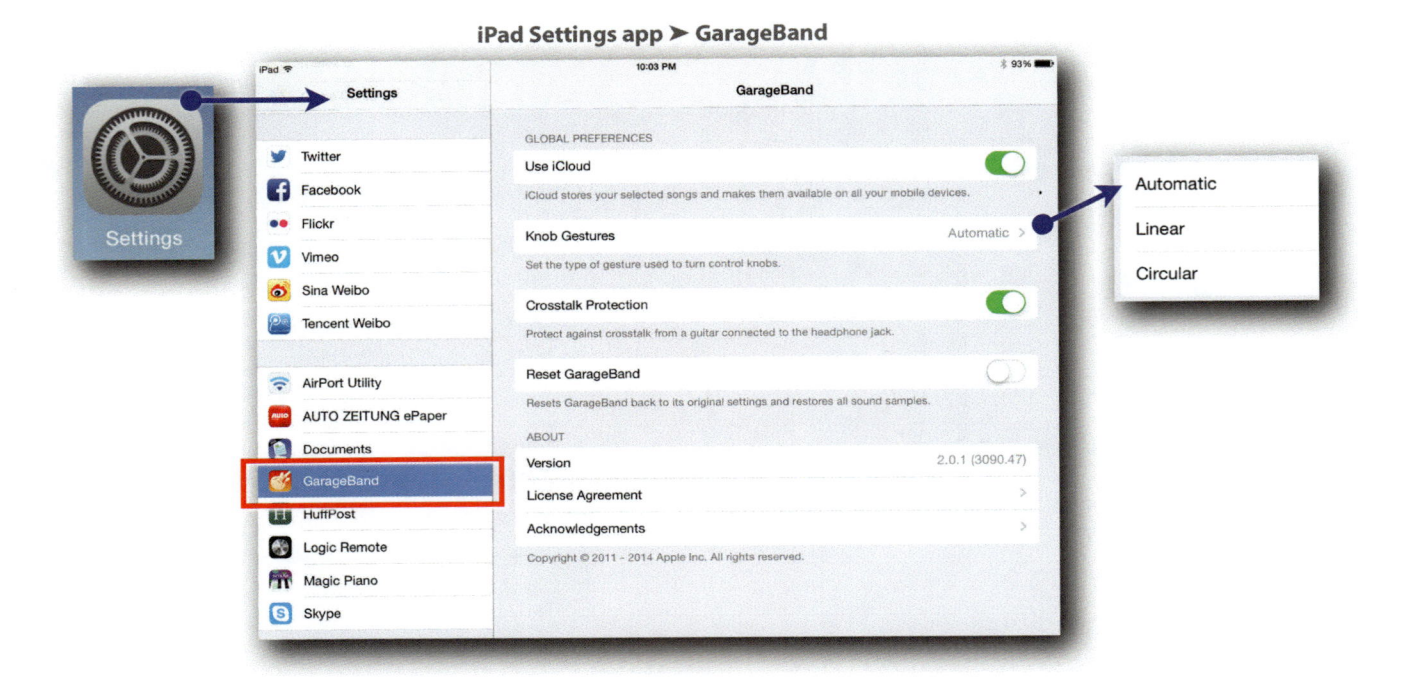

Audiobus Support

Since version 1.4, GarageBand supports the third party app "Audiobus" (from A Tasty Pixel). This enables you to play and record music apps (that support Audiobus) directly into GarageBand. Minimum requirements: iPhone 4S, iPod touch 5th generation, and iPad2.

https://itunes.apple.com/us/app/audiobus/id558513570?mt=8

Inter-App Audio (IAA)

Inter-App Audio is a feature that was first announced for iOS 6 but finally made it into the iOS 7 release. Here is a quote from Apple's Developer site that explains what it is:

> Inter-app-audio allows iOS audio applications that are remote instruments, effects or generators to publish an output which can be used by other audio applications. These applications which publish an output are known as nodes. Any application which connects and utilizes these node applications are known as a host.

What that means is that audio apps on your iPad and iPhone can "communicate" with each other. This is a big deal considering that just the exchange of files between iOS apps is very restricted. Inter-App Audio now allows the sending and receiving of real-time data between running apps.

Real Time Data Exchange

Please note that although the technology is called "Inter-App <u>Audio</u>", the exchange is not restricted to audio only. Also, this standard will most likely improve with more features and functionality as the technology matures. It is already embraced by many developers that updated their audio apps to support Inter-App Audio.

As of now, these are the types of data that are supported or announced:
- ☑ Audio
- ☑ MIDI
- ☑ Transport Controls

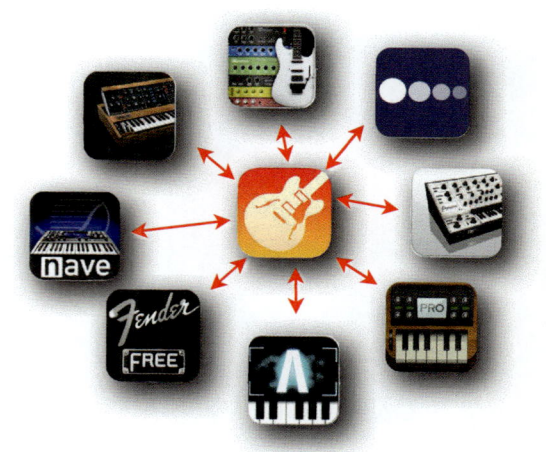

What about Audiobus

This concept of sending data between different apps, which is similar to Rewire on the desktop computer, was already available with the Audiobus app. Now, Inter-App Audio provides that functionality without the need of purchasing the Audiobus app. However, the Audiobus developer doesn't seem to be threatened by Apple's move because their app still provides features that are not available in Inter-App Audio (yet). One major advantage of Inter-App Audio is its zero latency with sample accuracy, since it's completely integrated into the OS as part of CoreAudio.

Routing Concepts

Here are four setups on how to record to an Audio Track in GarageBand (using the Audio Recorder or Guitar Amp Instrument):

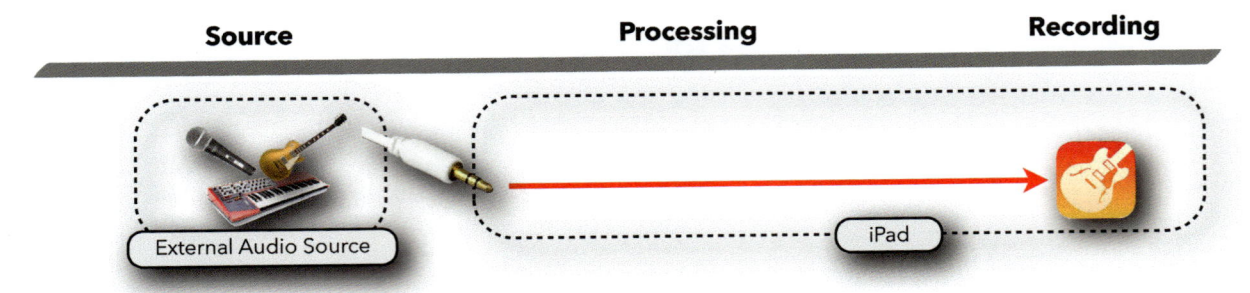

This is the standard procedure without using the Inter-App Audio feature. The input can be any external audio source (mic, guitar, synthesizer) that is recorded directly into GarageBand on an Audio Track.

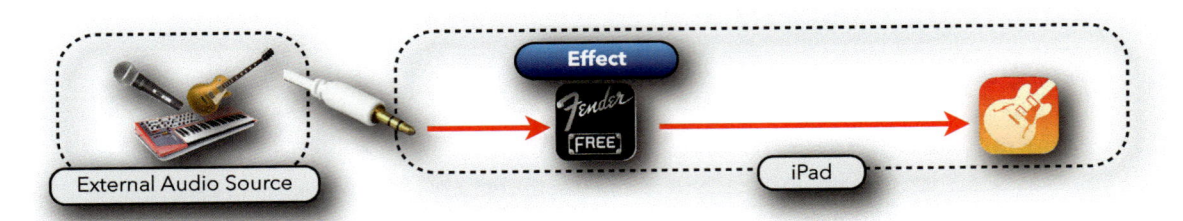

The input is again an external audio source. But now it is routed through an Inter-App Audio app (an **Effect** app) that processes the incoming audio signal. That app then sends the processed audio signal to GarageBand to be recorded on the Audio Track.

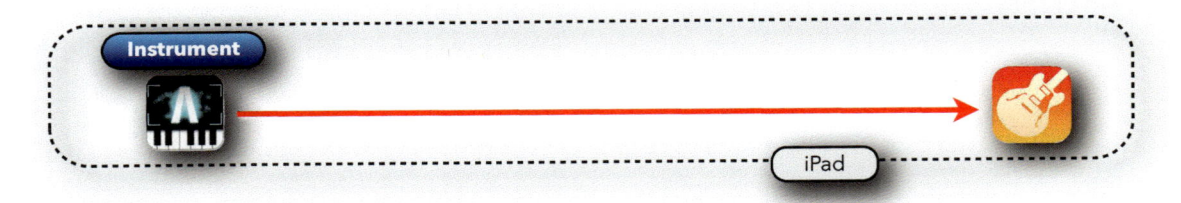

In this example, instead of an external audio source, you use an Inter-App Audio app on the iPad (an **Instrument** app) that produces its own audio output. This audio signal is routed internally on the iPad to GarageBand to be recorded on an Audio Track.

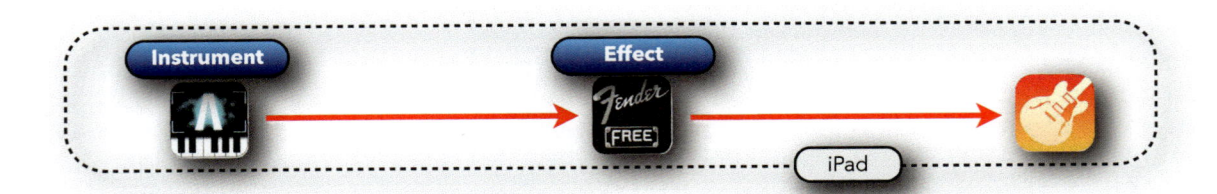

The audio source is again an Inter-App Audio app (an **Instrument** app) on the iPad. But now, it is routed through a second Inter-App Audio app on the iPad (an **Effect** app) that processes the incoming audio signal. That app then sends the processed audio signal to GarageBand to be recorded on an Audio Track.

Setup

Here are the steps on how to configure those setups:

Download Inter-App Audio Apps

Of course, before you can use the Inter-App Audio feature, you have to have apps on your iPad that support that feature. Search for the term "Inter-App Audio" in the App Store or on the Internet. There are also plenty of free apps available to first get your feet wet.

Configure Inter-App Audio

There are two ways to setup Inter-App Audio apps with GarageBand, from the Instrument Browser or the Input Settings Window.

➡ *Instrument Browser*

- ☑ Create a new Track. The Instrument Browser opens.
- ☑ *Tap* on the Inter-App Audio App ❶ icon in the Instrument Browser. This option is automatically available once you have at least one app on your iPad that supports Inter-App Audio.
- ☑ A new window opens that shows you all the Inter-App Audio apps on your iPad listed on two pages:
  - **Instruments ❷**: *Tap* on the Instruments tab to display all the Inter-App Audio apps that function as Instruments (produce audio signal)
  - **Effects ❸**: *Tap* on the Effects tab to display all the Inter-App Audio apps that function as Effects (process audio signal).
- ☑ *Tap* on an app and the following will happen:
  - The window closes.
  - GarageBand creates a new Track with the Audio Recorder Instrument assigned to it.
  - The Instrument View opens with that newly created Track ❹.
  - The Plug 🔌 Icon in the upper left corner ❺ that opens the Input Settings Window now displays an additional icon, the icon of the assigned Inter-App Audio app ❻ next to it.
  - If the selected app was an Instrument app (in this case "Alchemy"), then the Tracks view will display the app icon as the Tracks Icon ❼ and will also name the Track after the app ❽.

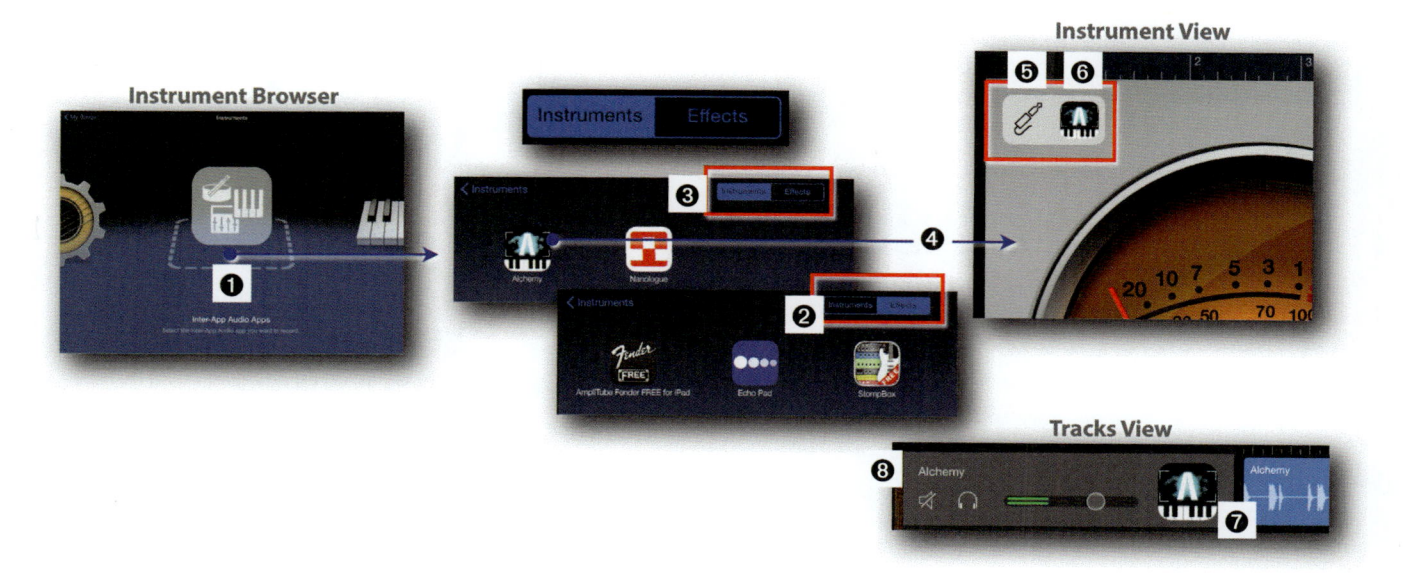

14 - More Stuff

➡️ *Input Settings*

As we have just seen, once you have at least one Inter-App Audio app on your iPad, then the Instrument Browser will display that special "Instrument" 🎹. The same dynamic behavior happens in the Input Settings Window ❶.

☑️ *Tap* on the Plug Icon 🔌 on the Audio Recorder or Guitar Amp Instrument. If you have at least one Inter-App Audio app installed on your iPad, then an additional Inter-App Audio Button ❷ will be displayed in the Input Settings Window.

☑️ *Tap* on the button to open the Inter-App Audio Window ❸ with two more buttons.

☑️ *Tap* on the Instrument Button to open the Instrument Window ❹. It displays all the Inter-App Audio apps that function as an Instrument Plugin.

☑️ *Tap* on the Effect Button to open the Effect Window ❺. It displays all the installed Inter-App Audio apps that function as an Effect Plugin.

You can select only one Instrument app and one Effect app per Track. Whatever apps are selected are displayed in the Inter-App Audio Window ❻ and in the Instrument View next to the Plug Icon ❼.

> Please note: You access the Input Settings from the Instrument View. This might be misleading when you think that settings are for that specific Track. That is not the case. The Input Settings are global settings that change the input for all Audio Tracks. Special Rule: One Input Settings for all Audio Tracks.

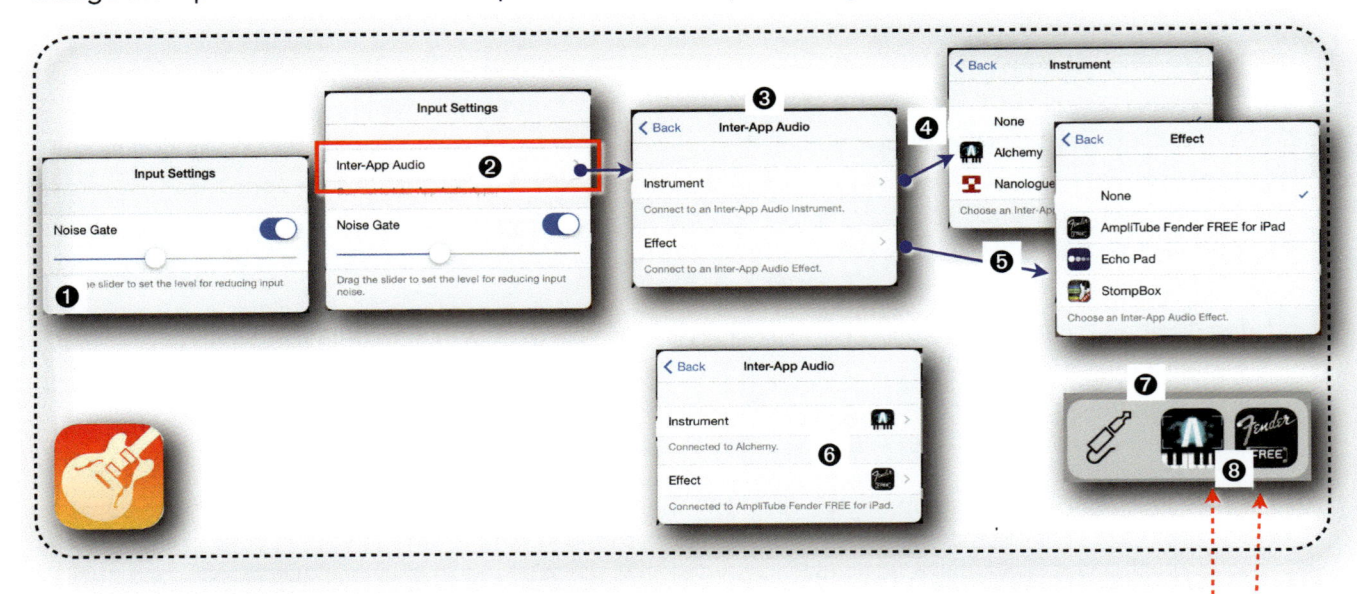

Operation

Once you've assigned one or two apps and their icon shows up next to the Plug icon ❼ on the Audio Track, then you can use those icons as buttons to switch to that app ❽.

Most Inter-App Audio apps have a special Control Panel with the following components:

▶ The Transport Controls ❾ function as GarageBand remote controls. That means you can start Record Mode from the Inter-App Audio app without switching back and forth to GarageBand. Some panels even provide a time display and tempo information.

▶ *Tap* on the GarageBand icon to switch back to GarageBand.

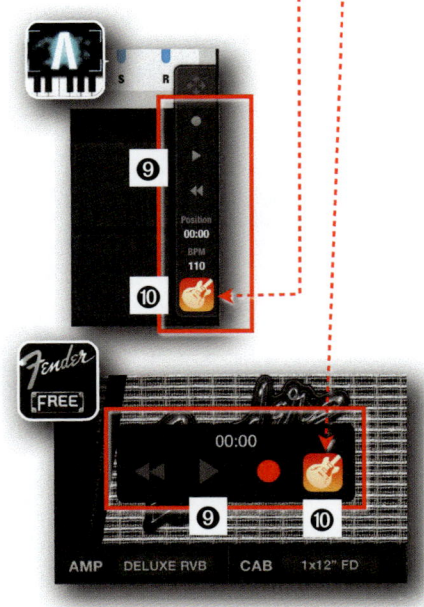

This concludes my "GarageBand for iPad - How it Works" manual.

If you find my visual approach of explaining features and concepts helpful, please recommend my books to others or maybe write a review on Amazon or the iBook Store. This will help me to continue this series.

To check out other books in my "Graphically Enhanced Manuals" series, go to my website at:

www.DingDingMusic.com/Manuals

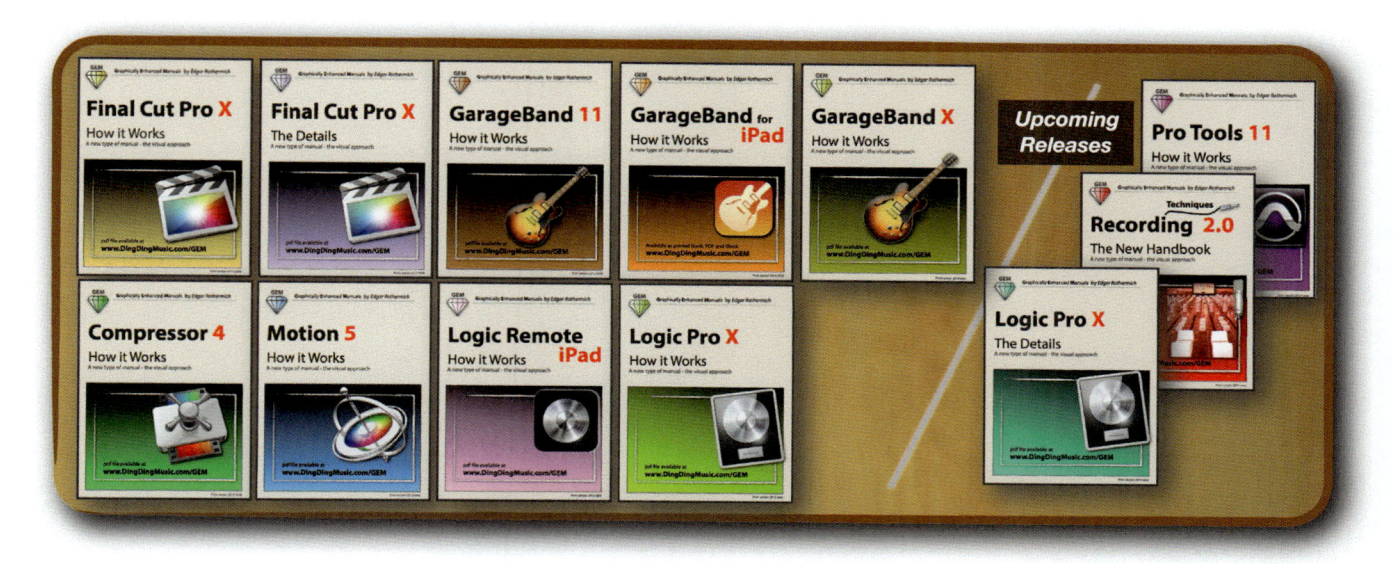

To contact me directly, email me at: GEM@DingDingMusic.com

More information about my day job as a composer and links to my social network sites:

www.DingDingMusic.com

Listen to my music on SoundCloud

Thanks for your interest and your support,

Edgar Rothermich

Printed in Great Britain
by Amazon